PRAISE FOR *THE EMPEROR FAR AWAY*

"A superlative choice for either casual interest or a more in-depth look at modern China." —*Library Journal* (starred review)

"A witty and endearing travelogue, and one which presents a view of the country which may surprise even seasoned China watchers . . . An excellent exposition on how China's hard-line stance on the immovability of its borders is affecting the lives of millions living on the fringes of both a country and a society." —*South China Morning Post*

"[A] lively and informative book . . . A breathtaking travelogue . . . An exciting and powerful examination of the vulnerable people who live in the path of the Dragon." —*Star Tribune* (Minneapolis–St. Paul)

"The book offers insight into an important aspect of China that will likely remain in the news for some time to come." —*The Christian Science Monitor*

"A swift-moving, colorful account of the bewildering array of fiercely independent ethnic groups within an uneasy Chinese 'home.'" —*Kirkus Reviews*

"[An] engaging travelogue . . . Narrated by this curious Englishman and peopled by a cast of natives, settlers, tourists, and ex-pats, this absorbing book is a tantalizing introduction to China's diversity and the ethnic and political dynamics at the extremes of its empire." —*Publishers Weekly*

THE EMPEROR
FAR AWAY

Travels at the Edge of China

David Eimer

BLOOMSBURY
NEW YORK · LONDON · OXFORD · NEW DELHI · SYDNEY

Bloomsbury USA
An imprint of Bloomsbury Publishing Plc

1385 Broadway	50 Bedford Square
New York	London
NY 10018	WC1B 3DP
USA	UK

www.bloomsbury.com

First U.S. edition published 2014
This paperback edition published 2015

ISBN	HB	978-1-62040-363-1
	PB:	978-1-63286-249-5
	ePub:	978-1-62040-364-8

Library of Congress Cataloging-in-Publication Data has been applied for.

2 4 6 8 10 9 7 5 3 1

Typeset by Hewer Text UK Ltd, Edinburgh
Printed and bound in the U.S.A. by Thomson-Shore Inc., Dexter, Michigan

For my mother and father

Shan gao huangdi yuan:
The mountains are high and the emperor far away

Traditional Chinese proverb

Contents

Part IV: DONGBEI – PUSHING THE BOUNDARIES

THE EMPEROR FAR AWAY

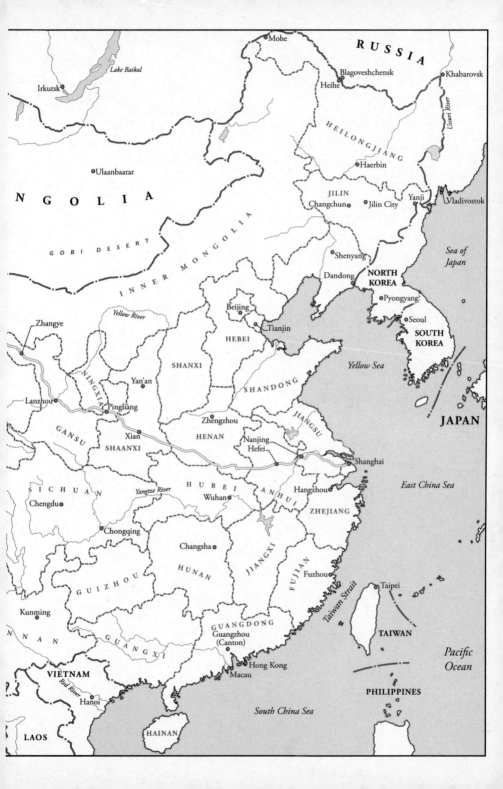

Introduction

For almost 400 years, the fort at Jiayuguan marked the end of the known world for the Chinese. Everything further west of this final outpost of the Great Wall in Gansu Province was beyond both their understanding and their control. Savage tribes and legends of demons which rose out of the desert sand waited to torment the travellers who ventured beyond the fort's high walls. Those who did journey on soon found themselves in a land which ethnically, culturally and geographically had everything in common with central Asia, while sharing nothing with the China they had left.

To be stationed here at the far frontier of the Chinese realm was to endure isolation on a grand scale. It was the equivalent of the British garrison guarding convicts in Botany Bay in the early eighteenth century, a place so distant as to be unimaginable. Even now, gazing out from the battlements, it is easy to understand the fear the soldiers must have felt. The constant wind that swirls through Gansu, sending the topsoil skimming through the air, is a portent on its own, rendering those exposed to it more susceptible to the lifeless landscape surrounding the fort.

The desert, too, is still the same unforgiving, gently undulating carpet of sand and rock it was in the fourteenth century. A road has been carved through it and there is now a railway line, leading towards neighbouring Xinjiang Province and the west of the current Chinese empire. But the vista from the fort has remained constant. To the north, shaded in delicate, distinct hues of brown, are the Beishan Mountains, which divide China from Mongolia and the

Gobi Desert. South lies the Tibetan Plateau, guarded by the Qilian range.

In Imperial China, Gansu was a border province ringed on three sides by past and future enemies. That made Jiayuguan the ideal place for the beginning of my travels to the extreme edges of China, because the fort still marks an unofficial internal boundary. It is the point where the China of the Han Chinese, who account for almost 92 per cent of the country's population and whom the outside world thinks of as 'Chinese', begins to give way to its colonial conquests in the west. From here on, the Han cease to be the majority ethnic group and live alongside people who remain reluctant citizens of their country.

There are around 100 million people in China who are not Han. They belong instead to fifty-five officially recognised ethnic minorities scattered mainly across the borderlands: a vast area that takes up almost two-thirds of the country, much of which was absorbed into China relatively recently. There are another 400 or so groups with fewer than the 5,000 people needed for them to be acknowledged formally as minorities by the ruling Chinese Communist Party (CCP).

Some chafe under Chinese control. The Tibetans and the Uighurs of Xinjiang have fought the Han ever since they started pushing into their homelands. Other ethnic groups resisted Chinese attempts to subjugate them too. The nascent CCP acknowledged that unhappiness with Beijing's rule as far back as 1922, promising the minorities they would have the right of self-determination, and even the option to secede from China, when it took power. That pledge had been forgotten by the time of the communist takeover in 1949, resulting in a legacy of distrust and tension that remains today.

Many of the minorities are a mystery even to the Chinese. Living thousands of kilometres away from the Han heartlands, they inhabit regions of geographical extremes: the remote deserts of the west and north, tropical jungle in the south-west and the Siberian-like taiga that still covers the far north-east of China. Speaking different languages and sometimes following religions viewed with suspicion by the CCP, most have much stronger ethnic and cultural ties with the peoples of the countries across the nearby borders than they do with the Han.

Those links ensure that China's distant frontiers are places where nationality is a nebulous concept, where the passport a person possesses is less important than their ethnicity. That in turn makes the borderlands inherently volatile. They are areas where the old Chinese adage 'The mountains are high and the emperor far away', meaning Beijing's hold over the locals is tenuous and its influence unwelcome, still resonates.

An urge to explore those distant reaches and meet the people who live in them brought me to China for the first time in 1988. From the moment I laid eyes on a map of the Middle Kingdom, I was determined to reach Kashgar. A fabled former staging post on the Silk Road, it lies at the very heart of Asia in the far west of Xinjiang. It took me six weeks to get there, struggling west from Hong Kong by train and bus, hampered by my non-existent Mandarin and encountering wide-eyed stares from people who had never seen a westerner in the flesh before.

China had begun to open up to foreign travellers in the early 1980s, but few ventured east of Thailand back then. Everything from my sideburns and stubble to my sunglasses and jeans marked me out as I made my way towards Xinjiang. It was impossible to avoid attention. Followed down the streets of obscure towns by their residents, or surrounded by silent, staring groups of people while eating, I began to crave anonymity.

Only when I arrived in Turfan, a desert town in eastern Xinjiang famed for having recorded the highest temperatures in all China, did I find a place where I wasn't so obviously a foreigner. The majority of the population are Uighurs: the Muslim ethnic minority native to Xinjiang whose roots are in the Caucasus and central Asia. I felt far more at ease with them than I did with the Han. For the first time since my arrival in China, I was among people who needed to shave every day. And with my tan I could even pass as a Uighur, in the dark anyway.

One night, I met a Belgian backpacker who told tantalising tales about Kashgar. He spoke of an ancient oasis, complete with camels, mosques and smugglers, which rose out of the desert like a hallucination of the past. I was entranced already by the romance inherent in Kashgar's very name, but my desire to visit was perhaps enhanced by the hashish he'd acquired there. Travellers to South-east Asia couldn't walk down the street without being offered drugs, but in China in the late 1980s a joint was as alien as I was.

Getting to Kashgar was not easy, though. Located so far west it is just a day's journey from the borders with Pakistan, Afghanistan and Tajikistan, or a bus ride north to Kyrgyzstan, there was no train linking Kashgar to the rest of China at that time. The couple of flights a week on the then national airline CAAC, known to foreigners as 'China Airways Always Crash', were too expensive an option. Unless you were rich or a senior government official, you had to travel by road across the Taklamakan Desert, a 330,000-square-kilo-metre stretch of sand and scrub that sits in the middle of Xinjiang.

After three long days on a bus more suited to a suburban route, I arrived in Kashgar. In the nineteenth and early twentieth century, its proximity to British India had made it a battleground in the Great Game, the struggle between Britain and Russia for control of India and central Asia. Bearded and tanned British army officers posed as locals, real-life versions of John Buchan characters, while Russian agents headed south through the most distant stretches of the tsar's domain to counter their influence.

With the Cold War still spluttering on in 1988, the echoes of dead and dying empires continued to resound in Kashgar. You could find a bed at the Chini Bagh, the old British consulate, or the more comfortable Seman, the former Russian consulate. I chose to stay loyal to the Crown and so passed through the gates of the Chini Bagh into a mudbrick-walled compound of low-rise, distressed wooden buildings on the edge of the old town.

Peter Fleming stopped at the British consulate on his way to India from Beijing in 1935, a seven-month journey recounted in his book *News from Tartary*. Then, the gates were guarded by Gilgit Scouts on loan from the Indian Army with whom Fleming played polo in the mornings. His nights were spent chatting over bridge and whisky with the consul, his wife and the Swiss skiing international and adventurer accompanying Fleming on his trip.

Times had changed, the Gilgit Scouts replaced by Pakistani traders. They slaughtered and gutted chickens in the filthy communal bathrooms and grilled mutton kebabs on open fires, which they ate with *naan*, the flat, doughy bread of Xinjiang. Unwise travellers who sampled them invariably spent the next day perched precariously over one of the Chini Bagh's squat toilets.

Two years before my arrival, the Karakoram Highway linking China to Pakistan had opened. In the summer, the traders came across the 5,000-metre mountain passes to sell what were then such unobtainable luxuries as western soap and shampoo, before loading up with as much cheap Chinese tat as they could carry back home to sell in their local markets. The ones staying in the room next to me also raided the remnants of the old consulate library, which I had discovered by chance in a cellar. They took the fading volumes with 'British Consulate Kashgar' stamps on their title pages, without offering me one as a souvenir.

Bound by their shared faith in Islam, the Pakistanis and Uighurs had a mutual dislike of the Chinese. In Kashgar, the Han and I were equally foreign. Yet they were more isolated, because the Uighurs were and still are far better disposed towards westerners than they are to the people who conquered them. Some 4,300 kilometres away from their capital by road, surrounded by hostile locals who spoke an incomprehensible Turkic language, the small numbers of Chinese civilians in the city then maintained a low profile, especially once the sun went down.

The longer I stayed in Kashgar, the more I began to realise that Xinjiang was a country within a country, one with far closer connections to its central Asian neighbours than to China. The Sunday market, the social event of the week, was an exhilarating mix of local tongues and minorities. Ethnic Kyrgyz and Tajiks from the surrounding countryside arrived on donkey carts piled high with watermelons, or trailing dispirited lines of sheep, to join the Uighurs and Pakistanis in selling their wares. The different languages vied with each other to such overpowering effect that I no longer felt I was in China.

Kashgar was my introduction to the huge, unwieldy and unstable empire that is China. The outside world tends to regard the country as a culturally and ethnically homogeneous entity. But until the CCP took power, China's leaders acknowledged their imperial role openly. The Qing dynasty, which ruled from 1644 to 1912, established a separate bureaucracy called the Lifan Yuan, or Court of Colonial Affairs, to manage the minorities who populated the far-flung regions it conquered. It functioned much like the former Colonial Office in the UK, which administered the British empire.

Shaking off the perspective that equates China solely with the Han Chinese is difficult. The Han-dominated CCP assiduously encourages a view of the country that relegates the other ethnic groups to the fringes. Just as they exist at the geographical edges of China, so they occupy an uneasy space at the margins of society. The Chinese like to think of themselves as one vast family with their unelected leaders, whether the emperors of the past or the CCP, as its patriarchs. China's minorities are at best distant cousins, linked to their relations by forced marriages rather than blood.

As such, they are present in small numbers at important family events. They march in the parades through Tiananmen Square which mark the anniversaries of the CCP's time in power. When China's version of parliament meets for its annual session each March, a photo of the token minority delegates in their colourful headgear and traditional costumes is always splashed across the front pages of the state-controlled newspapers. One old Tibetan joke says their official representatives have only three responsibilities: to shake hands when they enter, clap hands during speeches and raise hands to vote yes.

I returned occasionally to China after 1988. But only when I moved there in early 2005 to work as a journalist did I decide it was time to revisit Xinjiang. That prompted a more ambitious plan: to travel through the most contentious borderlands and examine the relationships between the different minorities and the Han. I wanted to find out why many still view the Chinese as representatives of a colonising power. Giving the different ethnic groups a voice – something mostly denied them in China itself – while journeying to some of the least-known corners of the world to do so is the principal motivation for this book.

Challenging the notion that China is a nation largely insulated from outside influences is another reason why I felt the need to go to the ends of China. Far from being cut off, the Middle Kingdom is inexorably bound to its neighbours. China's land border stretches for 22,117 kilometres, the longest such frontier on earth. Along with Russia, China borders more countries, fourteen, than any other nation in the world. In the north-east, south-west and west, China is surrounded by the most isolated countries of South-east Asia, the 'stans of central Asia, Afghanistan, Bhutan, India and Pakistan, Mongolia, Nepal, North Korea and Russia.

They are some of the most unpredictable states on the planet, and the conflicts that rage within them inevitably spill across the frontiers. To explore the border regions is to enter a very different China from the glittering mega-cities of Beijing and Shanghai, one that is often lawless and prone to violence. Now they are areas where some of the world's most pressing problems confront China directly. The war against terrorism and on drugs, people smuggling and the exploitation of the environment all have their own unique Chinese aspect.

Twisting history, the CCP does its best to insist that the borderlands have long been part of China. The party ignores how it, and the emperors who came before, took some of those regions by force as little as sixty-odd years ago. It maintains, too, that the minorities enjoy far more prosperous lives under its rule and are content to be part of China, even as its grip on the most restive areas, such as Tibet and Xinjiang, is dependent entirely on the presence of huge numbers of soldiers.

Part of the process of attempting to expunge China's colonial past, while simultaneously reinforcing Beijing's dominion, involves erasing physical memories of it. In Jiayuguan, only the heavily restored fort and a few crumbling sections of the Great Wall stand as a reminder of the time when it was a border town. The arrival of the fort, built in 1372 during the early days of the Ming dynasty, and the Wall was an acknowledgment that the emperor's influence stopped here.

Now, as in most Chinese cities, Jiayuguan's architecture is designed to impose a uniformity – one that, consciously or not, diminishes the role of the minorities in its history. Lined with the same bland white office blocks and apartment buildings that can be found all over the country, the streets are named after provinces and cities from the distant east, a none too subtle declaration of where power in China resides.

But many of the people who walk those streets are not Han. Jiayuguan has a significant population of Hui, a Muslim minority descended from the Arab and Persian traders who came down the Silk Road thirteen centuries ago. They are perhaps the strangest of all China's minorities. After hundreds of years of intermarriage with the Han, they are indistinguishable from them physically. Nor do they have a language of their own. They have spread all across China too, unlike most of the minorities who remain clustered in their traditional homelands.

Just their faith in Islam marks them out and the ten million Hui are the sole people classified as a minority because of their religion. Yet, despite their closeness to the Han – the Mandarins of the Qing dynasty distinguished them from more troublesome minorities by dubbing them HanHui – their presence is still an inconvenient hangover from the past. They are the most tangible evidence that Jiayuguan was once both a crucial junction on the Silk Road and China's far western edge, a place Marco Polo claimed to have passed through, the gateway to and from Muslim lands where Beijing had no remit.

Until the eighteenth century, the Chinese were content to stay put in Jiayuguan's fort. Only after the Ming dynasty was overthrown by the Manchus, who swept down from north-east China to take Beijing and establish the Qing dynasty, did China turn its attention towards the territories beyond Jiayuguan. Under Emperor Qianlong, the Qing decided they needed to put more space between them and the central Asian tribes they feared would invade.

Armies of Manchu Bannermen started moving west. By 1759, they had massacred around one million people and terrified everyone else into submission. But the Qing's control over the region the Chinese now call Xinjiang, which means 'New Frontier', was always unconvincing, as a series of revolts in the nineteenth century confirmed. Uprisings continue to this day.

Jiayuguan remains a place where China is still seeking to expand its frontiers further. Near by is Jiuquan, China's space city, from where an increasing number of rockets carrying satellites and the country's *taikonauts* blast off. In Jiayuguan, you can watch the Long March rockets blazing across the clear desert sky towards the stars, as wondrous a sight for the locals as the camel caravans with their cargoes of unknown treasures that passed through in the days of the Silk Road must have been.

Late one afternoon, I boarded a train moving slowly west to Urumqi, the capital of Xinjiang and China's far west, following the route of the Silk Road through the Hexi Corridor. Once known as the 'throat' of China, the Corridor is a bleak, 1,000-kilometre-long sand and pebble plain which the locals call *huang liang*, a phrase that translates as 'desolate'. A few small towns, former oases on the Silk Road, are dotted across it, but there are hardly any villages. Most of the land is too barren to be cultivated. It is scarred and fissured, as if it has been hacked at by an irritated giant wielding a monster hoe.

During the Silk Road's heyday, the Hexi Corridor was the conduit for the caravans headed via Xinjiang to far-off India and the Middle East with exotic new inventions like paper and gunpowder. Coming in the opposite direction, the spice merchants and monks and Muslims spreading the new religions of Buddhism and Islam knew that the Corridor was the final hurdle to be navigated before reaching the safe haven of Jiayuguan.

Centuries later, Emperor Qianlong's armies travelled through the Corridor on their way to claim Xinjiang for China. Now, it is ordinary Chinese who cross it. The train I was on had originated in Shandong Province, a thirty-one-hour ride away in eastern China, and few of the passengers were Uighurs, the people native to Xinjiang. Instead, Han men with bare chests and pyjama-clad women occupied every bunk, sat on the fold-down seats in the corridor or just stood staring out of the windows, while their children ran around playing.

Chatting, and sometimes singing, at all hours, they played cards, drank tea out of plastic containers which they topped up with hot water from thermos flasks and munched Chinese train food – instant noodles, processed sausages and sunflower seeds. Ignoring the no-smoking signs, they scratched, yawned and fingered their mobile phones constantly. They were the Han masses, heading west.

Part I

XINJIANG – THE NEW FRONTIER

We say China is a country vast in territory, rich in resources and large in population; as a matter of fact it is the Han nationality whose population is large and the minority nationalities whose territory is vast and whose resources are rich . . .

Mao Zedong speech, 25 April 1956, subsequently published in the *Selected Works of Mao Tse-tung*, vol. V (1977)

'Uighurs Are Like Pandas'

My friend Billy was always happy to explain why the Uighurs regard the Han as interlopers in Xinjiang. 'We don't have any connection with the Chinese,' he would tell me. 'We don't look Chinese, we don't speak the same language and we don't eat the same food. And we are Muslims, we believe in Allah. The Chinese believe only in money.' It was hard to disagree with him. With their thick hair, big eyes and prominent noses, no one would pick the Uighurs as citizens of the same country as the Han.

Soon after I arrived in Urumqi, I stood waiting for Billy outside a popular department store near the city centre. As usual, he was late. Meeting a Uighur often involves hanging around, because they run on different clocks to the Han. Billy set his watch to unofficial Xinjiang time, which is two hours behind Beijing. It isn't just a case of the Uighurs thumbing their noses at the Chinese, but practical too. Beijing insists on one time zone for all China, another attempt at asserting its mastery over the borderlands. In Urumqi, a 3,000-kilo-metre journey by car from China's capital, it means it is still light at nine at night and dark at eight in the morning.

The department store's workers were lined up outside the entrance like soldiers, while their managers barked instructions at them. Such parades are a common sight in China, whether in factories or outside hairdressers and restaurants. The daily drills are not so much about improving perfor-mance or customer service, which remains a vague concept outside of Beijing and Shanghai. Instead, they reaffirm the Chinese devotion to the Confucian order, where everyone has their place.

Teenage and twentysomething Han women made up the vast majority of the store's staff, confirmation perhaps that the Uighurs sit right at the bottom of Urumqi's hierarchy. Here in the capital of Xinjiang, where the 9.6 million Uighurs are the largest single ethnic group, the influx of Chinese immigrants in recent years has been such that the Uighurs now account for only 10 per cent of Urumqi's population.

Small-scale Han migration to Xinjiang began even before the formal incorporation of the region as a full province of China in 1884, prompted by the acute shortage of land in China's interior as the population multiplied. Parts of the territory were occasionally subject to Chinese rule during the previous 2,500 years. But only Emperor Qianlong had been able to control both the Dzungaria and Tarim basins that make up most of what is Xinjiang.

About the size of western Europe, it is a massive area which borders eight countries and accounts for over one-sixth of China's total landmass. Much of it is uninhabitable. The Tian Shan Mountains run along the northern frontiers with Kyrgyzstan and Kazakhstan, and divide the dry steppe of the Dzungaria Basin from the Taklamakan Desert which covers most of the Tarim Basin in the south. In the far north the Altai Mountains separate Russia and Mongolia from China. To the west and south, the Pamir, Karakoram and Kunlun ranges mark the frontiers with Afghanistan, Pakistan, Tajikistan, India and Tibet.

Until the Qing dubbed it Xinjiang, it had gone by a variety of names. The Han referred to it first as Xiyu, literally 'western region', and later as Huijiang, or 'Muslim territory'. To the West, it was Chinese Turkestan, a nod to the indigenous population whose roots lie far away in what are now Turkey and the former Russian Caucasus. The sand of the Taklamakan has preserved the bodies of a few of the earliest inhabitants of Xinjiang, who arrived during the Bronze Age. Those mummies have European features, red or brown hair and light-coloured eyes.

Their descendants are the Uighurs, who went on to intermarry with Persians as well as their central Asian neighbours. Xinjiang is home to at least fourteen different ethnic minorities, including Kazakhs, Kyrgyz, Mongols, Russians, Tajiks, Tatars and Uzbeks, but only the Uighurs regard it as their country. For them, Xinjiang is a Chinese-imposed name. The unknown numbers who want independence call it East Turkestan.

When he finally showed up, Billy looked much the same as before. Still quick to smile and slight with a narrow face, topped by messy black hair, and a scratchy goatee, he was in one of his collection of fake Chelsea shirts, a team he supported with a passion. His love of English football was one of the reasons we became friends, even though I supported a rival London club.

His preference for western clothes meant that Billy didn't wear a *doppa*, the distinctive square-cornered hat many Uighur males sport. Taking an English name was another expression of his fondness for the West. Many Han, especially those in the big cities who work or come into contact with foreigners regularly, have alternative English names, but few Uighurs do. It suited me that he did. His real name, like those of many Uighurs, had far too many 'x's in it for me to pronounce properly. It was much easier, and safer, to call him Billy.

We caught a taxi to Yan'an Lu, the main street of Urumqi's biggest Uighur neighbourhood. I thought it ridiculous that so many Uighurs were concentrated in just one area of the capital of their homeland. But Han and Uighurs do their very best to avoid living side by side, and the sheer number of new Chinese arrivals has forced the Uighurs to cede much of Urumqi to them. Around People's Square, the heart of the city, the only concession to Urumqi's heritage is that the names of the shops are displayed in both Chinese characters and the Arabic script the Uighur language is written in.

Ramadan had just started, but at the open-air restaurant we had lunch in the Uighur diners were tucking into their food heartily. 'Out in the country people take it more seriously, they're more religious there,' said Billy, as he ordered *polo*, the rice and lamb dish that is a staple all over central Asia, kebabs, the freshly baked *naan* bread the Uighurs eat with every meal, and yoghurt sweetened with sugar.

Uighurs are traditionally more relaxed about their faith than their Pakistani and Afghan neighbours. In part, that's because Islam was a relatively late arrival in Xinjiang, taking hold only in the tenth century. Until then, the locals were mostly Buddhist and it took centuries for all to become Muslims. But even in Urumqi, most Uighur women wear headscarves and long skirts or trousers, while the city's mosques are always busy.

Religion is at the heart of why Beijing has always regarded the Uighurs, along with the Tibetans, as the most recalcitrant of China's minorities. As well as periodically rebelling against Chinese rule, the Uighurs steadfastly refuse to integrate with the Han. They scorn Chinese culture and Mandarin in favour of their own language, which is very close to Uzbeki and similar to Kazakh and Kyrgyz, while their music and folklore also have their roots in central Asia.

But it is their adherence to Islam which especially frustrates the Han. As far back as the eighteenth century, the Qing railed against the hold Islam had on the people of Xinjiang. Officials petitioned Emperor Qianlong to ban what they described as a 'perverse doctrine'. The CCP, which regards all organised religions as a threat, because of their potential to focus opposition to its rule, adopted a more rigorous approach. In the 1950s, it created the China Islamic Association which appoints all imams. It means that the party is able to monitor what is being said in the mosques, as well as who is attending them.

Beijing has progressively tightened restrictions on the Uighurs' right to worship since then; anyone under the age of eighteen is now banned from attending a mosque. Billy wasn't religious, but like most Uighurs he was upset about the rule. 'When I was young, we all went to the mosque with our fathers. Now the children can't do that.

They can't study the Koran in school and they can't study it in the mosque. Their parents have to teach them about it. The Chinese say we have the freedom to practise our religion, but they are stopping young people from learning about it.'

While we ate, I asked Billy about his family. I still felt guilty over what had happened to them when we first met in July 2009, in the immediate aftermath of some of the worst ethnic violence in China for twenty-five years. Almost 200 people, mostly Han, died and around 1,700 were injured after an initially peaceful protest by Uighurs in Urumqi turned into a vicious race riot with Uighurs indiscriminately attacking Chinese across the city. Han mobs took to the streets on the following two days to exact revenge. Billy had introduced himself to me by showing off the wounds he had received fighting them.

Talking to a foreign journalist was risky then for a Uighur. The next day, we were spotted by one of the low-level Han officials who oversaw Billy's neighbourhood. A shrill woman in her mid-thirties, she approached us demanding to know what we were doing. When we walked away without answering, she tried to rip my press card from around my neck, saying I might be a spy. That night, Billy's parents received a visit from the police who told them he shouldn't be talking to westerners. It had frightened them.

Now, we were much more cautious. I bought a local sim card for my phone, rather than using my Beijing number which was known to the authorities, and we established a cover story. I was an old friend from Shanghai, where Billy had studied, in town as a tourist. And in an effort not to stick out so much, I was also growing a moustache. I didn't want to attract the attention of the police, who might wonder what a westerner was doing in a Uighur neighbourhood.

My dark hair, along with my skin quickly turning brown under the desert sun, made a moustache seem like good camouflage, especially as nearly every adult Uighur male sports one. Beards are frowned upon by the CCP, which associates them with religious zealotry, and Uighurs working for the government are prohibited from growing them. So a moustache, like the *doppa* so many of them wear, is a compromise, a way to express both their faith and identity. Billy approved of the fledgling growth above my top lip, even if I found it off-putting each time I looked in a mirror.

Billy's family were originally from Kashgar, the Uighurs' spiritual capital. His parents had come to Urumqi in search of better jobs, and his father was a cook in a restaurant. Billy was the middle of three sons. Uighurs, like all minorities, are exempt from the one-child policy that was introduced in 1980. It is a huge cause of resentment among the Han, along with the fact that the minorities need to score fewer points on the *gaokao*, the national university entrance exam, to go on to higher education.

One Han shopkeeper in Urumqi expressed that bitterness after the 2009 riots by saying 'Uighurs are like pandas.' It was a sly comparison with the dwindling numbers of China's iconic national animal and the way they are cosseted by the authorities. Many Chinese can't understand why the minorities aren't more grateful for such apparently preferential treatment. But it is only in the last thirty-odd years that the Han have been restricted to having one child, and they still vastly outnumber the other ethnic groups. The questions on the *gaokao*, too, are in Mandarin, which most of the minorities don't speak as their first language, let alone write.

Billy, though, was one of the Uighurs who had benefited from the special policies for minorities. He spent two years at Xinjiang University, before transferring to a college in Shanghai. After graduating, he worked briefly for a property company in the north-east of China, but soon returned to Urumqi. 'You can't get good Uighur food there,' he said of the east. At twenty-seven, Billy had never held down a job for very long and was still looking for the main chance he was convinced was out there for him. His latest scheme was operating an ad hoc airline ticket agency with a friend.

Like all Uighurs his age, Billy attended an all-Uighur junior school, before going to a mixed high school. Now the government has banned Uighur-only education and insists that all of Xinjiang's ethnic groups attend the same schools as the Han. It is another source of resentment for the Uighurs. 'At Chinese school, you only learn Chinese history, no Uighur history,' Billy explained. 'And it's very hard to find a book in China on Uighur history. We have to hear it from our parents and grandparents.'

Along with many other locals, Billy was convinced that making Uighur kids attend Han schools was a deliberate attempt by the authorities to dilute Uighur identity. 'I've been walking down the street and heard two Uighur kids speaking Chinese to each other. Chinese! What do you think of that? It makes me really sad. It's the result of making them go to Chinese school. If our language dies out, then so will the Uighur nation,' said Billy.

During the twilight days of the Qing dynasty, the Chinese also tried to make Uighur children learn Mandarin, going so far as to keep the reluctant pupils in school by chaining them to their desks. It was part of an attempt to sinicise the Uighurs which has never really stopped. In what has been described as the Confucian Man's Burden, the Han felt it was their duty to civilise their conquered subjects. Essentially, that meant making them more like the Han. In the parlance of the time, the barbarian minorities were either *shufan*, cooked and therefore tame, or *shengfan*, raw and savage.

Defiantly uncooked, the Uighurs needed to be grilled. Han officials flooded into the region and demanded an allegiance and respect that was enforced by the sword. Intermarriage with Chinese immigrants was encouraged, but the matches made were few and far between. The Qing's time was almost past, though, by the time Xinjiang became a full province of China, and the locals never took to Confucius. When the Han finally rejected thousands of years of imperial rule in 1912 and the Qing dynasty collapsed, Xinjiang split once more into the fiefdoms which were its natural state whenever the Chinese weren't around.

Even today, few Uighurs speak and write fluent Mandarin. I thought it would surely help future generations if they knew the language properly. Billy dismissed that with a wry smile. 'I speak and write good Chinese,' he pointed out. Indeed, Billy was one of the Uighurs who, if the CCP's propaganda is to be believed, should be reaping the benefits of government investment in Xinjiang. Huge amounts of money have been pumped into the region in an effort to quell Uighur unrest by raising their living standards.

Who benefits from that largesse is a different matter, because it is the Han who control the local economy. Chinese companies claim they cannot employ Uighurs because so few of them speak Mandarin, or else they insist the Uighurs prefer to work with each other. Either way, the result is economic apartheid. Just 1 per cent of the work force of the booming oil and natural gas industries, which account for over half of Xinjiang's GDP, are Uighurs.

That disparity between the prospects of the locals and those of the Chinese migrants fuels the conflict between them. There are now eight million-plus Han in Xinjiang, or over 40 per cent of the population, up from just 220,000 in 1947. For the Uighurs, it is the equivalent of 25 million Poles arriving in the UK, or 120 million Mexicans migrating to the USA, and taking charge of the economy, while refusing to employ the natives and demanding they learn to speak Polish or Spanish.

'The government has sent more money to Xinjiang, but they've also sent more Han and they're taking all the work. Their lives are getting better and ours are getting worse and worse. It's the same in all cities in Xinjiang. Of course we feel angry about it,' said Billy. Nor is there any sign of that hatred diminishing. While I was in Urumqi, a Uighur man drove an electric cart into a crowd in the city of Aksu in western Xinjiang, and detonated a bomb that killed seven people.

With little chance of being employed by a Han company, most well-qualified Uighurs like Billy look for work with the Xinjiang government. Local authorities are huge employers all over China. But jobs with them are especially prized at the edges of the country where state-owned companies, which in Xinjiang means Chinese-staffed ones, are far more prevalent than the private enterprises found in the eastern cities. The fact that Billy didn't attend the mosque was another point in his favour. Under Chinese law, no government worker can practise a religion of any kind.

Yet Billy held back from applying for positions which would guarantee him, and his family, a better life. He claimed it was because he despised the Han. 'I hate them, I do. I've hated them since I was a kid,' he said in his mild way. Listing the litany of complaints the Uighurs have against the Chinese like an imam intoning the Koran, Billy seemed to have lost all hope for the future and thought Uighurs who crave an independent state were just dreaming.

'A lot of Uighurs say they want independence. They look at Uzbekistan and Kazakhstan and wonder why we're not like those countries. It's only Uighurs who don't have their own country with our own traditions and cultures. But we lost our place a long time ago. The Han are too strong. They have all the power and all the weapons,' Billy said. 'I think two things will have happened in twenty years' time. Either the Uighurs are over, finished, and we are assimilated, or another country like the US helps us. Maybe if the Americans fight China we can get our own country.'

Many Uighurs express similarly apocalyptic sentiments: that it will take either China's economy collapsing, or a world war, for them to gain independence. It is an unlikely scenario. Xinjiang acts as a strategic shield between China and central Asia and Russia and, more importantly, has vast reserves of coal, oil and natural gas that are immensely valuable to China, the most energy-hungry country in the world. Losing them would be a huge blow, one which Beijing would do anything to prevent.

It is for that reason that Xinjiang has effectively been ruled by the gun since the communist takeover. In September 1949, the residents of Urumqi were ordered to the airport, or face being shot, to greet the first planeloads of soldiers from the People's Liberation Army

(PLA). Their commander was General Wang Zhen, who would later rise to be vice-president of China. A Long March veteran and diehard Maoist, Wang was notorious for his unreconstructed opinions. After the pro-democracy protests in Tiananmen Square in June 1989, he suggested exiling what he described as 'bourgeois-liberal intellectuals' to Xinjiang.

Wang oversaw the massive increase in Han migration that occurred after 1950 at the behest of Mao Zedong. It was empire expansion on a grand scale with millions of former PLA troops and their defeated opponents in the nationalist army heading west. Mao recognised that as long as the Chinese remained a tiny minority in Xinjiang they would always be vulnerable to Uighur insurrection. Ensuring that didn't happen made Wang infamous. Even some Han historians acknowledge that as many as 60,000 Uighurs died during the 1950s, both resisting Beijing's rule and in what Mao called the 'stamping out of superstition'.

Over sixty years later and Urumqi is still full of soldiers. Slow-moving convoys of the Wujing, the People's Armed Police, an offshoot of the PLA, rumbled down the roads at all hours. They were not as visible as they had been in July 2009, when I watched them marching ten abreast through the deserted streets chanting 'Protect the country, protect the people, preserve stability.' But they still guarded significant intersections in steel helmets with their AK47s to hand.

There were newly formed police SWAT teams too, tucked down side-streets in vans waiting to move if there was trouble. My hotel overlooked one of their barracks. In the morning, I'd lean out of the window and watch them doing press-ups or practising unarmed combat in their all-black uniforms. They were mostly Han, with a smattering of Uighurs, including a lone young woman with a ponytail.

After lunch, Billy and I walked along Yan'an Lu, heading deeper into Uighur Urumqi. North, west and east of People's Square,

Urumqi looks much like any Chinese city. There are only a few Uighur pockets near the former main bazaar, now a market for tourists, where the minarets of mosques poke into the sky alongside the apartment blocks. But the further south you go in Urumqi, heading towards the desert that surrounds it, the more Uighur it becomes.

By the time we reached a district called Saimachang, we could have been in any one of the small oasis towns that run along the fringes of the Taklamakan Desert in the far south of Xinjiang. On the main street, sheep were being butchered and the meat sold, alongside piles of watermelons and tomatoes. Billy pointed to them proudly. 'Han people think Xinjiang is just a desert and that we ride camels. They don't know we grow so much fruit and vegetables. It's because they only show Xinjiang on TV when something bad happens.'

Food is almost as important to Uighur identity as Islam. Streetside bakeries making *naan* dominate any Uighur neighbourhood. The bakers knead the dough and sprinkle it with water, before sticking it on the sides of the *tonur*, the bread oven. When ready, it is removed with two skewers with their ends bent into the approximation of a fish hook. In Urumqi, *naan* comes in every conceivable variety: plain or with elaborate patterns imprinted on the bread, sprinkled with sesame seeds or rice, and sometimes with lamb embedded in it.

No one was going hungry in Saimachang. Instead, it is jobs and money that are in short supply. Kids with bright eyes shining out of dirty brown faces offered to clean shoes, while groups of young men lounged around in ill-fitting camouflage uniforms. Ostensibly security guards, they are hired by the local government in an effort to reduce the absurdly high Uighur unemployment statistics. Billy told me they were paid 1,000 yuan (£100) a month.

Old men with white beards sat stoically on the steps of the tenement buildings that line the narrow alleys off the main street. The women were dressed much more conservatively here than elsewhere in Urumqi. All but the very young wore headscarves and long dresses that covered every inch of their bodies bar their hands. But even if just their large eyes were visible, no one was in the dreary all-black worn in the Middle East, Afghanistan and Pakistan. Uighur women love bright colours, and their dresses and hijabs were a kaleidoscope of patterns in lilac, turquoise, pink, red and yellow.

'They're not from Urumqi. Most of the people here are from the country, from the south,' said Billy as we walked the alleys. Southern Xinjiang is the Uighur heartland where agriculture is the main industry. But much of the south is made up of the Taklamakan Desert and is far from suitable for cultivating anything. So more and more Uighurs are choosing to follow the example of Han farmers elsewhere in China and moving to the cities in search of better-paid work.

Lacking both education and fluency in Mandarin, most of them fail to find jobs. Many of the 2009 rioters were newcomers from rural areas. Saimachang was where I had come two days after the violence, to find that almost all the men under fifty had been taken away by the police. Now, its residents are subdued to the point of hopelessness. Hanging grimly on at the very edge of Urumqi, Saimachang is an outpost in enemy territory – the site of the Uighurs' last stand in a city where they have been all but vanquished by the Han.

2

The New Silk Road

B illy drank alcohol only on special occasions, so most evenings in Urumqi I went alone to the one western-style bar in the city. It was owned by Hiro, a stocky, long-haired Japanese guy with a goatee, and Manus, a laidback Irishman who was tall and thin with a shaved head. Both were eight-year veterans of Urumqi who had first arrived as language teachers.

Their bar functioned as a gathering place for the city's tiny foreign community, who were mostly students or taught English, and passing travellers. But, uniquely for Urumqi, it was a place where Uighurs and Chinese drank side by side. The bar attracted a crowd who could be described as Urumqi's bohemians, people whose work brought them into contact with westerners or those who had rejected the local entertainment options.

Uighurs patronise dance clubs no Chinese will step into for fear of being stabbed, and which are dangerous too for foreigners who try it on with the Uighur women. Han head to the karaoke joints or the Chinese bars, where whisky is bought by the bottle and mixed with green tea and endless games of liar's dice are played, with the losers downing their drinks in one as punishment. One of my Han friends in Beijing used to tell me that the Chinese don't really like western alcohol and only drink it as a sign of status. He thought the dice games were a way of forcing each other to consume it.

At Hiro and Manus's bar, though, everyone was thrown together. Chinese customers had no choice but to play Uighurs at pool if their names came up on the blackboard. Americans and Europeans, as well as a few Africans, drank foreign beers, talked endlessly of their China experiences and chased the local women regardless of whether they were Han, Uighur, Mongolian, Kazakh or Uzbek. It was integration on a tiny scale, but so divided is Urumqi it seemed startling.

That alone ensured the bar aroused suspicion among the authorities. 'The cops don't like us and would rather we shut down. They don't like the idea of foreigners gathering in one place and they don't like the fact that a lot of Uighurs drink here,' said Hiro. Smart, fast-talking and more than a little burned out by his eight years in Xinjiang, Hiro was one of the rare foreigners who can speak fluent Uighur. He needed to, just to mediate the disputes that erupted almost nightly between the bar staff.

'I'd prefer to employ Han waiters, to be honest. The Uighurs don't work as hard and they're always arguing with each other. If they can't agree among themselves, how can they expect to get anywhere? Uighur means "union", but they never have been united. It was the Chinese who created Xinjiang. Before 1949, it was just a series of city states,' said Hiro. It was true. Only in the 1930s did the natives of Xinjiang begin using the term 'Uighur'. Until then, they identified themselves by their home region. They were 'Urumqilik', which in Uighur means someone from Urumqi, 'Kashgarlik' or 'Hotanlik'.

Hiro had no time for the wide-eyed solidarity expressed by the few foreigners who embrace the Uighur cause. Nor was he impressed by my efforts to pass as a local. 'You look too clean. You look like a westerner with a moustache. If you really want to look like a Uighur, you need to stop washing your hair,' he told me. It was harsh, but he was right. Personal hygiene isn't always a priority for Uighurs, and the closest I had come to being taken for a native was when taxi drivers asked me if I was from Kazakhstan.

But there were other people who drank in the bar who also looked nothing like the Uighurs, and they had been born and bred in Xinjiang. I was most intrigued by six-foot-tall Fei Fei, whose extraordinary high-angled cheekbones and slanted eyes marked her out as pure Manchu, and Kamil, a Chinese Tatar. With his blond mullet haircut, pot belly and taste for loud shirts, he looked like he should be propping up a bar in Vladivostok.

So Russian did Kamil appear it was only when he opened his mouth and Mandarin came out that I remembered he was a Chinese citizen. Hearing him speak was disconcerting. It reminded me of how foreigners are sometimes wheeled out on Chinese TV shows to perform in perfect Mandarin, while the live audiences stare at them as if they are chimpanzees holding a tea party. Certainly, I used to gaze at Kamil and Fei Fei like they were rare animals in a zoo. Tatars and Manchu have intermarried so much there are very few left who look as they did, and Xinjiang is the only place they can be found.

Descendants of their Russian cousins who wandered across the border centuries before, the Tatars are now one of China's smallest minorities. Fewer than 5,000 of them are left, living mostly around Yining in the Ili Valley near the frontier with Kazakhstan. Also resident in the Ili Valley are the 200,000 Xibe. Closely related to the Manchu, and like them originally from north-east China, the Xibe are the ancestors of soldiers sent to garrison Xinjiang in the eighteenth century.

Unlike the Manchu, who assimilated with the Han they had conquered to the point that their tongue is now virtually extinct, the Xibe have retained their version of Manchu. Xinjiang is now the sole place where you can hear an approximation of the language of the Qing dynasty emperors, a geographical irony given that it is thousands of kilometres away from the Manchu homeland.

Kamil seemed to spend most of his time drinking or destroying all-comers on the bar's over-subscribed pool table, but he somehow managed to run a successful import and export company. China's Tatars are known for being bright. Ninety-five per cent of them go on to higher education, the highest proportion of any ethnic group in China, and Kamil had spent four years at Moscow University.

In contrast, Fei Fei was the outdoor type. A star basketball player for Xinjiang in her youth, she took Han tourists on adventure tours to the Altai Mountains and spent her free time scaling peaks in Tibet. So rare is it to encounter full-blooded Manchu people that many of her clients mistook her for a Mongolian, even though she had the pale skin and oval face desired by all Chinese women. I told her jokingly she would have been a princess in the Qing dynasty. Fei Fei answered seriously that her family were once very rich and powerful and had owned a huge estate in the north-east.

Spending a night at the bar was to rewind back through the centuries to when Urumqi was a crucible of races and religions. It was a modern-day version of the caravanserai, the inns along the Silk Road where merchants and travellers from the Middle East, central Asia, India and China had spent their nights telling tales around open fires. Indeed, some of the bar's customers were the same traders from central Asia and Russia Kamil did business with.

Lured to Urumqi not by the promise of rare spices and exotic inventions but by the low cost of more prosaic items like furniture and household appliances, their increasing presence in Xinjiang is a sign a new Silk Road is emerging. It is one where the cheap clothes and goods churned out by the factories in the south and east of China head west via Urumqi, while the natural resources of central Asia travel in the opposite direction.

Come dawn, though, and the bar's cosmopolitan atmosphere seemed fantastic, a mix of races that belied the reality of life in Urumqi. It was as if the desert sun illuminated the true nature of the relationship between the Chinese and the Uighurs, while the night sky cloaked it, because there was a palpable tension on the streets during the day. You could see it in the eyes of the police sitting in their vans scanning passing pedestrians, and the security guards who stood outside the banks and big shops.

Whenever there were Han and Uighurs in the same vicinity their mutual loathing was obvious. So polarised are they that they look straight through each other, as if that Uighur selling sweet apples or the Chinese newspaper vendor didn't exist. But in the centre of

Urumqi the Han and Uighurs have to walk the same streets every day, and there is always the sense that it would take very little for the barely suppressed hatred on both sides to explode.

One afternoon, Billy took me to meet his friend Mardan. He looked like a caricature of a Uighur: big-eyed and dark-skinned with a curving nose, thick black hair and a moustache that straggled down both sides of his mouth. We met him on the edge of Saimachang, where he was waiting for us at the wheel of a Chery, a cheap Chinese car, his shiny grey shirt and trousers set off by eye-catching red fake-leather shoes.

He was what the Chinese call a black, or unlicensed, cab driver and rented the car for 70 yuan (£7) a day. 'I can make 1,000 yuan [£100] a week if I am lucky,' said Mardan, whose name means 'brave' in Uighur. He hardly spoke Mandarin, despite his years in Urumqi. 'I didn't have much education. I just went to middle school, not high school. This is the best way for me to make money.'

His job is a direct consequence of the 2009 riots, which prompted a big rise in car ownership among the local Han and created a subsequent glut of inexpensive, second-hand motors like the one Mardan drove. Fearful of what could happen if there is a repeat of the violence, the Chinese residents of Urumqi no longer want to take public transport to work, or let their children walk to school. Many of the Han victims of the riots were attacked on buses. I interviewed one young woman in hospital whose face was a swollen, purple mess of cuts and bruises. She had been dragged off a bus coming from the airport and beaten half to death.

Mardan knew something of the rage that drives people to commit such an appalling act of violence against a defenceless woman. His cousin was one of five Uighurs who stabbed a Han man to death on Yan'an Lu during the disturbances. He had agreed to talk to me about it but was twitchy about doing so in a public place, so we drove through Saimachang until we found a quiet alley to pull into.

Like Mardan, his cousin hadn't graduated from high school. He was twenty-four and unemployed at the time of the riots. His only previous job had been working in the kitchen of a restaurant. As Urumqi erupted in anger, so did he. 'He was in the wrong place at the wrong time. He went out with his friends and lost control,' said Mardan, who was clearly reluctant to describe the exact horror of what his cousin had done. 'The whole family are heartbroken. He was a good boy, he went to the mosque. He'd never been in trouble before.'

Embarrassed about recalling the details of his cousin's role in the attack, Mardan was also fatalistic about it. 'It has happened. We can't change it.' The only bright spot from the family's point of view was that he had escaped being executed. At least twenty-five Uighurs were given death sentences after the riots, but Mardan's cousin had avoided that by turning himself in to the police. He had no choice, because one of his friends was already in custody and had offered up his name.

Now he was serving life in a prison in Aksu, nearly a thousand kilometres away. It was too far for his family to visit, even if they were allowed to. 'We haven't heard from him since he was arrested. He's not permitted to write,' said Mardan. His parents had seen him at his trial, but weren't able to speak to him. They had hopes they could get him out of prison in a few years by paying compensation to the dead man's family. I didn't say what I thought, which was that it would take an awful lot of money for the victim's family and the authorities to agree to release a Uighur convicted in those circumstances.

The 2009 protests were triggered by the murder of two Uighurs working in a factory in southern Guangdong Province, near Hong Kong. They had been falsely accused of raping a Han woman, and her co-workers had set upon them. The news of the killings reached Xinjiang quickly via text messages. Along with the internet, mobile phones have made it far harder for the CCP to censor unwelcome news. The only way to do so is by severing all access. Within hours of the riots breaking out, it was impossible to make a call to Xinjiang, or send or receive a text.

Beijing, though, blamed the disturbances on its usual Uighur suspect, Rebiya Kadeer. Once a highly successful businesswoman and a member of the National People's Congress, China's rubber-stamp version of parliament, she was held up by the Han as a role model to other Uighurs. But Kadeer fell foul of the authorities after criticising the CCP's policies in Xinjiang. She was imprisoned for six years before being allowed to go into exile in Washington DC, where there is a large expatriate Uighur community.

Since then, Kadeer has become the president of the World Uighur Congress. A Munich-based coalition of exiled groups agitating for an independent Uighur state, the Congress is the most visible face of opposition to Chinese rule in Xinjiang. In response, Beijing has consistently pilloried Kadeer as a separatist and terrorist, and was quick to accuse her and the Congress of orchestrating the riots. Kadeer insists she wants to establish an independent East Turkestan through a peaceful, non-violent and democratic process.

For the CCP there is no greater crime than separatism. The crowning achievement of Mao and the party was to unite China; to advocate dividing it is heresy. Ever since the start of the twentieth century, Chinese intellectuals had argued that a lack of nationalist sentiment was the reason why China had been bullied and exploited by the former colonial powers throughout the previous century.

By the time Sun Yat-sen became the first president of China in 1912 after the Qing dynasty had been overthrown, that argument was enshrined in the theory of *minzuzhuyi*, or nationalism. Sun described the Manchu, Mongols, Uighurs, Tibetans and other minorities as 'alien' races, whereas the Han were descended from Huang Di, the great Yellow Emperor and the father of Chinese civilisation. Only by standing together at all times could the Han maintain their supremacy.

It is a doctrine which, by claiming that the Han are all one big family, automatically excludes the minorities from being considered wholly Chinese. But rather than admit that, or recognise why the

Uighurs regard the Han as invaders, it is far easier for Beijing to make scapegoats out of Kadeer and the World Uighur Congress. Blaming external forces has become the way the CCP deals with internal unrest, a convenient means of both stoking Han nationalism and avoiding acknowledging that some minorities would rather not be Chinese. To do anything else would be a tacit admission of how their policies towards them have failed.

After meeting Mardan, I had my first and only Uighur language lesson. I was hesitant about travelling through the Uighur-dominated countryside of Xinjiang speaking my bad Mandarin. If nothing else, I thought uttering a few phrases in Uighur would make the locals laugh and so be better disposed towards me. But as soon as I met my tutor, whose English name was Jenny, I realised that humour wasn't on her agenda.

Short and stout with thick black eyebrows, Jenny taught Uighur at a local university. She was a hard taskmaster. In China, teachers are used to being obeyed, and students at both schools and colleges are much more respectful than they are in the West. As she rattled through a basic primer of Uighur words, phrases and numbers so quickly I didn't have time to write them down, my constant interruptions to get her to repeat what I had missed made her both cross and scornful.

'You're not concentrating. I thought you wanted to learn,' she admonished me. I asked her not to speak so fast. Jenny responded by enunciating the strange sounds so slowly that I felt like the stupid boy in class again. Unsure of the spelling of some of the words, I asked her to write them for me. She did so, but in Arabic script. I told her I had enough trouble with Chinese characters, so she could forget me learning Arabic.

I was as keen to hear about her life as I was to study her language. Uighur society is far less strict than the Middle East, but it is still a Muslim culture and most women don't speak to men they don't know. Nor are Uighur males happy with foreigners talking to them. Jenny, though, didn't wear a headscarf and was used to dealing with overseas students, so I thought it was a good opportunity to hear a Uighur woman's point of view.

First, I asked why she didn't cover her head. 'I am a member of the CCP, so I don't follow Islam,' she said. The eighty-two million-odd members of the CCP are a self-electing elite; you are invited to join. Jenny had been recruited while she was a student. She was the first Uighur in the party I had met and a rarity, because only 6 per cent of the CCP are from ethnic minorities. 'I was asked to join when I was nineteen. You can't really say no. It's helped me get tenure at my university. I wouldn't have got that if I wasn't a member.'

Tenure for Chinese academics means the chance to buy a cheap apartment on campus, subsidised healthcare and a guaranteed salary whether you are teaching or not. In China, those are coveted benefits. Despite its professed socialist policies, the CCP does not provide its citizens with free education or healthcare, while the cost of buying a flat has spiralled in recent years as China's economy has boomed. School fees, medical bills and mortgages swallow up a large part of people's incomes.

Jenny had paid a high price for her relatively comfortable life too, even if she claimed it didn't matter to her that the party's rules meant she wasn't allowed to wear a headscarf or pray in the mosque with her family. 'It's not a problem. Maybe it would be if I came from the countryside, where people don't have much education and believe in Islam much more,' she said.

She was still single at twenty-eight, an age when most women in Xinjiang are married. I wondered if her adoption of a more liberal lifestyle made it harder for her to find a partner. 'I had a boyfriend, but we split up,' said Jenny with a fierce glare. 'Was he Uighur?' I asked. 'Of course, I wouldn't go out with or marry a Chinese guy. It's not that I think they're worse than Uighur guys – I think all men are quite similar. It's because I come from a different culture.'

We had wandered far from the reason for our meeting, and Jenny was growing more disaffected by the minute. I had jotted down a few notes of our conversation. Jenny snatched my notebook from me, ripped out the page where they were written and tore it into little pieces which she tossed into an ashtray. Not content with that, she took my lighter and set fire to the scraps. 'We're here to study Uighur,' she told me. 'Not to get me into trouble.'

Ever polite, Billy smiled when I told him about my combative lesson and resisted interrupting as I attempted to order dinner in Uighur. But he was also single. He had a different problem to Jenny: his lack of regular work and cash didn't make him a great catch. It was a rare night out for us, as Billy preferred to be with his family after dark. I was leaving Urumqi soon, though, and had offered to take him to his favourite restaurant as a farewell.

Joining us was Murat, Billy's younger brother. His thinning, receding hair made him look older than Billy, but he had the same skinny frame and narrow face. Instead of English, his foreign language was Russian. It was a sensible choice because Russian remains the lingua franca of central Asia. While Billy watched Chelsea on the internet and dreamed of emigrating to London or Washington, Murat worked as a translator and fixer for the increasing numbers of people from the countries surrounding Xinjiang who come to Urumqi to shop.

'Most of my customers are Russians who live in Kazakhstan, as well as Kazakhs and Uzbeks. They buy everything from construction machinery to clothes and electronics. I negotiate with the sellers, arrange the transportation and get a percentage of each deal,' he explained. With prices for almost everything at least 50 per cent lower in China, and rapidly expanding road, train and flight links with the surrounding region, Murat had no shortage of clients and made more money than anyone else in his family.

Much of his work takes place at the Hualing Wholesale Mall, Urumqi's modern-day equivalent of the bazaars that once lined the route of the Silk Road. It is the biggest market in Xinjiang: two vast buildings, each one 800,000 square metres, side by side in the north of Urumqi. Billy, Murat and I arrived to find Uighur beggars sidling up to the approaching shoppers, who were mostly Russians and Kazakhs, interspersed with the odd Pakistani or Indian.

Inside, a dazzling variety of merchandise was spread across four floors. Whether you want a duvet or a dishwasher, a sofa or a stereo system, Hualing has one, and at prices that make shopping in bulk attractive. Most of the customers were dragging around wheeled suitcases and bags stuffed with their purchases. Others needed the trucks parked around the back to take away all they had bought.

On the third floor, we found one of Murat's regular contacts, a television retailer named Wang Guanghui. Han, but born in Urumqi, Wang sat in his shop drinking green tea, surrounded by TVs playing a mixture of movies and Chinese soap operas at different volumes. 'In Kazakhstan, TVs are double the price they are here. Most of my customers will buy ten at a time. But some are just ordinary people. They come and buy a TV and then take it back on the bus,' he said.

Many of the Han working at Hualing come from inland China's major manufacturing centres, such as Wenzhou, Yiwu and Dongguan. They are cities that are now as famous to traders in Asia as Kashgar and Xi'an were during the heyday of the Silk Road – the places where the merchandise Wang and the other traders sell originates. 'Ninety per cent of the people who run the stores here are Chinese. The Uighurs don't know how to run a business like this. They don't have the connections in the east to get the goods,' said Wang.

Murat was one of the lucky few Uighurs whose language skills enabled him to work as a middleman at Hualing. But most of his compatriots never set foot in the place. To them, it is as remote as the Forbidden City in Beijing – just another example of how the Uighurs are being excluded from economic life in their homeland. Outside, the beggars were still lurking in hope as we walked to the back of the market where trucks with licence plates from as far off as Germany waited to be loaded with goods bound for the West. It was a new Silk Road all right, but not one the Uighurs would be travelling down.

3

Exiles

The Uighurs might not be profiting from the new Silk Road, but a few are using it to escape China. I wanted to follow them and investigate the Uighur diaspora in central Asia. My timing was off, though, when I visited Yining, a city close to Kazakhstan thriving on cross-border trade. After arriving on the overnight train from Urumqi, I hopped in a taxi to a hotel, only to find my way in blocked by the Wujing, who sent me packing before I was out of the car. It transpired that my first choice of lodging had been taken over by a high-ranking member of China's politburo.

For the officials of Yining, a tiny city by Chinese standards of just 250,000 people, the presence of the fourth most senior politician in the country was the equivalent of the pope, the Queen of England and the president of the USA all arriving at the same time. Over the next few days, crossing roads became a tedious process as the police held up both pedestrians and cars while he moved around Yining in a convoy of police vehicles and black SUVs, all travelling at speeds that contravened even China's lax traffic laws.

Trailing around town, it took me two hours to find a place to stay. Some hotels were booked out by the officials and media accompanying the special guest from Beijing. Others weren't licensed to take foreigners, and wouldn't bend the rules with so many police on duty for the visit. Eventually, I found a home on a road named after Stalin, a legacy of the time when China and the Soviet Union had been allies and Yining sat near the frontier between their respective empires.

Ninety-five kilometres from the border with Kazakhstan, Yining has been fought over for centuries by Russia, China and Mongolia. As late as 1962, Soviet and Chinese soldiers were exchanging fire across the frontier. That history has left it with a muddled identity. To the Chinese it is Yining, but the Uighurs call it Ili, the name of the river that runs through the south of the city. The Russians and Kazakhs refer to it as Gulja, a name it acquired when the tsar's forces briefly occupied it in the late nineteenth century.

Normally tranquil, with a smattering of faux-Russian architecture and tree-lined streets which provide much-needed shelter from the ferocious summer sun, Yining sits in the Ili Valley. The river that gives the valley its name ensures it is the most fertile part of Xinjiang. Yining's suburbs are expanding fast, but they give way to fields of wheat, corn, lavender and green pastures full of grazing sheep that stretch all the way to the frontier with Kazakhstan. Looming over them are the snow-tipped Tian Shan Mountains, which divide China from central Asia.

Like many small cities in China, Yining is really just an overgrown country town, the donkey carts that act as taxis in the older districts only adding to the rustic feel. But Yining's proximity to the border means it and the surrounding area are home to the greatest concentration of the 1.25 million ethnic Kazakhs in Xinjiang. As such, it is the capital of the province's Kazakh Autonomous Prefecture. It is a title that dates back to the 1950s, when Xinjiang was carved into autonomous areas. Each of the region's minorities was given a prefecture or county ostensibly run by a local authority staffed by their own people.

Predictably, the Uighurs are not part of this scheme. None of the areas of Xinjiang where they are a majority are designated as Uighur autonomous districts, although the entire province was renamed the Xinjiang Uighur Autonomous Region in 1955. This glaringly obvious ruse to restrict Uighur influence verges on the ridiculous in many places. In the vast Mongolian prefecture that extends south from the centre of Xinjiang to the border with neighbouring Qinghai Province, the Uighurs outnumber the Mongols seven to one.

With every senior ethnic minority official shadowed by a Han CCP cadre who holds the real power, the prefectures and counties are merely for show. They are a classic example of divide and rule, a way of separating the Uighurs from the other ethnic groups and preventing any joint rebellion. It has been an effective tactic in Xinjiang, because the Uighurs' antipathy towards other minorities, even their fellow Muslims, is notable. Whenever I asked why that was I got vague answers blaming their different lifestyles. 'We are traditionally farmers, while the Kazakhs and Kyrgyz are nomadic people,' one Uighur told me.

Angelina, a Uighur woman I got to know in Yining, was more honest. 'A lot of Uighurs are jealous of the Kazakhs and other minorities because they all have their own autonomous areas. They think the other minorities get treated better than we do.' She said it with a shrug which could have been her way of expressing a view on the boundless capacity of the Uighurs to feel sorry for themselves, or her agreeing with their sentiments. It was hard to tell.

Introduced by a mutual friend, a Uighur living in exile in Australia, we met for the first time outside Yining's most fashionable department store. The advertising billboards which covered its façade were all of smiling Han faces, something which can't have been lost on the Uighur and ethnic Kazakh shoppers. Unlike the perpetually late Billy, Angelina was dead on time. She strode confidently up to me, her long hair in a ponytail and slim and elegant in a white dress that showed off her brown legs. She shook my hand and suggested we go to a nearby park to talk.

Despite being born and raised in Yining, Angelina was not your typical small-town girl. At twenty-six, she seemed much older than her years. As we strolled through the park, passing middle-aged Han women pushing their grandchildren in buggies and groups of teenagers in the baggy tracksuits that are school uniforms in China, it became apparent that her experiences were far removed from those of most Uighurs.

Angelina's divergence from the path of provincial life began when she was fourteen. Her excellent exam results meant she was one of eighty Uighurs selected from across all Xinjiang to attend high school in a big city in the east of China. It was a chance to gain a far better education than she could expect in Yining; the catch was she had to leave her parents and travel more than 3,000 kilometres from home to obtain it.

It had been akin to going to boarding school in a foreign country. 'I remember when we arrived and one girl from Kashgar started crying immediately. Then we saw the food and we were all unhappy. I really missed Uighur food and I missed not being at home for the Muslim festivals too,' said Angelina. From the time she arrived at the school, she hardly saw her mother and father. 'I got to go back home once a year, but my parents weren't able to come and visit me. It was too far.'

Adapting to her new Chinese classmates was no easier. 'The Han kids thought we were foreigners when we first arrived. They came and said "Hello" to us in English. They didn't know anything about Xinjiang except that it was very poor. They would ask us if we went to school on camels and if we had television.' Nor were there many opportunities to dispel the stereotypes held by their Han counterparts. 'We didn't have much contact with the Chinese kids. We were taught on our own, we ate different food because we were Muslims and we lived at the school while they went home each day,' said Angelina.

Her reward for four years of isolation in Han China was a place at one of the country's top universities. After graduating, she had not been keen to return to Xinjiang. 'I wanted to stay and find a job suited to my degree. But my parents didn't agree. They wanted me to come home because I had been away for eight years and they missed me. So I did. I felt sad for the first few months I was back in Ili. I missed the east and the big cities. I suppose I had got used to the life there.' Angelina said it in a rueful tone that made it obvious that she still chafed at living in a backwater like Yining.

Now she had a job which although important by local standards, and one I agreed not to reveal, was a poor match for a woman of her intelligence. She was pinning her hopes on being transferred to

Urumqi, which was close enough to home to keep her parents happy but would allow her to enjoy urban life again. More importantly perhaps, it would improve Angelina's chances of finding a husband.

'Girls who are my age here should be married. My mother says I should be and I want to be, but I don't have a boyfriend. It's hard for me to meet someone I can talk to on an equal basis. A lot of the boys here haven't got much education,' she said. 'I'm not interested in looks. I never look at a man because he is handsome. I only want a man with a good heart and someone who has a similar background to me.'

Smart, pretty but single women are an increasingly common phenomenon in China. Girls do better than boys at school and university, and more and more of them are establishing meaningful careers for themselves. But the Chinese concept of face, where preserving one's dignity and reputation is more important than anything else, along with the way males are traditionally more valued than females, means it is a rare man who is willing to marry a woman with a better degree and a higher salary than his. To do so would mean losing face in front of not just his family and friends, but his wife's as well.

Many women I knew in Beijing bemoaned their single status. Angelina's predicament was far worse. Few Uighur men in rural Xinjiang graduate from high school, let alone university, and Angelina, despite her bare legs and uncovered head, was still traditional enough only to be interested in marrying a fellow Uighur. I wondered if I should offer to introduce her to Billy, a fellow graduate, but decided against it. I wasn't sure feckless Billy and the hard-working and serious Angelina would be a great match.

We walked on in silence; it was hard to know what to say. Angelina deserved to find a decent man and a life outside Yining and I hope she has. Like many Uighur stories I heard, hers was more tragic than anything else. For all her achievements, her time on the east coast had made her as much of an exile as the Uighur in Australia who introduced us, only Angelina was still stuck in her hometown. Now she was regarded as exotic by her own people, yet as a Uighur she remained an outsider in the Han society her education had prepared her for.

At least Angelina was not living in what is essentially a ghetto, like most of the Uighurs in Urumqi. In the Ili Valley, the Chinese make up less than half the population and are outnumbered by the ethnic Kazakhs and Uighurs in the area. For the first time since my arrival in Xinjiang, I was reminded of Kashgar in 1988 and the way both the Han and western visitors had been the foreigners in town.

The main market was a genuine central Asian bazaar. Porters transporting goods on trolleys or their backs pushed through the crowds of shoppers crying out '*Boish boish*', the Uighur equivalent of 'make way', while the stalls were a chaotic jumble of gold, carpet and clothes. Some vendors squatted on the floor hawking cheap household items, as well as pirate DVDs from Uzbekistan which were either Bollywood-style musicals or blood-drenched gangster movies.

Surrounding the market were dark, fly-ridden restaurants. The only dishes on offer were *laghman*, the thick noodles found all over central Asia, *polo* and lamb kebabs grilled over glowing coals by young men who fanned the smoke away constantly with pieces of stiff cardboard. Little Mandarin was spoken in those places and I was grateful now for the snippets of Uighur I'd picked up from Jenny in Urumqi.

Some Han shopped for bargains at the market and I noticed how they avoided eye contact with me. Normally, the Chinese are unrestrained when it comes to staring at foreigners they encounter in remote parts of their country. It was my moustache that caused the unusual reticence. The locals might not have been fooled by the hair that sat above my upper lip, but it was a good enough disguise for the Han to assume I was a Uighur and so I was treated as if I was invisible.

I was delighted at not being taken for a foreigner, although such is the diversity in appearance of Yining's different ethnic groups that a moustache isn't really necessary to pass as a local. Most men did have a black growth of hair curling around the top of their mouths, while many of the women were dark-skinned, brown-eyed beauties in jeans, T-shirts and headscarves who could have been Turkish or even Pakistani. But there were also people with complexions paler than mine and blue or green eyes topped by blond or red hair, testimony to the wild mix of genes the Uighurs have inherited from their many ancestors.

Yining's residents were far more religious than Urumqi's Uighurs, and Ramadan was strictly observed. Outside of the market area, the only restaurants open during the day were Chinese ones. Come sundown and there was a rush of customers to the Uighur places, which made it difficult to find a table. Nor did they serve alcohol, and there are no bars in Yining. Instead, anyone out on a spree heads to the karaoke bars. They are places where one can both croon sentimental love songs and drink, and are staffed by young women who walk a thin line between hostesses and hookers.

One of them was located on the fourth floor of my hotel. Half-cut men breathing fumes of *baijiu*, a noxious white spirit that is China's equivalent of vodka or tequila, would stagger out, arms around the heavily made-up young Chinese ladies in short skirts and garish high heels. Such girls are called *xiaojie*, literally 'miss' but now a China-wide euphemism for a prostitute. At night, some would ride the lifts on their way to make room calls, jabbering into their phones in thick accents from far-off provinces like Henan and Sichuan and spitting the shells of sunflower seeds on to the floor.

Apart from karaoke, the main entertainment option was to head to the banks of the Ili River, where a sad little funfair overlooked the fast-flowing waters. Its rusting rides piped out snatches of patriotic songs like 'The East is Red', and were operated by controls straight out of a 1950s science-fiction movie. Most people just perched by the river chatting, flirting, smoking and watching the foolhardy Uighur teenagers who tried to swim to a sandbank in the middle of the river without being swept downstream by the strong current.

After a dismal night by the Ili, which ended when a drunk Uighur threw up over my shoes, I was glad to see Angelina again. This time we met on a street called Ahemaitijiang, the Chinese name for Ahmet Jan. He had been one of the leaders of the East Turkestan Republic (ETR), the short-lived result of the last widespread Uighur uprising in Xinjiang and the only democratic regime ever to run the region.

Founded in Yining in 1944, the ETR existed for five brief years after Uighur anger at the troops loyal to Chiang Kai-shek then occupying Xinjiang turned into a full-scale rebellion. The CCP was overjoyed with the ETR for overthrowing its enemy, and Mao himself wrote to them lauding their achievement. But by 1949, with the nationalists all but defeated, the CCP no longer had any need for allies. In August of that year, Ahmet Jan and most of the ETR government perished in one of the mysterious plane crashes that punctuated the Mao era. Their victims were always potential opponents to the Great Helmsman's rule.

Ahmet Jan's death did mean he avoided the purge of the ETR that followed the CCP takeover of China. He is still officially a revolutionary hero, rather than a separatist, and one of the few Uighurs from any period to be acknowledged publicly by Beijing. Yet, in a supremely cruel historical irony, the street that honours his name was the site in 1997 of one of the most controversial confrontations between the Uighurs and the Han since 1949.

Ramadan had ended the day before and with typical insensitivity the local authorities had chosen the last day of the most important Muslim religious festival to arrest the leader of Yining's *mashrap*. Part social clubs, part local forums and part venues for religious education, *mashrap* sprang up in large numbers in Uighur communities in the 1990s. Their formation was prompted both by despair over worsening economic prospects and by the fear that Uighur identity was being fatally diluted by the Han presence in Xinjiang.

They quickly aroused the suspicion of the Chinese, who saw them as an expression of the Uighurs' desire for independence, and the police moved to close them down. In Yining, though, the *mashrap* movement was especially strong, and most continued to meet in secret. The arrest of its leader was greeted with dismay, as was the detention of two *talib*, the Uighur term for students of Islam. Next morning, thousands marched down Ahemaitijiang Street calling for their release. The protest soon morphed into a general outpouring of Uighur grievances, according to Angelina who was thirteen at the time.

'There were many people chanting "There is only one God, Allah" and some carried banners. They were protesting about religious freedom and calling for fair treatment and for jobs. They weren't being violent, or fighting the Han,' said Angelina. 'But the soldiers opened fire on them. I remember my father was out on his bike and he came rushing back after he heard the shots. Many men died, no one knows how many. It was very bad what the government did.'

Worse were the reprisals meted out to those suspected of taking part in the demonstration. Uighurs who subsequently escaped to Kazakhstan revealed a horrifying picture of further instances of the PLA opening fire on unarmed people, as well as of public executions of prisoners whose hands were bound with wire. Some human rights organisations put the number of dead in the hundreds. Many more were imprisoned, while thousands fled across the frontier.

Rebiya Kadeer, then the most prominent Uighur in China, publicly criticised the brutal crushing of the Yining protests. It was the beginning of her downfall; she was imprisoned on trumped-up charges of leaking state secrets two years later. Other Uighurs decided on a more militant response. A subsequent spate of bomb attacks was attributed to a shadowy separatist organisation called the East Turkestan Islamic Movement (ETIM). Now Beijing delights in comparing the ETIM with Al-Qaeda, and uses its existence as a justification for all its punitive efforts in Xinjiang.

Following the events of February 1997, it took years for relations between the Uighurs and Han in Yining to stabilise. They deteriorated again after the 2009 Urumqi riots. Angelina categorised them now as 'so-so', although she socialised occasionally with her Chinese work colleagues. But she was not optimistic about the future, and believed the authorities thought the same. 'There are a lot more police and soldiers in Ili now. They're worried there will be more trouble here.'

Our walk had begun on a beautiful, sunny summer afternoon. Soon, though, a vicious, howling wind arrived, turning Ahemaitijiang Street into a dustbowl. The sky grew dark and the air murky as people scurried for cover with their heads down, or covered their faces with newspapers or bags, to avoid being stung by the dirt being propelled through the air. It was apocalyptic weather signalling impending rain, and our cue to leave.

As we drove off down the street where so much blood had been spilled, I struggled to comprehend what had happened here in 1997. I had the same problem whenever I cycled past the intersection on the Beijing street where large numbers of people were killed by the PLA during the Tiananmen Square protests. There was nothing to remind you of the deaths of so many innocent people and they are never referred to by the authorities; what took place has simply been omitted from the official record.

Ignoring the history they don't like, or manipulating the facts of it, has long been party policy. Mao was fond of claiming inspiration from Qin Shi Huang who, in 221 BC, became the first emperor to unite China. But he is also remembered for burying 460 Confucian scholars alive – a demonstration of his contempt for the study of what he regarded as obsolete and irrelevant facts from previous eras.

Just like Emperor Qin, Mao sought to submerge the past, and the present CCP carries on his work. That has had a devastating effect on minority identities, one almost as harmful as the slow death of many of their languages as the study of Mandarin only is enforced in schools across the frontier regions. As long as the CCP continues to censor all books published in China, the Uighurs have no way of recording their version of what has happened to them. All they can do is pass on the gruesome memories of events such as the Yining slaughter to their children, like a hereditary disease that taints generation after generation.

Early the next morning I went to the bus station looking for transport to Korgas, the border town with Kazakhstan. One minivan was going. The driver and I sat and smoked, while he waited for more passengers. After an hour he gave in and started the engine and we took off down a bumpy two-lane highway flanked by tall pine trees, which we shared with overloaded trucks and lines of sheep being cajoled along by ethnic Kazakh farmers.

Korgas was a madhouse. Kazakhs and Russians who had arrived on overnight coaches from Urumqi were loaded down with TVs, microwaves and large bags full to bursting with clothes. We all fought to squeeze through the narrow steel barriers that led to passport control. Around us, local Kazakhs offered to change yuan or US dollars into tenge, the Kazakh currency, acted as porters or simply hung around looking shifty, while the Wujing on duty did their best to ignore our presence.

Things were more relaxed on the Kazakh side of the frontier. An ethnic Russian in the high-peaked hats that are one of the most obvious legacies of Soviet rule in central Asia – along with decrepit Lada cars, vodka and statues of Lenin – stamped my passport and sent me on my way with a cheery 'Good luck'. I found a ride to Almaty with a Chinese woman and a Kazakh returning from a business trip to Yining. It took just over four hours through a landscape of largely uninhabited barren, brown hills, the driver hammering his battered Audi down unsealed roads at a speed of 130 kilometres an hour.

Almaty is the unofficial capital of central Asia – by some distance the most international and prosperous city in the region. Running uphill from north to south along steep streets, Almaty has one magnificent, wooden Russian Orthodox cathedral, a couple of pleasant parks and several monolithic buildings in the Socialist-Realist style. Dominating the suburbs are endless lines of uninspired Soviet-era apartment blocks.

It reminded me of cities I had been to in the Russian Far East, and not just because Russian is still the local language and, like Russia, the price of everything is three times as expensive as it is across the border in Xinjiang. Almaty is isolated and seemingly down at heel and that comes as a shock after China, where even the centre of a remote city like Urumqi has an increasing number of gleaming high-rise shrines to steel, concrete and glass.

Yet Kazakhstan is far more developed than its neighbour in less showy ways. Home to a bewildering number of minorities, some 131 in total, Kazakhstan is a genuine multi-ethnic society. In sharp contrast to Xinjiang, there is no segregation of the races in Almaty. Dark, oval-eyed Kazakhs and blond ethnic Russians are the most numerous people, but there are also Uighurs, Uzbeks, Tatars, Turks, Chechens, Ukrainians and even Koreans. And while Kazakhstan isn't a paradise of equality, the different minorities all work together, live side by side and sometimes date and marry each other.

Kazakhstan's Uighur community is around 300,000 strong. They are the country's fifth-largest minority and one of them, Karim Massimov, is the second-most powerful politician in the country. A former prime minister, Massimov is now chief of staff of the Presidential Office, a role created just for him and one which makes him Kazakhstan's administrative head.

Admittedly, Massimov doesn't advertise his ethnicity and, as a Mandarin-speaking former KGB officer, he makes a rather unlikely Uighur. Yet he is still one, and I enjoyed seeing photos of him with his broad face and impressive 'tache standing next to senior Chinese politicians at official talks. His presence acts as a rebuke to China, because the chances of a Uighur, or any member of an ethnic minority, attaining such a powerful position is so inconceivable as to be fantasy.

My Uighur contact in Almaty was equally improbable. Kakharman Khozhamberdi was a tall, sturdy man with an upright bearing and swept-back black hair that belied his sixty-plus years. He looked like a military man and had been a tank commander in the old Soviet army. But he is also a vice-president of the World Uighur Congress, the Rebiya Kadeer-led organisation the Chinese claim is responsible for inciting all unrest in Xinjiang.

True to the Uighurs' reputation for disunity, Khozhamberdi was no fan of Mr Massimov. 'I don't really like him,' he told me when we met in a park in the west of Almaty. 'He's too close to China and doesn't stand up for the Uighurs.' We sat side by side on a bench in the afternoon sun. Opposite us, small children jumped around on a bouncy castle while their parents gossiped.

Khozhamberdi was a fourth-generation Kazakh Uighur, whose family were originally from Yining. They left in 1883 after the city had been returned to the Chinese, part of the first wave of Uighur migration to what was then Russia. Many more Uighurs followed, along with ethnic Kazakhs, Kyrgyz, Tajiks and Uzbeks. Large numbers crossed the frontier in 1962, after losing their land to Han migrants. Others left to escape religious persecution during the Cultural Revolution of the 1960s and 1970s and, traditionally, there is always a spike in Uighur refugees after major protests.

But it is increasingly difficult to flee Xinjiang. 'The border is much better guarded now and only a few hundred make it out each year,' said Khozhamberdi. 'They're allowed to stay for a year or two, unless they have relatives here, then they go on to other countries like Turkey, Norway or Germany. I think they should be allowed to stay permanently, like they used to be able to do. But the government doesn't want to do anything to offend China. You know, politics is complicated and China is so powerful. That makes it very difficult for the Uighurs in central Asia.'

Completely integrated into Kazakh and Soviet society, Khozhamberdi traced his conversion to the Uighur cause back to a day out in Moscow in the late 1970s. 'I met a friend in Izmailovsky Park. He asked me if I wanted to buy some different books to the ones on sale in official shops. I thought he was talking about dirty books – you know, pornography. But it was a samizdat copy of *The Gulag Archipelago*.'

Reading Solzhenitsyn's account of life in the chain of prison camps that stretched across the Soviet empire made Khozhamberdi start to doubt communism, even as he continued his army career and rose to be a colonel. Like Solzhenitsyn, who served part of his sentence in a labour camp in Kazakhstan, Khozhamberdi discovered religion relatively late, in his case the Muslim faith of his ancestors. Now he believed it is the fundamental cause of the tension between the Uighurs and the Chinese. 'Islam is the reason why the Han and the Uighurs will always be separate,' he told me.

His sole experience of Xinjiang was a brief trip in 1994. His high profile as a Uighur activist means he can never return. He had even been arrested a few times in Almaty, for leading anti-Chinese demonstrations. It was as if Khozhamberdi had turned himself into an exile because, despite his staunch Soviet background and his family's hundred-plus years in Kazakhstan, he no longer regarded himself as a Kazakh. 'I consider myself a Uighur first. Kazakhstan is my home but Xinjiang is my homeland, my spiritual home,' he stated.

Turning it into a separate state was now his mission, or maybe dream. 'I really want an independent East Turkestan. I see a lot of contradictions in China, a capitalist country run by communists. I think the CCP will fall eventually and China will collapse, and Xinjiang and Tibet will secede. I mean, even the Han Chinese don't like the CCP. What we need to do now is look to the West for support,' he said.

I had heard it all before, from every articulate Uighur prepared to talk about such a sensitive topic. Perhaps the doubts in my mind about the reality of Xinjiang ever becoming its own nation showed on my face, because Khozhamberdi paused and smiled at me, looking more like the grandfather he was in private than the politician that is his public persona. 'When I was young, I never thought the USSR would collapse and that Kazakhstan would be an independent, successful country,' he said. 'But it happened. History is like that.'

4

The Great Game Again

Leaving Almaty proved far harder than I had anticipated. A public holiday resulted in Kazakhstan's borders being closed for three days. Instead of moving on, I found myself in Astana Square listening to a concert of Beatles songs being performed in honour of Constitution Day. 'Come Together' was turned into a heavy-metal anthem, while the British ambassador, in what was clearly above and beyond the call of diplomatic duty, did a passable version of 'In My Life', accompanying himself on piano.

I plotted my escape over cold herring and numerous vodkas in the company of Almaty's tiny community of foreign journalists. My plan was to head west to Kyrgyzstan, just a few hours' drive away. From Bishkek, the capital, I would turn south-east and make my way down to the border with Xinjiang. Then I could travel across Xinjiang's Kyrgyz autonomous prefecture to Kashgar, where my China adventure had begun back in 1988.

First, though, I needed a Kyrgyz visa. Again, my timing was bad. I was told it was Kyrgyzstan's turn to be celebrating a national holiday soon, and that the Kyrgyz consulate would be shut for days. But it has a reputation for being hopelessly corrupt, so early one morning I joined the queue outside hoping I could persuade the consul to give me an express visa before the consulate closed down for the holiday.

Three other westerners stood in line. Alicia, Philippa and Sebastian were in their early twenties and on a fifteen-country odyssey around Asia and Africa making a documentary about camel milk. They enthused about its potential to lift nomadic communities out of poverty, and cure everything from anaemia to tuberculosis. 'Camel milk is the new oil,' Alicia said. 'It's only a matter of time before the rest of the world finds out about it and tries to get a piece of the action.'

True or not, and I had my doubts, I was impressed by the way the trio operated. Alicia was American and arty, responsible for the vision of their film and for shooting it. The well-spoken and pretty Philippa hailed from Shrewsbury in England and was the practical one who arranged their schedule, while Sebastian, a gregarious, bearded Swede, had a gift for getting people to talk. Together, their different personalities seemed to fuse, turning them into a formidable and determined three-headed unit.

They travelled in a way that was alien to me, utilising social media for almost all their needs. The budget for their documentary had been raised by crowd-funding, where individuals pledge small amounts of money via the internet. They spurned hotels, couch-surfing their way around the world and using Twitter to find contacts and helpers in each country they arrived in. Facebook and a blog enabled them to provide daily updates to their followers. Compared to their wired journey, I felt like a Victorian traveller setting off into the interior armed only with a pen and paper.

After three hours, I arrived at the front of the queue and came face to face with the Kyrgyz consul, an unhappy-looking middle-aged man. My request for a same-day visa was greeted with a flat *nyet*. It would take him five days to issue an express one. I told him I needed to be in Bishkek the next day. He shrugged. I offered to pay extra to get the visa today. '500 tenge,' was the reply. I handed over the money, about £20, the visa fee and my passport. He slapped a sticker in it which said 'Kyrgyz Republic', scribbled my passport number on it and handed it back.

By lunchtime the next day I was in Bishkek, after another high-speed drive through endless grasslands, where goats and sheep grazed, that ran towards the mountains in the far distance. Along the way, I asked the Kazakh driver if Bishkek was nice. 'No,' he replied. At passport control on the Kazakh side of the frontier, the official paused before stamping me out of the country and asked me if I was sure I wanted to leave.

I was beginning to detect a theme. As we drove into Bishkek's eastern suburbs, bouncing down crumbling roads lined with decaying apartment blocks and swerving past cars dating back to the time of Gorbachev and *glasnost*, I wondered if I was in the right place. 'It doesn't look like the capital, does it?' said the driver. Even in the centre of town, only a few statues and a couple of forlorn squares offer a clue that this is Kyrgyzstan's first city.

Bishkek never managed to dispel my first impressions of it as an extended, unlit sink council estate. It is small and undeveloped, a city of corner shops and kiosks, with far fewer ethnic Russians than Almaty. At night, much of it becomes an open-air pub. Groups of men in the tracksuits which have supplanted traditional nomad garb as the national dress in urban areas gather to swig vodka in parks and squares, or wherever there is space to sit. Anyone unable to afford the £1.50 needed to buy a bottle can slake their thirst with a 10p shot of firewater at a street stall.

Getting drunk is what many people do in Bishkek. But there are different ways of achieving oblivion. So while the poorer locals drink outside, richer residents can imbibe in a handful of bars that charge western prices. They exist primarily to fuel the US Air Force personnel based at Manas, Bishkek's airport. Since 9/11 and the NATO intervention in Afghanistan, Manas has become a gateway for the men and supplies needed to combat radical Islam in the region.

Both Kyrgyzstan's former masters in Moscow, who also maintain military bases in the country, and the Chinese are disturbed by the US presence in Bishkek. The fact that there are significant numbers of American soldiers in two countries bordering China – Afghanistan and Kyrgyzstan – only reinforces the paranoia that is deeply embedded in the CCP's psyche. Ever since the former colonial powers forcibly established mini-colonies in ports like Hong Kong and Shanghai in the nineteenth century, Beijing has been wary of any foreign activity close to its frontiers, seeing it as a potential prelude to another attempt to carve up the Middle Kingdom.

But the 'stans of central Asia have always been a crossroads of conflict, an area where major powers tussle for power and influence. In the nineteenth century, they were one of the battlegrounds for what Kipling called 'The Great Game', the tug of war between the British and Russian empires for control of the region and so of India. The game had reached into Xinjiang, and now history is repeating itself. This time around, it is a three-sided fight, with the combatants being the US, Russia and China. The prizes are the oil, natural gas and minerals the 'stans hold.

Sandwiched between Russia and China, and with Washington offering much-needed cash in return for access to Bishkek's airport, Kyrgyzstan is not much more than a pawn in the battle for central Asia. It is mineral-rich but mountainous, making access to those precious metals difficult. Nor does it have the huge reserves of oil and natural gas that enable Kazakhstan and Uzbekistan to bargain effectively with the new Great Game players.

Kyrgyzstan is also more unstable than its neighbours, principally because relations between the different ethnic groups are far from harmonious. The small Uighur and Hui communities complain of Kyrgyz discrimination against them, as do the ethnic Russians. In the months before I arrived, the country had teetered on the edge of civil war with anti-government protests in Bishkek. There were also violent clashes close to the border with Xinjiang between the Kyrgyz and ethnic Uzbeks, who are the majority in the south of the country.

Militant Muslim groups are rumoured to operate there, including the remnants of the Islamic Movement of Uzbekistan, an organisation which fought alongside the Taliban in Afghanistan and has recruited a few Uighur fighters in the past. That alone is enough reason for China to seal its frontiers with Kyrgyzstan whenever trouble breaks out. When I arrived, the border crossing near Osh, the country's second city and home to most of the ethnic Uzbeks, was still shut following the fighting in the south.

That left only the border post at the Torugart Pass, a sliver of land sitting high in the Tian Shan Mountains. All frontiers in central Asia open and close on the whims of officials who live far from them and who never have to use them. The Torugart Pass crossing is more unpredictable than most. It is officially open for Chinese and Kyrgyz citizens only, unless you have a permit and onward transport on the Xinjiang side of the frontier arranged in advance.

A local travel agency told me they could arrange the papers and a car to get me to Kashgar once I was across the border. But it would take them a few days. Unwilling to stay on in unlovely Bishkek, I arranged for the permit to be delivered to the small town of Naryn, which lies on the route to Xinjiang, where I had been told I could easily arrange a ride to the frontier.

Rural Kyrgyzstan's peaks and alpine lakes are a delight after Bishkek. The road to Naryn twists through the Khrebet Kara Katta Mountains, one of a string of ranges that criss-cross the country. We followed a river that sparkled in the sun, travelling as high as 3,000 metres across lush green hills where men wearing *kalpaks* – the patterned felt hats with high crowns and turned-up brims that are Kyrgyzstan's national headgear – rode horses beside flocks of sheep.

Above them, eagles with wings spread wide floated on the thermals searching for stray lambs to pounce on. In the winter, wolves come down from the mountains to hunt, according to one of the other passengers in my shared taxi. There were yurts scattered across the grassland, as well as antique-looking mobile homes mounted on car tyres, outside which women in headscarves cooked on open fires and dogs lazed.

The road was peppered with gaping holes, but the driver didn't let that slow him down. Instead, we careered across its whole width in the quest for the fastest passage. His car was a typical, beaten-up central Asian taxi: cracked windscreen, non-functioning dials on the dashboard, worn tyres and doors that could be opened only from the outside. Shared taxis have taken the place of public transport in Kyrgyzstan; all the bus terminals I saw were derelict shells of buildings that served only as meeting points to find a ride in a private car.

Naryn is no more than a staging post, an extended village strung along a road at the bottom of a mountain valley. I stayed with one of the many families who rent out rooms in their homes. They lived in a low-rise Soviet-era apartment block with a corrugated-iron roof and walls covered in sickly yellow pebbledash. There were precarious balconies that looked like they were about to fall off and rotten wooden windows, but the bed was surprisingly comfortable and the breakfast of cheese, ham and fresh bread the best I ate in Kyrgyzstan.

From Naryn, I headed further south to Tash Rabat, an old Silk Road caravanserai said to date back to the tenth century. It is more of a fort than an inn: a grey stone edifice partially sunk into the steep hillside of a valley. The gates were chained shut but I clambered on to the roof, still riddled with the holes that allowed the smoke from the fires of the travellers and merchants to escape.

Yurts are the only accommodation option now. As the sun sank, I realised it was going to be an uncomfortable night. Tash Rabat is 3,000 metres high, and it was the beginning of September and already nippy in the early evening. Hazira, who rented me a bed, agreed. 'It's too cold to be sleeping in a yurt,' she said as we sat in her warm mobile home drinking black tea. 'I'll be closing for the winter next week and moving into my house.' She was right; not even the stove fired by cow dung that Hazira lit could keep me warm in the early hours.

Scraping the ice off the car's windscreen, we left at first light, driving past trucks so overloaded with hay it bulged far over their sides, as if the vehicles had been given Afro haircuts. Further on, the road to the border was being rebuilt by Chinese migrant workers. They were small-time players in the new Great Game, filling in potholes in the middle of nowhere, but still part of it. Repairing roads is an easy, cheap way for China to win friends among the locals, while trucks from the motherland will rumble down the refurbished highway with goods to sell.

Their foreman was from Heilongjiang in China's far north-east and was first puzzled then pleased to be hearing a foreigner speaking his language. With the Torugart Pass getting closer, I was increasingly anxious about whether my door back into Xinjiang had been slammed shut because of some event I had no knowledge of. I asked the foreman if the border was open. He nodded and said, '*Mei wenti*' – no problem.

As we climbed higher into the Tian Shan Mountains, the peaks became craggier and some were topped with snow. We ran past a lake of glistening, deep-blue water. The border fence appeared on the right-hand side of the road and soon a line of trucks with Chinese characters emblazoned on them. Kyrgyz passport control was an unheated shed. Then it was a short, steep climb around the final few tight bends up to 3,700 metres and the Torugart Pass itself.

An iron pole lowered across the road separated Kyrgyzstan from China. Smoking and dozing in the car, I waited a couple of hours for my pick-up to arrive from Kashgar. It came in the shape of two smiling Uighurs in a Toyota. The pole was raised and I was back in the Middle Kingdom, descending swiftly into red sandstone hills and Xinjiang's Kizilsu Kyrgyz Autonomous Region.

Only the fact that we had exchanged mountain pasture for a more austere, desert-like landscape gave me a clue I was back in Xinjiang. The villages closest to the border are all Kyrgyz, with the men wearing the same *kalpak* hats I saw in rural Kyrgyzstan. Like the majority of their cousins across the border, few of China's 160,000 ethnic Kyrgyz are still nomads. They have abandoned their yurts for mudbrick houses and life as farmers, although they remain known for their prowess on horseback.

Most are relatively new arrivals in Xinjiang. Some came across the border in 1916, when Russia started calling up Muslims for army service and central Asia rose in revolt against the tsar. Others followed in the wake of the 1917 Russian Revolution. They have not strayed far from their ancestral homeland, and are mainly concentrated in this remote and stark north-western pocket of Xinjiang.

The Uighurs, though, are the most numerous ethnic group in the Kyrgyz territory and, as we dropped lower and reached the fertile plain that surrounds Kashgar, the *kalpak* hats gave way to the familiar *doppa*. The ETIM, the original Uighur separatist group, first emerged in these villages outside Kashgar, after protests over mosque closures in the nearby town of Baren turned violent in April 1990 and were put down by the PLA. That provoked the cycle of repression and resistance that has defined the last twenty-five years in Xinjiang. It was time to see how Kashgar had fared during that grim period.

5

Return to Kashgar

Revisiting the places that captured your heart when you were young is always unwise. You hope they remain trapped in time and that their magic is still potent. But invariably they have changed, just as you have, leaving you questioning your memories and wondering if they are wishful thinking or merely imagined. My return to Kashgar was a disappointment foretold. Trying to tune into the resonance of 1988 was like searching for a signal on an antique radio, and all I got was faint hisses and crackles.

I knew already Kashgar was no longer the isolated oasis it had been when I first visited. The railway arrived in 1999, there are daily flights and even the tortuous bus journey from the east of Xinjiang now takes only thirty hours and not the three days I endured. I was aware, too, that there would be far more Han Chinese than before, and that the city is undergoing the same rapid development happening all over China, which means expanding roads jammed with new cars and a rising skyline.

Yet I was still unprepared for its transformation. On my first morning, I returned to the Chini Bagh, where I had stayed in 1988. Then it had consisted of the same wooden one- and two-storey buildings in flaking green and yellow paint that housed the British consulate in Kashgar from 1890 to 1948. Now a newish hotel covered in off-white tiles stood around a car park. The gates and mudbrick walls that had surrounded the compound were gone, and security guards occupied a kiosk close to where the Pakistani traders once grilled their bowel-loosening kebabs.

Kashgar's consulate was the most remote of Britain's diplomatic outposts in Asia, a three-week ride on horseback from India. The people who passed through included some of the most remarkable figures from the colonial past. The half-Chinese Sir George Macartney, whose same-named ancestor was Britain's first ambassador to China in the eighteenth century, served as consul here between 1890 and 1918. Sir Percy Sykes, who effectively ran Persia during the First World War, relieved Macartney briefly in 1915.

Great Game players, both legendary and unsung, were regular visitors. Francis Younghusband stayed a winter. He went on to lead a British invasion of Tibet in 1903–4, only to experience an epiphany on the roof of the world that transformed him from an empire-builder into a soldier-mystic. In 1918, Colonel F. M. Bailey was at the consulate en route to an extraordinary series of adventures in central Asia. They included helping to propagate the revolt among Muslims which resulted in so many Kyrgyz crossing into Xinjiang after the Russian Revolution.

Bailey was such an effective spy that he was recruited by the Cheka, the forerunner of the KGB, to hunt himself, the British agent who was stirring up the peoples of central Asia against their new communist masters. He was also a noted naturalist, just as Sykes and Eric Shipton, the last British consul in Kashgar, were part-time explorers. In the days of empire, it was possible to serve your country and collect rare butterflies on the Tibetan plateau, conquer unclimbed mountains or cross unmapped deserts.

A traveller in a more modest way, I felt a pleasing sense of solidarity with those men, simply by virtue of having stayed in the same place they had, even if Beijing, rather than London and Moscow, is now the imperial power in this part of the world. But I doubted whether Bailey, who could have stepped out of the pages of a John Buchan thriller, would have approved of how I and many of the other guests at the Chini Bagh spent our nights smoking hash on the balconies of our rooms. He would have been a whisky-and-soda man, although I suspect Younghusband in his later incarnation would not have been averse to a joint to aid his spiritual journey.

While we were sitting stoned under the stars on one of those hot summer evenings, the British among us came up with the idea of a party to celebrate the Chini Bagh's unique history. A Union Jack was found at the bottom of a backpack and draped over the balcony rails and we held open house, drinking beer from the bottle, until there was a knock at the door and the police arrived.

They weren't concerned about the reek of hashish in the still desert air; it was the flag that was the problem. They had heard, probably from our teetotal and less imperially minded Pakistani neighbours, that we were gathering in honour of the Chini Bagh's past. The Union Jack was clear evidence of our separatist tendencies. It took some time to convince them it was a joke, and that we had no intention of reclaiming this little bit of Kashgar for Britain.

Eventually, they left smiling, but only after we had taken down the flag and promised not to display it again. It was an early lesson in how the Chinese authorities regard anything that could remotely be conceived as a threat to Beijing's dominion over its furthest-flung territories as nothing less than treason. Luckily for us, we were foreign tourists and so allowed a little leeway.

If we had been Uighurs gathering to commemorate Kashgar's past status as the de facto capital of the only truly independent state ever established in Xinjiang, then we would have been arrested and quite possibly executed for our splittist activities. That state was created in 1864 by Yakub Beg. An Oliver Cromwell-like figure, Beg took over almost all of what is now Xinjiang through a combination of military cunning and sheer ruthlessness, before imposing strict Islamic law on the region. His country, which he called Dzetyshaar, or 'Seven Cities', died with him in 1877, but not before the British and Russians had paid court to him as its ruler.

With no physical traces left of the Chini Bagh I had known, my uncertain recollections were all I had to remind me of 1988. But when I walked around the back of the hotel, I found that not all of the past had been obliterated. One small part of the consulate was still standing. A sign outside stated the building was a 'Cultural Relic', although that hadn't stopped the hotel converting it into a restaurant. As I peered into the dining areas full of Chinese tourists whose chopsticks were whirring over their dishes, I realised that one of them was my former sleeping quarters.

Stained lino covered the old wooden floors, but the elaborate ceiling cornices were still there, as were the doors leading to a small stretch of the balcony I had spent so much time lounging on all those years before. The view from the terrace then was of the tight little alleys of the old town. I looked out now on to salmon-pink apartment complexes and a bright-red office block with Chinese characters atop its roof. But I was happy just to be standing there, transported back to being twenty-one and footloose.

Discovering that my former digs had survived the wrecking ball infused my return to Kashgar with some much-needed meaning, because almost everything else I remembered had disappeared or was in the process of going. In 1988, the old town covered most of the city centre, an intricate mesh of winding, cobblestoned lanes, some no more than lines of simple mudbrick homes. But other alleys housed elaborate, three-storey structures with terraces and window frames decorated with brightly coloured arabesque patterns, accessed by wooden doors that opened to reveal small courtyards.

Plunging into the old town was both disorientating and invigorating. Barbers and dentists, their profession indicated by signs displaying rows of teeth, *naan* bakeries, blacksmiths, knife makers and carpet weavers, silk shops, restaurants and small mosques were scattered throughout. Donkey carts clattered down the alleys, where the smell of spices mingled with the smoke billowing off the grills outside the restaurants as skewers of lamb were barbecued in their dozens. Mobile butchers wielding wicked-looking knives hacked up the carcasses of sheep to provide the raw material for the kebab men.

Now those shops and houses are vanishing fast and whole streets are like the film-set version of a town – a single row of buildings with vacant land behind them where the alleys have already been levelled. 'I think in three years there'll be nothing left of the old town. It won't exist,' a Uighur who was still clinging on to his small general store told me. 'No one is happy about it but it is the government, so what can you do?'

Its demise began in the wake of the devastating Sichuan earthquake of 2008, an event that allowed the city authorities to claim that Kashgar's oldest buildings were no longer safe to live in. Yet the old town had already survived two millennia, while the schools and apartment blocks thrown up as cheaply as possible in Sichuan Province by corrupt contractors crumbled to the ground when the 2008 quake struck, leaving almost 70,000 people dead.

Most locals believe tearing down the old town is less about making Kashgar safe for its residents and more about wiping out the past – an effective means of emphasising Han control over the Uighurs' spiritual and cultural capital. It is no coincidence perhaps that the 220,000 residents of the old town are being moved to hutch-like flats on Kashgar's outskirts, where it will be much easier to monitor their activities.

Only the great Id Kah Mosque, the largest in all China, is certain to survive the destruction. In every sense it is the heart of Kashgar, the one building that can't be demolished unless the Chinese want to incite a Xinjiang-wide uprising. From first light on, as darkness gives way to an orange-streaked dawn sky, the square in front of it starts to fill up. Old men fingering prayer beads and women covered from head to toe join vendors selling ice cream and prayer mats, kids running around and tourists snapping pictures. People pray at all times, while families promenade before heading to the nearby restaurants for dinner.

During major Muslim festivals, 50,000 people or more pack into the Id Kah and the square. There are so many worshippers that the surrounding roads are blocked when they fall to their knees as the loudspeakers boom out the prayers. It is a peaceful demonstration of how Kashgar remains a Uighur city, even as much of it is being systematically obliterated, a once great Silk Road city being reduced to rubble to fit the CCP's narrative.

Mosques in China are often hybrids of traditional Islamic and Chinese architecture, a concession to the long-held Han distrust of religions from far-off countries. Many appear to be Buddhist temples, until you notice the silver or golden crescents perched on the pagoda roofs. But there is no mistaking the Id Kah's denomination. Sand-coloured, it is partially hidden by trees which make it appear smaller than it is until you venture inside and realise how far back it extends. There is a classic simplicity to its lines, with perfectly proportioned minarets at the corners flanking the arched entrance and walls neither too high nor too low.

The Id Kah dates back to the mid-fifteenth century, although other mosques occupied the same site for hundreds of years before. Having survived numerous conflicts over the last five centuries, it stands now in defiance of the changes around it, like one of those forts in an old western movie surrounded by hostile Indians. The latest challenge is a row of recently built, Chinese-owned department stores across the road. They incorporate a faux-Islamic styling, yet they stand taller than the minarets of the Id Kah.

Their presence allows for a symbolic stand-off – grandiose new shrines to the Han religion of commerce opposite the Uighurs' ancient place of worship. I was confident the Id Kah would still be there the next time I came to Kashgar, while the department stores would go the way of most modern Chinese architecture and age rapidly and disastrously, before being pulled down and replaced.

So much of old Kashgar has gone that I was at a loss to know what to do with myself. But I hung around anyway, reluctant to move on after investing so much in my return. I spent a lot of time with Lin Lin, a thirtysomething woman from Beijing who was staying at my hotel while scouting locations for a TV show. Rather more sensitive to Uighur culture than most Chinese, she took care to wear a head-scarf and it was only when you saw her delicate features and pale skin close up, or heard her melodious Mandarin, that you realised she was Han.

Lin Lin liked to cultivate an air of mystery. She had an enticing, cat-like, self-contained nature. A keen shopper, she dragged me to the various markets around Kashgar in search of pashminas, silk and jewellery. The only place she didn't buy anything was the Sunday market. In 1988, it had been a frantic clash of peoples and tongues. Now Uighurs and ethnic Kyrgyz and Tajiks still bargain over camels and sheep and goats tied tightly together, but they do so confined inside a much smaller, rigidly demarcated area. I preferred the chaos of before.

At night, we ate in the Uighur places near the Id Kah, leisurely meals of lamb skewers, *naan*, *laghman* noodles and the black Xinjiang beer. She would appear uninterested when we returned to the hotel, saying 'Good night' and disappearing to her room, only to call later and ask me to come over. I didn't mind being summoned. Lin Lin was travelling on TV company money and her room was much more comfortable than mine. It had two double beds and after we'd slept together, I was always sent to the spare one with a warning not to make any noise. Cats are light sleepers.

6

Three Borders

When Lin Lin returned to Beijing, I had no excuse to stay in Kashgar. I decided to make my way south along the Karakoram Highway to Tashkurgan, close to the borders with Tajikistan, Afghanistan and Pakistan. It was another exercise in nostalgia; I'd travelled the same route when I departed China in 1988. But Tashkurgan's proximity to three frontiers was too tempting to pass up, so I caught an early-morning bus and said a bleary-eyed, not very fond, farewell to Kashgar as we edged through the traffic towards its southern suburbs. I knew I wouldn't miss the city it has become.

Outside Kashgar, the bus ran in between fields of wheat and corn and past fruit farms where watermelons grew in rows and pear and peach trees stood in neat lines. An hour past the small town of Upal and we were on the Karakoram Highway proper, climbing through a valley of towering stone cliffs stretching for mile after mile, along with army trucks, construction vehicles and tour-group jeeps.

There was a police checkpoint at Ghez I didn't remember from before, and we all trooped off the bus to have our identity cards or passports scrutinised and our names recorded. A fellow passenger told me all Uighurs now need a permit to travel beyond Ghez, unless they live in the Tashkurgan area. They are being kept away from the restive Muslims across the nearby frontiers.

Past Ghez, giant sand dunes rose, and then the magnificent Karakul Lake, ringed by snow-capped peaks and green pasture with yaks and yurts reminiscent of Kyrgyzstan, appeared. The two highest mountains in China outside of Tibet, Kongur Tagh and Mutzagh Ata, look down on the still, glacial lake from above 7,500 metres. So clear is the water that it reflects the surrounding landscape like a giant mirror.

Unlike Kashgar, Tashkurgan had not changed much. It is still an overgrown truck stop, with a large PLA base on its outskirts, despite being the capital of Xinjiang's Tajik Autonomous County. Ethnic Tajiks make up the majority of the population, along with Uighurs, a small community of civilian Han and the odd Pakistani trader. Soaring, menacing mountains surround the town. Tashkurgan, a collection of grimy, hastily constructed buildings, seems fragile and temporary in their presence, as if it could be blown away by the strong winds that drone down the few streets at night.

At 3,600 metres, it is cold even in September. People were already buying winter fuel at a depot where women with blackened faces wielded sledgehammers to smash up boulder-sized lumps of coal, before shovelling it into sacks. Every other shop sold the thick green PLA overcoats that are the winter uniform of farmers and migrant workers in the parts of China where the mercury plunges. In another month, Tashkurgan would become a place to hibernate in until spring arrived.

Tajikistan's easternmost province, Gorno-Badakhshan, is just sixty-five kilometres away by rough road, close enough for China to have contested the borderline until 2002. Travel to it is not encouraged by Beijing. The frontier is closed to foreigners and only a couple of buses a month run there. Eastern Tajikistan is almost as lawless a place as Afghanistan, which borders the south of Gorno-Badakhshan. It is home to its own band of Islamic groups fighting for a separate state, while the heroin ferried out of Afghanistan north to Russia and Europe passes through the region as well.

Despite their radical relatives across the border, there is none of the tension between Tajiks and Han that characterises the Chinese–Uighur relationship. Nor, unusually, are the Tajiks resented by the Uighurs. With just 41,000 people in Xinjiang, they are too small a presence for the Uighurs to feel challenged. They have assimilated a little too. Among themselves the Tajiks speak Sarikoli, a Persian-based dialect, but most can also understand Uighur.

They are easy to spot with their sharp, Caucasian-like features and lighter hair, eyes and skin than most Uighurs, although everyone in Tashkurgan has the wind-burned face and red-spotted cheeks that come with living at altitude. The women wear black pillbox hats, with elaborate pink or red patterns around the sides and a veil pinned back to reveal their faces, along with black skirts over long leggings. Ismaili Muslims, they owe their allegiance to the Aga Khan, like their cousins in Gorno-Badakhshan, the Afghans in the Wakhan Corridor to the south and the people of Pakistan's Hunza Valley.

While crossing into Tajikistan is difficult, it is impossible to travel from China into the Wakhan Corridor and Badakhshan Province in the far north-east of Afghanistan. The border was closed after the communist takeover in 1949 and has remained shut. Just seventy-five kilometres long, it is the shortest of China's frontiers and the most remote. Like a crooked finger pointing east, the Corridor is sandwiched between both mountain ranges and countries. To the north are the Pamirs and Tajikistan, in the south the Hindu Kush Mountains separate it from Pakistan, while at its eastern end the 4,900-metre Wakhjir Pass leads into China.

Long ago, the Wakhan Corridor was part of the southern Silk Road route that connected the Middle Kingdom to India. Marco Polo is said to have entered China via the Corridor, if he came at all. For 2,000 years, the mule trains braved the snow and ice as they struggled over the high, desolate mountain passes on their way to Tashkurgan. From there, they headed east to Yarkand, where camels replaced the mules, to begin the long pull across the southern fringes of the Taklamakan Desert towards Gansu Province and Jiayuguan. Then it was a short journey south to Xi'an, the ancient capital of China and the beginning and end of the Silk Road.

With Afghanistan and Tajikistan all but closed, Tashkurgan is now a transit point for people travelling to and from Pakistan. South of town, the Karakoram Highway leads up to the 4,700-metre Khunjerab Pass and the highest paved road border crossing in the world. I travelled that way in 1988, hitching rides on trucks and tractors to Karakul Lake and on to Tashkurgan before catching a bus to Sost in the Hunza Valley.

Back then I managed to cross the frontier without a Pakistani visa. The Chinese guards didn't bother to check if I had one and once in Sost, a five-hour drive from the actual border, I apologised profusely to the Pakistani officials for flouting the rules so flagrantly. Over a leisurely cup of tea, they agreed finally to give me ten days to get to Islamabad where I could rectify my mistake.

Security is much less lackadaisical now. Before I could even leave Tashkurgan, I had to stop at the army base and buy a permit just to get me to the Khunjerab Pass. I was with Lao Yu, a Han migrant from Sichuan Province eager for extra cash. He quoted an outrageous price to drive me to the border and back, but accepted half with good grace and we set off towards the end of China in the far west.

Apart from a few Pakistani and Chinese trucks moving slowly up towards the frontier, we had the road to ourselves. On our right, the dull grey, jagged peaks of the Pamir Mountains rose above the snow-laden clouds and separated us from Tajikistan, a natural barrier far more formidable than any border fence. Tiny settlements of box-like houses, grazing yaks and sheep and the odd Tajik farmer trotting slowly along on a horse were the only signs of life.

An hour beyond Tashkurgan, we came to the largest village we would pass through. Lao Yu pointed to the mountains on our right. 'Afghanistan is over there,' he said. Until very recently, the border and the Wakhjir Pass were accessible only by a dirt track and the soldiers posted there patrolled on horseback. When winter closed in, they could not be relieved till the following spring.

So isolated is the frontier that, even when it was open, just a handful of westerners journeyed across it. Francis Younghusband went through on Great Game business after his stay in Kashgar. An 1873 agreement resulted in the British and Russians designating the Wakhan Corridor as the dividing line between their empires. Both sides monitored the Corridor to make sure there were no unauthorised incursions.

The last westerner known to have crossed the border was the Briton H. W. Tilman. A much decorated soldier in both world wars, Tilman was born too late for the Great Game but was still a character out of a *Boy's Own* annual. A noted mountain climber, often in the company of Eric Shipton, the last of Britain's Kashgar consuls, he was the sort of man who shinned up 7,000-metre peaks in a Norfolk jacket and a pair of stout walking boots. In 1947, after a failed attempt on Mutzagh Ata, Tilman travelled alone into the Wakhan Corridor via the Wakhjir Pass in search of the source of the Oxus River.

Reading about Tilman's exploits had induced romantic visions of me following in his footsteps, ghosting up the track disguised as a local and slipping past the PLA guards to reach the frontier. I knew that wasn't actually possible, but I still wanted to see how far I could travel along the track, or at least get close enough to know where it began. Lao Yu, though, wouldn't even consider it.

'I'll be in trouble and so will you. The army are building a new road to the border and there are checkpoints and cameras now,' he said. I pondered the irony of the fact that the Chinese–Afghan frontier has been all but ignored by Beijing since 1949, yet I'd arrived just at the time when they had decided to take an interest in it. That sudden surge in activity has been prompted by the presence of NATO soldiers in Badakhshan Province. The new road will enable the Chinese side of the border to be reinforced speedily, and in strength, should they decide to march east to Xinjiang.

Gazing at the seemingly impenetrable crags which shielded the new road from view was the closest I got to Afghanistan. We carried on towards the mountains in front of us, which mark the beginning of the Karakoram Range. Somewhere over 4,000 metres, we reached the snowline and my ears started to pop. From then on, Lao Yu negotiated a series of switchback curves as we ascended the last few hundred metres to the Khunjerab Pass.

Another checkpoint and then we were at the frontier. A double line of barbed wire rose above the snow lying knee-deep on either side of the road, and there was a giant arch which hadn't been there in 1988. On the far side of it were two Chinese, one PLA officer and a Wujing soldier, and a bearded Pakistani in mirrored sunglasses and camouflage. I strolled up and asked if I was in Pakistan now. They nodded in assent.

We shared cigarettes and I fielded the inevitable questions about where I was from and what I was doing. The officer told me the soldiers did one month at the pass and then one back in Tashkurgan, even when the border closed for winter. He was the chattiest PLA man I have ever encountered, at least while on duty, and spoke good English. 'I have to – that's how we communicate with the Pakistanis,' he said. But I didn't envy him his posting. It was frigid, even in the midday sun, and I was shivering in three layers of summer clothes.

On the way back, Lao Yu gave me the benefit of his thoughts on the Uighurs. Five years of working in Tashkurgan had enriched his pocket, while leaving him severely prejudiced against the natives. He had no problem with the ethnic Tajiks. 'They're fine, they don't cause trouble.' Instead, it was the Uighurs he disliked. For Lao Yu, they were *jiade*, or fake, Chinese people. I thought most Uighurs would agree with that, except they would qualify it by saying they were also unwilling Chinese citizens.

Lao Yu was just getting started. *Meiyou wenhua* was the phrase he repeated over and over again in connection with the Uighurs. It literally translates as 'having no education', but has a wider meaning implying that the person, or people, lacks civilisation and culture. 'They think they can be like the Kuomintang and have their own state like Taiwan, that's how stupid the Uighurs are,' he said with a nasty sneer.

'You know why they're so stupid? You know the person we call an uncle? For a Uighur, that's their elder brother not their uncle. They all marry their brothers, sisters and cousins and that's why they are so stupid.' I didn't know how to respond. During my time in China, I'd listened to many Han complaints about the Uighurs. How they are lazy, prone to petty crime, unwilling or unable to learn Mandarin, ate too much lamb and are overly religious. But Lao Yu's theory that the Uighurs are incestuous was new to me.

In the evening I played pool with Majid, a Uighur art student from Kashgar who was in Tashkurgan to sketch the Pamirs, and wondered if I should broach the subject with him. I decided against it. Majid was sparky and inquisitive and didn't look or sound inbred to me. We were in one of Tashkurgan's pool halls, essentially a shop holding a few tables with rock-hard cushions and patched baize. In all small towns in rural Xinjiang, as in many other parts of country China, pool is the only entertainment option outside of drinking beer in a restaurant.

I have lost at pool all across China. Once, I shot a few frames in Beijing with a giggly sixteen-year-old farmer's daughter from Henan Province who had just been crowned the World Nine-Ball Pool Champion. She was barely taller than her cue, but thrashed me off the table. Majid wasn't in her league, but he still beat me while a crowd of young Tajik and Uighur lads looked on smiling and offering advice.

Majid wanted to be an art teacher, preferably abroad. 'I'd like to go to London,' he said with a cheeky grin. I told him he should try. 'It's hard enough to get a permit to come here. It's almost impossible to get a passport,' replied Majid. He was right. Most Uighurs under the age of fifty have as much chance of obtaining a passport as they do of winning one of China's lotteries. Old people with relatives overseas can travel, but a twenty-three-year-old like Majid would need both connections at home and a powerful sponsor in his destination country to leave.

He spoke English, which is perhaps why he felt he could be outspoken despite the audience watching us play. I didn't have to ask leading questions to get Majid to talk about the situation in his homeland. 'Most Uighurs want independence, but Xinjiang has too much oil and gas for the Chinese to let that happen. It's cruel, because if we were independent then all our resources would enable us to develop very quickly. We could sell them and use the money to raise our living standards. But there's no hope of that. Uighurs have tried to be independent many times and it has never worked,' he said.

Neighbouring countries like Kazakhstan are resource-rich too, but also extremely corrupt, so that little money trickles down from the government to the people. Majid brushed that fact aside, as easily as he pocketed balls. 'Maybe, but we'd still rather be like them,' he said. 'You know why Uighurs are jealous of the ethnic Kazakhs and the Kyrgyz and even the Tajiks? It's because if they have a problem here, they can always go to Kazakhstan, Kyrgyzstan or Tajikistan. We don't have that option. If there was a Uighurstan, none of us would be here.'

7

Uighurstan

Talking to Majid reinforced how frustrating it must be not to have a homeland, while living alongside people with their own countries next door. It had been easier for the Uighurs before 1991 and the break-up of the USSR, when central Asia was still subsumed within the Soviet empire. Now, there are five 'stans, three of which border Xinjiang, and they are a permanent reminder to the Uighurs of what they lack the most.

The closest thing to a Uighurstan lies in the far south of Xinjiang, where the former oases of the southern Silk Road are strung along the edge of the Taklamakan in a long slow curve. Those towns are the Uighur heartland, the places with the fewest Chinese migrants. Exploring them would be my long goodbye to Xinjiang, as I travelled back towards Han China along a route dating back thousands of years.

I spent a disappointing time in Yarkand, searching vainly for an echo of the trade terminus it once was. Most of the city's historic buildings were knocked down in the 1960s and 1970s during the Cultural Revolution, with even the so-called old town no more than a cluster of rebuilt alleys. Only the Altun Mosque, a smaller version of the Id Kah in Kashgar, and the mausoleums of Yarkand royalty survived the Red Guards' fury. They sat in a square, overlooked by restaurants and carpet shops.

Yarkand was important not just as a Silk Road stop, but because it is where Xinjiang starts to bleed into India and Tibet. Until 1949, when the Chinese closed the border with India which lies some 300 kilometres south of Yarkand, caravans of Buddhist traders from Leh in Ladakh were regular visitors, along with Hindu merchants. Now much of what was formerly north-east Ladakh is a disputed no man's land, occupied by China but claimed by India as part of its territory.

Known as Aksai Chin, it is a region where high-altitude desert, saltwater lakes and untouched peaks combine in a landscape that could be a science-fiction writer's dream of a far-off planet. Barely inhabited, save for PLA soldiers, and barred to foreigners, Aksai Chin can be reached only via Highway 219, which snakes south from Xinjiang for almost 2,100 kilometres, across passes as high as 5,400 metres, before it reaches Lhatse in Tibet.

The construction of 219 caused a war. The Chinese started building a road linking Xinjiang with Tibet in the early 1950s. Only after it had been completed in 1957 did New Delhi discover it passed through Aksai Chin, which India regards as belonging to its state of Jammu and Kashmir. The tensions that arose out of 219 running through contested territory played a major part in setting off the 1962 Sino-Indian War.

Soon after leaving Yarkand, I passed the turn-off for 219. My road south to Hotan was not nearly as rugged as that highway, but all around me was the unnerving country that makes up southern Xinjiang. The few villages here are merely tolerated by the desert, which in turn is watched over by brutal, elemental rock formations. Through the dust-caked right-hand window of the bus, the Kunlun Mountains, which form a natural barrier between Xinjiang and Tibet, were barely visible in the far distance. But the Taklamakan was everywhere, a vast sand sea stretching away towards each compass point.

A stiff wind picked up grains of sand, lifting them over the new railway line, linking Kashgar to Hotan, which runs alongside the highway, and blowing them across the road in steady waves. Skinny poplar trees, ubiquitous to every oasis in southern Xinjiang, rose ahead at infrequent intervals to indicate we were approaching a small settlement, the only relief from the harshness of the land surrounding us until the outskirts of Hotan appeared.

Hotan will never be the spiritual home of the Uighurs; that honour is Kashgar's alone. There is no equivalent of the Id Kah Mosque, or of Kashgar's vanishing old town. Yet Hotan has a far better claim to be the capital of Xinjiang than either Kashgar or Urumqi, because its population is still overwhelmingly Uighur. The railway's arrival will inevitably change that, but for now the Han remain a tiny minority. Their smooth pale faces are an anomaly in a city where men flout the CCP's 'no beards' policy and many women shield their faces from view.

Far fewer people understood Mandarin in Hotan than anywhere else I'd been in Xinjiang. It made getting around difficult, as not only did the taxi drivers fail to understand what I was saying, but they couldn't read an address either. Most ignored or didn't know the Chinese names given to the streets anyway. They navigated around the city via landmarks like the Juma Mosque and the nearby main market, which spilled out of its allocated space in the north-east of town on to the surrounding streets.

Every inch of the pavements around the bazaar was occupied by someone selling something. Piles of vegetables and fruit, clothes hurled on to carts which the women customers stood three deep in front of as they rooted through them, and everywhere mobile food stalls. There were giant vats of *polo*, baby chickens turning slowly brown in primitive rotisseries, kebabs and lamb on the bone, as well as the sticky walnut cake beloved by the sweet-toothed Uighurs.

If food determines a city's status, then Hotan is the heart of Uighurstan, the undisputed culinary capital of Xinjiang. Much of what is on the menu is unique to the south, like the *gosh kurdah*, a big pastry filled with lamb and potato reminiscent of a Cornish pasty. Best of all are the rough hunks of lamb cooked slowly on a hook in a *tonur*, so the flesh comes apart with a gentle pull of the fingers. Served with a fresh *naan* embedded with thin strips of red onion, they combine to create a delicious and unexpected local version of a roast-lamb sandwich.

On Sundays, the residents of Hotan and the surrounding area gravitate to the market as if they are being summoned to the mosque. Early in the morning, the roads leading to it are a mêlée of motor-bikes carrying whole families, donkey carts and the three-wheeled electric vehicles with rug-covered benches in the back that serve as buses in the outlying villages. By the afternoon, such is the press of people packed tightly together in the bazaar's alleys that moving in any direction becomes a struggle.

What is on offer gives a clue to Uighur life in southern Xinjiang. Tools, used washing machines and spare parts for carts and bikes mingle with butchers' stalls where sheep dangle from hooks. Luxury items like silk and gold jewellery are sold from hole-in-the-wall shops. Medicine men stand on the back of their carts, armed with a microphone, extolling the virtues of herbal cures and ageing pharma-ceutical products.

There are none of the tour groups, either Chinese or western, which have turned the Sunday market in Kashgar into a mere attrac-tion. Instead, the white skullcaps worn by devout Muslims bobbed along in front of me as I inched through the crowds. They were more numerous than the *doppa*, a hat which indicates Uighur identity rather than faith in Islam. Most of the women were covered up in both the bright colours I'd seen elsewhere in Xinjiang and the more fundamentalist all-black. When the call to prayer wailed out from the nearby Juma Mosque, everyone dropped to their knees and turned west towards Mecca.

Unlike deracinated Kashgar, daily life in Hotan recalled the Xinjiang I experienced in 1988. The Han have only a toehold here, and I was elated by that after seeing the Uighurs shunted to the fringes of their traditional capital. I strolled around town with a smile on my face, stroking my moustache like a pantomime villain and gorging myself on street food at every opportunity.

Of course, I was dreaming. The new railway line alone is evidence of Beijing's vision of a Hotan that will be far less Uighur-dominated. One afternoon, I was snapped out of my reverie as I returned from a trip to the country. On the eastern outskirts of Hotan, close to the Jade Dragon River, my taxi became snarled up in a chaotic traffic jam. Cars were pointing in opposite directions on the same side of the road and backed up all the way to the other side of the river.

Ahead, police prevented anyone moving. We sat immobile for an hour until the first of a convoy of more than fifty PLA vehicles appeared. The soldiers wore steel helmets and stared out at us from the back of the trucks with expressionless faces. Their officers gestured and shouted at anyone who came too close. We were being held up to let them pass, and the Uighurs waited in silence as what looked more like an occupying force than the people's army went by.

I realised then that Hotan isn't just the unofficial capital of Uighurstan; it is the current front line in Beijing's battle to subjugate all Xinjiang. Not long after my visit, eighteen people died when the police station close to the bazaar was stormed by a group of Uighurs armed with petrol bombs and knives. They tore down the Chinese flag and raised a black one with a red crescent on it, before being killed or taken prisoner.

Uighurs said the attack was prompted by the city government trying to stop women from wearing all-black robes and especially veils, an ongoing campaign by the Chinese across all Xinjiang. They claimed, too, that men were being forced to shave their beards. The Xinjiang government said the assault was an act of terrorism and that the attackers had called for a jihad. But no evidence was produced to demonstrate any tangible link between Uighur nationalists and the militant Islamic groups in Afghanistan, Pakistan and central Asia.

Beijing, though, reveals little substantive information about the separatist groups it claims are operating in Xinjiang. Over the years, their names have mutated – the East Turkestan Islamic Organisation, the East Turkestan Islamic Movement, the Turkestan Islamic Party – as if their very existence is in question. Every so often, the Chinese media run a report saying a remote training camp has been overrun, or weapons confiscated. But no proof is ever offered of those raids, no captured rifles displayed.

Undoubtedly, there are Uighurs fighting for independence with bombs and guns and some have received guerrilla training in Pakistan or Uzbekistan. Yet their numbers are tiny. Nor have the restrictions imposed by the CCP on the Uighurs' practice of their faith spurred a rush to embrace radical Islam. Many are now more determined to demonstrate their loyalty to their religion. But growing a beard or wearing a veil is hardly akin to the extremist beliefs which provide Al-Qaeda and other Islamic terrorist groups with their motivation.

Going in search of the source of the Uighurs' religious identity took me further into the desert than I'd ever been before. After Hotan, there are no more cities. From here on, southern Xinjiang is a collection of tiny towns clinging to the edge of the Taklamakan and populated overwhelmingly by Uighur farmers. Niya was the first of them, a dusty one-camel settlement whose inhabitants are so sleepy not even the presence of a foreigner arouses much excitement.

Ninety kilometres north of Niya is Mazar Iman Jafar Sadiq, the holiest shrine in all Xinjiang, the Mecca of East Turkestan. Isolated out in the desert, far from the corrupting power of civilisation, it was a Buddhist pilgrimage site long before the Uighurs converted to Islam. Like Glastonbury in Britain, it straddles the ley lines and transmits a mystical charge, one that transcends mere religions.

No buses travel there so I asked Mahmut, a local Uighur, to drive me. Just outside town, we ran into a checkpoint. I was told I needed police permission to visit the shrine. We reversed down the road and Mahmut made a couple of calls. 'You can pay 300 yuan for the police permit, or give me an extra fifty and I'll go round the checkpoint,' he said. I chose to line Mahmut's pocket rather than those of the local authorities.

Jolting down a dirt track brought us into a field running parallel with the road we had been turned back from. After crawling through giant ruts of mud, Mahmut spun the steering wheel left and we regained the road with the checkpoint out of sight behind us. For the next few kilometres, we both kept checking the mirror to see if our unauthorised manoeuvre had been spotted.

Not far on, we joined the Tarim Desert Highway, which runs through the middle of the Taklamakan, linking the north of Xinjiang with the south. It was built in 1995, to ease access to the oil that lies beneath the sand all around here, as well as to enable the PLA to move swiftly south in the event of a Uighur uprising. A smooth two-lane road, it is flanked by reeds and scrub bushes, planted in an effort to stop the desert encroaching. Beyond them, sand dunes rose up in the distance till they seemed to touch the few clouds floating in the blue sky.

The Taklamakan has been described as the worst desert on earth, home just to the ruins of a few scattered cities that were once the capitals of long-forgotten mini-states populated by the Uighurs' forebears. They crumbled back into the sand when the rivers which flowed into the region started to retreat towards their sources in the Kunlun Mountains. Even here, on a modern highway still close to Niya, there were no people or animals to break the monotony of the endless dunes.

Only a few oases exist in the desert proper and we arrived in one of them soon after turning off the highway. Kapakaskan is a farming village surrounded by irrigation channels, its mudbrick houses dotted along a poplar-lined road that leads to Mazar Imam Jafar Sadiq. A makeshift barrier blocked our way and we went in search of the shrine's gatekeeper. He was a fiftysomething farmer with a *doppa* on his head, short and unshaven and slow in his movements and speech.

'You can't go, the police don't want foreigners here,' he said. I pleaded I had travelled all the way from Hotan just to see the Mazar.

Mahmut confirmed that and there was a brief, muttered conversation in Uighur I didn't understand. Finally, the gatekeeper relented and wrote down my passport number and accepted the entrance fee. 'Don't take any pictures,' he told me.

Cars, minibuses and even a coach were parked in front of the entrance to the shrine. 'People come from as far away as Urumqi to pray here,' said Mahmut. A green gate in a tall arch of sand-coloured bricks, with minarets on either side, led into a courtyard, where there were *tonur* ovens and kebab grills. Blankets were stacked for the pilgrims who stay overnight. One side of the courtyard was taken over by a small mosque.

A few hundred metres away in the open desert is the shrine itself. The footprints of previous pilgrims pointed the way along a path adorned with sticks thrust into the ground and crude little arches made out of tree branches, all decorated with scrappy bits of cloth. Offerings unique to Xinjiang's Muslims, they date to the time when the Uighurs' ancestors migrated here as animists, in thrall to shamans and the natural world rather than Buddha or Mohammed.

Climbing up the hill which the shrine sits atop, I passed worshippers on their knees chanting prayers with their hands held in front of them. In the distance, wave after wave of the largest sand dunes I had ever seen rippled north towards the horizon. They appeared grey, almost muddy, and far more sinister than the photogenic ones I saw on the way from Niya.

Despite the dramatic approach, the shrine itself is unremarkable – a simple and small white-stone mausoleum opposite a makeshift tent that acts as a prayer hall. White, green and blue flags surrounded the tomb, snapping back and forth in the strong wind while people waited their turn to pray. The presence of so many pilgrims is the only tangible indication of the supreme spiritual hold the shrine has over the Uighurs.

Who is interred here is unknown. The actual Imam Jafar al-Sadiq was a Muslim saint, descended from the Prophet himself, and is buried in Medina. His name was most likely appropriated around the eleventh century, as the Uighurs who had converted to Islam fought those who stayed loyal to Buddhism. Aurel Stein, the Hungarian-British archaeologist who pillaged his way across northwest China in the early part of the twentieth century, speculated that the tomb honours the remains of Muslim leaders from Hotan and near by who were martyred in the battles.

An old man in a white robe with a long, straggly beard approached me as he left the prayer tent, his wife, son, daughter-in-law and grandson in tow behind him. He placed his right hand on his heart, greeted me with '*Salaam Aleikum*' and asked me if I was from Pakistan. I shook my head and said I was '*Angliyelik*', Uighur for English. He was from Hotan and had been to the shrine before. 'It is the first time for my grandson,' he said, smiling.

Their seven-hour journey to pray together puts the CCP's efforts to separate the Uighurs from their religion in profound context. Just as the Taklamakan has resisted all efforts to tame it, so the Uighurs' devotion to Islam remains unchanged. Matched against the antiquity of the shrine, the CCP's restrictions appear entirely futile, the equivalent of the spindly reeds that line the Tarim Desert Highway trying to hold back the sand.

But even here, there was an example of Han insensitivity towards people of faith. On my way back, I looked into the prayer hall of the mosque in the courtyard. As I did so, a group of Chinese arrived. There were two men, a woman and two young girls. One of the men produced a camcorder and started filming the girls as they skipped across the patterned red rugs in their trainers. A watching Uighur clicked his teeth in disapproval. Their parents probably didn't even know to tell their children to take their shoes off inside a mosque.

Chance encounters while travelling sometimes have an impact out of all proportion to their apparent significance. My meeting with Ma Zhilin was innocuous enough, but we were fated to spend the next few days together on an ill-starred journey. By the time we parted, I never wanted to see him again. But I couldn't have guessed that when he came up to me at Niya's bus station after hearing me enquire about a ticket to Cherchen, the next town on the trail back to inland China.

'I'm going to Cherchen too. There are no more buses today but we can get a shared car. There are two other people who want to go as well,' he said. Ma was small and wiry with a homemade haircut and a wind-beaten face relieved by bright, curious eyes. In his old army jacket, stained blue sweater and trousers that swung around his ankles, he could have been any one of the hundreds of millions of country Chinese who toil with their hands for a living. He was returning to his village outside Golmud in neighbouring Qinghai Province, the final stop on my journey, after working at a gold mine in the mountains near Hotan.

Ma is a common surname among the Hui people and he was Hui, although he didn't go out of his way to advertise his Muslim faith and was always keen to differentiate himself from the Uighurs. The most notable thing about him was the deep, dirty cut running between the thumb and forefinger of his right hand. Extremely angry and obviously painful – Ma cradled his crocked hand whenever he could – it needed antibiotics and stitches. But when I suggested he get medical help, he just said, '*Mei wenti*,' no problem.

Sitting shoulder to shoulder with him in the cramped car taking us to Cherchen, I had no inkling Ma was a jinx. He was over-solicitous, in the way Chinese people not used to the company of foreigners can be, forever pressing on me the expensive, for China, cigarettes he smoked and suggesting we share a room when we got to Cherchen. But I was accustomed to that and he knew the route over the Altun Mountains to Golmud well, so I thought it would do no harm to have a companion.

Like Niya, Cherchen was another speck of a town surrounded by the desert that was growing more tedious by the day. The late-afternoon sun had retreated behind high clouds when we arrived and a gusty wind was lifting the sand on the streets into the air, shrouding the shoddy buildings in a nasty brown haze. Cherchen is a place only to pass through, infamous for its long association with China's prison system. During the Qing dynasty, it was the site of a penal colony where opponents of Manchu rule were banished. Now Cherchen is home to a *laogai*, one of the forced-labour camps that house those who have offended the CCP.

It lies on the outskirts of town, its watchtowers and wire fence shielded from view by tall poplars. There are over a thousand similar labour camps in China, holding almost seven million prisoners, and they function as farms, factories and mines. Most of the inmates are now ordinary criminals. In Xinjiang, though, some are Uighurs convicted of political crimes, as well as dissidents from other parts of China. The prisoners do twelve hours of manual work a day, subsisting on a mostly meatless diet of watery soup and rancid vegetables.

Xinjiang's *laogai* are run by the Xinjiang Production and Construction Corps (XPCC). Better known in China as the *bingtuan*, the XPCC is one of the most secretive organisations in the country. It was established in 1954, when soldiers from the defeated nationalist armies, demobilised PLA troops and workers willing to go west in return for better salaries were recruited to form a paramilitary reserve to the PLA that was also designed to take control of Xinjiang's economy.

Based in Shihezi, a small city close to Urumqi, the XPCC is in effect a parallel regional government, running whole towns and industries, including the lucrative tomato and cotton farms scattered across rural Xinjiang. The *bingtuan* has its own university, newspaper and TV station and currently accounts for around 10 per cent of Xinjiang's GDP. An unknown amount of that comes from the sweat of *laogai* labour.

We went through a *bingtuan* settlement an hour outside of Charklik, the last town of any size on the southern Silk Road. Miran was previously known as the 36 Regiment Farm, and began its existence as a *laogai*. For the Han sent there either as prisoners or guards in the 1950s, it must have been like landing on the moon. Miran sits in the largest county in China: 200,000 square kilometres of windswept nothingness, where the Lop Desert meets the Tarim basin and the Taklamakan. So vast and under-populated is the area, the Chinese tested their nuclear weapons here until 1996.

Miran's residents seemed to be all Han, living in neat little houses surrounded by the cotton fields which justify the town's existence. The presence of so many Chinese in the middle of nowhere was a sure sign I was in *bingtuan* territory. Just 6 per cent of the 2.5 million employees of the XPCC are Uighurs, while the 700,000 seasonal workers it hires annually to pick cotton are mostly recruited from outside Xinjiang.

Charklik had been a lunch stop. Ma and I arrived in the early afternoon, after a miserable night in Cherchen. I had planned to sleep in Charklik, leaving early the next morning to ensure I crossed the Altun Mountains and reached Huatugou, the first town in Qinghai Province, the same day. But Ma was keen to keep moving. He dug me out of a restaurant and hustled me back to the bus station, where a minibus was slowly filling with passengers.

'The driver says we'll be able to get a ride to Huatugou tonight no problem,' said Ma. That wasn't a surprise. The more people the driver carried, the more money he made and he didn't care if we ended up stranded. Ma was insistent, though. 'We can be in Golmud tomorrow,' he said. I was running short of cash and there are no ATMs between Hotan and Golmud, so against my better judgment I climbed in.

After leaving Charklik, the camel caravans following the southern Silk Road travelled across the desert for almost a thousand kilometres, skirting the Altun range, until they arrived in Gansu Province and the start of the Hexi Corridor. Now a road over the mountains into Qinghai is the quickest way back to Han China. It passes through some of the loneliest country I have ever seen. From Miran on, there is nothing save a wasteland of sand and rocks to the left and deserted peaks on the right.

Pushing on at a steady speed, we entered a narrow canyon with a sheer drop on the left-hand side down to a dried-up river bed. Then we started the ascent proper, looping upwards until we reached a plateau surrounded by the spectacular, snow-dusted summits of unnamed, unclimbed mountains. At almost 4,000 metres high, with the desert far below us, we shut the windows to keep out the chill and sat swathed in cigarette smoke.

Our journey's end, Shimiankuang, appeared as a vision of hell amid a starkly beautiful mountain wilderness on the border between Xinjiang and Qinghai. Shimiankuang means 'asbestos mine' and that is what it is, an open-cast pit around which a grim village has sprouted like the weeds which pop out of contaminated water. Its inhabitants walked the rutted dirt streets swaddled in padded jackets and trousers to keep out the vicious wind, bent forward like old men to make better headway.

All wore surgical-style cloth masks over their mouths and noses, in a vain effort to keep out the asbestos dust that was surely and slowly shutting down their lungs. The shops were windows in the crude brick boxes that passed for homes, through which could be glimpsed cigarettes, bottles of beer and instant noodle packets. There was a police station, the only building of any quality, and a mobile-phone mast, while patriotic music from the 1980s blasted out from antique loudspeakers mounted on poles.

Before I had even retrieved my pack from the minibus's roof rack, a car pulled up and four of my fellow travellers jumped into it. Only as it drove off did I realise it was the promised transport to Huatugou. 'You'll have to stay the night,' said the minibus driver with a broad smile. He pointed out a shack which offered beds. 'There's a bus in the morning,' he said as he strode away.

For once, Ma was lost for words. It was past seven in the evening and we were stuck in a mountain village where invisible and deadly dust danced on the wind and the temperature was dipping remorselessly towards zero. Hope came in the shape of one of our fellow passengers, a young Han geologist from Chengdu in Sichuan Province, returning home via Golmud after two years of prospecting for minerals in Xinjiang.

'A classmate of mine from college is working in Huatugou,' he said. 'He's coming to pick me up. He'll give you a lift.' We settled down to wait, huddling out of the freezing wind behind the wall of the police station. After an hour during which it got dark and progressively colder and there was no sign of the classmate, a car stopped and offered to take us to Huatugou for 50 yuan each. Ma said it was too expensive. The geologist insisted his friend was on his way. So I stayed with them.

Eventually, the classmate arrived with another chum in a pick-up truck. There were smiles and handshakes all round, and I thought I still had a chance of a late dinner in Huatugou. But the road was bad and after twenty-five kilometres of pitching in and out of deep potholes, the driver turned off it in an effort to avoid what he said was a particularly rough stretch. It was a terrible decision. Apart from the light of a waning full moon and the truck's headlights, we were running blind across mud made dangerously soggy by the streams gushing down from the mountains.

Riding our luck for twenty minutes, crawling along at walking speed, we were close to regaining the road when the truck lurched violently to the right and stopped moving. Its front and rear right wheels were sunk so deep in soft, sticky mud they had almost disappeared. For the next two hours, we dug the wheels out with a shovel that was in the back of the pick-up. We collected stones to give them something to grip on, while the driver revved the engine madly in an attempt to get us moving. We tried to manhandle the truck out. Finally, we jacked it up to see if that would lift the wheels out of the cloying mud. Nothing worked.

Midnight approached with everyone sitting in the truck trying to stay warm. The geologists and the driver carried on talking about ways to extricate us, as if the last couple of hours hadn't made it obvious we were going nowhere until another vehicle hauled us clear. Ma and I looked at each other and, for the only time in our travels together, I agreed wholeheartedly with what I could read in his eyes. Without saying a word we slipped out of the truck, grabbed our bags and made for the road.

Guli was our saviour, a Uighur housewife in a headscarf driving a red hatchback. She went past as we reached the road and I shouted at her to stop, although the words came out of my mouth as a high-pitched scream. Amazingly, she pulled up. We sprinted to the car and explained our situation. I offered 100 yuan, and she agreed to turn around and drive us to Huatugou. My last sight of the geologists was of them illuminated by the truck's headlights, still trying to excavate the wheels as if they were digging deep for minerals.

Huatugou was a village until oil was discovered beneath its mountain mud. Now, it is a scruffy, fast-growing town. As we approached, the winking lights of the derricks pumping away around the clock looked like stars which had descended from the night sky. Then we turned on to the main street and ran headlong into a swirling gale that flung debris at the windscreen. When Guli dropped us off, we were enveloped by huge clouds of dust coming from the partially constructed buildings all around.

Most of the hotels refused to take foreigners. While Ma disappeared quickly to a bed in a dormitory by the bus station, I walked the unlit, empty streets for what seemed like for ever before finding a place that condescended to admit a westerner. Lying on the bed at three in the morning in a room with no hot water and too tired and cold to take off my clothes, I cursed myself for not ignoring Ma and staying the night in Charklik.

Yet I couldn't really blame him. Like so many ordinary Chinese I'd met, the future wasn't something he planned for: things just happened, good or bad, whether you liked them or not. Mostly, they were bad. You lost your job, your salary was cut or you were injured working like Ma had been. Maybe the local government and a property developer conspired to take the land your family had lived on for generations in return for a pittance. China is a cruel and unpredictable country, so it is understandable why most of its people concentrate on the immediate – the next meal, the next bus ride – and leave the rest to fate.

Five hours later, I was at the bus station. Ma was waiting for me. 'The tickets for the morning bus to Golmud are sold out, but I've found someone who'll take us in a car,' he said. I decided it was time to end our brief acquaintance, and turned around and walked out. My ride to Golmud was uneventful, and I know for sure that if Ma had been with me we'd have broken down or had a puncture or been delayed somehow. Ma was a Jonah, and proof that it is nearly always better to travel alone.

Part II

TIBET – THE WILD WEST

We can see that for Chinese with respect to barbarians, to slaughter them is not an unbenevolent act, to deceive them is not untrustworthy and to steal their land and wealth is not unrighteous.

Wang Fuzhi, seventeenth-century Han philosopher

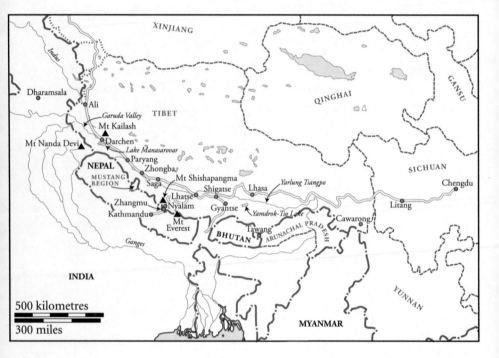

XINJIANG

Dharamsala

Ali

Garuda Valley
Mt Kailash
Darchen

TIBET

QINGHAI

GANSU

Mt Nanda Devi

NEPAL
MUSTANG
REGION

Lake Manasarovar
Paryang
Zhongba
Saga

Mt Shishapangma

SICHUAN

Chengdu

Zhangmu
Kathmandu

Lhatse
Nyalam
Mt
Everest

Shigatse

Gyantse

Lhasa

Yarlung Tsangpo

Yamdrok-Tso Lake

Litang

Cawarong

Tawang

BHUTAN ARUNACHAL PRADESH

Ganges

INDIA

YUNNAN

500 kilometres

300 miles

MYANMAR

8

The Tibetan Borderlands

Samphel's home was a temple of Tibetan resistance to Chinese rule. The two-room house was squeezed between other similar dwellings in an unpaved alley in the lee of Litang's monastery. One room was given over to prayers, the other served as the living room, kitchen and bedroom for Samphel, his mother and two brothers when they were around. Outside, a satellite dish rusted slowly in the tiny yard.

I perched on a low stool opposite his mum, a smiling, fat woman with cropped hair who constantly spun the prayer wheel she clutched in her left hand. Samphel sat next to me, tall and broad-shouldered in his crimson monk's robes. A TV tuned to Radio Free Asia's Tibetan channel murmured softly in the background. On the far wall, pictures of the Dalai Lama and the former Panchen Lama, the second most senior monk in Tibet, hung side by side.

Almost all Tibetans refuse to recognise the current Panchen Lama, who was selected by the CCP after it rejected the Dalai Lama's choice of a six-year-old boy as the Panchen's next reincarnation. Three days after the Dalai Lama named him in May 1995, he was taken away by the Chinese authorities and hasn't been seen since. 'He is under arrest,' said Samphel, bringing his two wrists together to indicate someone handcuffed. His replacement lives in Beijing and makes occasional, stage-managed visits to Tibet during which he invariably praises the religious freedom enjoyed by Tibetans under the CCP's benevolent reign.

In Litang, there is little sign of such tolerance. 'We have to hide the pictures and our satellite dish when the police come to check the houses,' Samphel told me. 'They do the same up at the monastery.' Earlier that day, I had been astounded to see a near-life-size photo of the Dalai Lama in the prayer hall of Litang's monastery. It was propped up next to the empty throne all Tibetan monasteries maintain in case he should ever return from exile in Dharamsala in northern India.

Just possessing a picture of the Dalai Lama can lead to arrest for any Tibetan. If the monastery was found to be displaying one, then the senior lamas would likely disappear and the other 600 monks consigned to yet more of the re-education classes the CCP requires them to attend on a regular basis. Listening to Radio Free Asia for the latest news of the Dalai Lama's activities, or the statements of the Tibetan government-in-exile, is a punishable offence too. But many of Litang's policemen are Tibetans, and I suspected the monastery received advance warning when they were about to make their rounds.

'Do you eat *tsampa*?' asked Samphel. He offered me a paper cup half full of the barley flour which is the staple dish of Tibetans. He poured in some yak-butter tea – yaks rather than cows provide many Tibetans with meat and milk – and I used a chopstick to churn it into the sticky, porridge-like paste it needs to become before it can be consumed. We ate it with *gori*, doughy Tibetan flatbread, drinking hot water to wash it down. A diet of *tsampa* alone swiftly becomes tedious. But the last time I had eaten it was in a restaurant in Beijing, where Tibetan dancers circled the tables of the mostly foreign and Han diners. It tasted better in Litang.

As we ate, Samphel told me about his life. He was nineteen and a student monk. 'I want to teach Tibetan history and language at the monastery,' he said. In a mix of fractured English and passable Mandarin, he told me how happy he was to speak with a foreigner. 'I envy your lifestyle and the fact you can talk in your mother tongue with freedom.' Like all people in China his age, Samphel had attended a Mandarin-speaking school, but Tibetan was his first language. He asked if I had met the Dalai Lama or been to Dharamsala. 'One of my brothers lives there,' he said. Samphel's siblings were monks too.

He dug out a prized photo taken in Barkhor Square, the heart of the Tibetan capital Lhasa. In jeans and a T-shirt and with a broad grin on his face, Samphel looked like any carefree teenager on holiday rather than the serious monk sitting next to me. I wondered why he was in mufti, rather than his robes. 'The Chinese don't like monks going to Tibet. I had to go dressed in normal clothes,' he explained.

That trip was the only time Samphel had visited Tibet as China defines it. Officially, his hometown of Litang is in the far west of Sichuan Province. The actual border with Tibet is another 160 kilometres away across the grasslands and mountains that encircle the town. But this is still the Tibetan Plateau, the roof of the world, which stretches for almost 2.5 million square kilometres in all directions, and Litang is over 4,000 metres high. I had come from much lower Chengdu, Sichuan's capital, and the sudden jump in altitude had left me with a headache and gasping in the thin air.

To the Tibetan government-in-exile in Dharamsala and its numerous supporters overseas, Tibet extends far beyond its present-day frontiers, pushing into the neighbouring provinces of Qinghai and Gansu to the north-east, Sichuan in the east and Yunnan in the southeast. Their version of Tibet dates back to a 1914 interpretation of the borders, and is almost double the size of the land Beijing currently recognises. It includes the areas in the neighbouring provinces, like Litang, which are historically part of Amdo and Kham, pronounced 'Cham', two of the four regions Tibet is divided into.

Those borderlands are designated Tibetan Autonomous Prefectures, as opposed to Tibet itself, which is classified as an Autonomous Region like Xinjiang. The prefectures are overwhelmingly populated by Tibetans. So many live in them, around three million, they outnumber the 2.7 million Tibetans who reside inside Tibet. Another 150,000 or so are in exile, mostly in India and Nepal.

Tibetans in the borderlands regard themselves as still living within Tibet – the Dalai Lama was born in an area of Qinghai that is traditionally part of Amdo – even if both Kham and Amdo functioned as semi-independent states largely outside of Lhasa's control in the time before Beijing ran Tibet. They ignore the fact that their country's frontiers have fluctuated, just as the fortunes of the Tibetans have, and many still identify themselves by the region they come from. 'The Chinese say we are Sichuan people. But we are Khampa,' stressed Samphel, his voice rising as he used the Tibetan word for those from Kham.

His vehemence didn't surprise me. Litang has long been associated with a particularly militant form of Tibetan nationalism. As well as being the hometown of the seventh and tenth Dalai Lamas – the present one is the fourteenth – Litang was the site of a fierce battle in 1956. The Khampa had risen up against the Chinese who had marched into Lhasa five years earlier and ended Tibet's brief period of de facto independence. Litang's monastery was besieged for a month, before the PLA resorted to bombing it from the air. The revolt went on to become a Tibet-wide uprising. It ended in defeat three years later, resulting in the Dalai Lama escaping into exile.

Exactly how many Tibetans were killed during the 1956–9 rebellion is unknown. Exile groups in Dharamsala put the number at around 85,000, based on what they say are captured Chinese documents. Many historians dispute that figure, but there is little doubt that tens of thousands died and that thousands more were subsequently imprisoned in the harshest of conditions. For a country with such a small population, Tibet paid a very high price for its refusal to bow to Beijing.

Litang remains a place the CCP is deeply suspicious of. Since March 2008, when protests against the Chinese erupted in Lhasa, prompting demonstrations elsewhere across greater Tibet, it has been periodically barred to visitors. Many other parts of western Sichuan are permanently closed. Tibetans in the autonomous prefectures suffer the double indignity of being under Chinese sway and not considered to be living in Tibet itself – reasons for many to resist Beijing's rule.

Foreigners had been banned from Litang until a few days before I arrived, because monks from all over Tibet and the borderlands were gathered at the monastery for debates. Samphel had returned for them; he was temporarily studying at another monastery. He thought 3,000 had come to Litang, enough to spark fears among the authorities that disgruntled lamas might publicly express their dissatisfaction with China's occupation of Tibet.

Litang's annual horse-racing festival had been cancelled again as well. The week of races and horse-trading is the social highlight of the year for the locals, but has taken place only once since 2008 and then just for a single day. Even if they aren't waving pictures of the Dalai Lama, the nomads from across Kham who descend on Litang for the festival have a habit of fighting over the race results.

Many nomads had travelled to Litang anyway and their tents were pitched outside town on the grassland. Grazing yaks stood as unofficial sentries, while wild-looking horses whinnied and mean mastiffs barked ferociously at the approach of a stranger, straining at the ropes and chains that tethered them. I learned quickly that it is best to announce your arrival at a nomad settlement by yelling from afar '*Tashi Delek*', the Tibetan for 'Hello', so that the nomads can keep any loose dogs under control.

They looked nothing like any Tibetans I had encountered before. The long-haired men were haughty and appeared almost piratical, with gold teeth glinting out of their brown faces and knives tucked into the belts or sashes that held in place their *chuba*, the thick woollen cloak worn by rural Tibetans at all times of the year. Every so often, they swung themselves easily up on to the horses and galloped them around bareback. Their women had pony-tailed hair dangling almost to their waists, and were bundled up in so many layers their bodies seemed shapeless.

Herding yaks and horses and moving across the grasslands in groups a few families strong, camping in set places depending on the time of year, the nomads are romantic figures but have a distinct edge to them. It is easy to see why they make the Chinese wary. Even now, they are still *shengfan*, or uncooked in the old Han classification of barbarians – people who have resisted all efforts to tame them. At night, when they roared into Litang on motorbikes decorated with Buddhist symbols, the long red tassels on their handlebars flying in the wind, police cars shadowed them.

Outside its few towns, Kham has always been a wild west. Before 1951 and the Chinese occupation of Tibet, it was a place where every man carried a gun or a sword and outlaws flourished by robbing both passing travellers and the locals. Many of those high-plateau highwaymen were people fleeing the bonded labour that all Tibetans – apart from the aristocratic landlords, officials and monks – spent part of each year performing in lieu of tax.

Old Tibet was a feudal society, one where most people lived in desperate poverty. In 2009, as part of the CCP's efforts to remind Tibetans of what their lives had been like before 1951, a new public holiday was introduced, the ponderously titled 'Serf Liberation Day'. Yet few of the former 'slaves' appear keen to celebrate it. By harking back to those times, the Chinese are just reinforcing the idea that Tibetans have always been subjugated by someone, while reminding them that Beijing is the new landlord.

Nothing about the nomads camped outside Litang suggested they were ever serfs, even if they remain poor by any standards. The knives in their belts are testament to the reputation the Khampa have among their fellow Tibetans for being especially unruly. It was the nomads of Kham who played a major part in the war of 1956–9. They launched brave, foolhardy and ultimately hopeless attacks on horseback armed with swords, antique rifles and amulets around their necks which they believed would deflect the PLA's machine-gun bullets.

China still uses its superior technology to subdue Tibet and the autonomous prefectures. With 90 per cent of its 50,000 residents Tibetan, Litang is a town under permanent surveillance. CCTV cameras monitor every street, while a large contingent of Wujing are based conveniently close to the monastery. For Samphel and many others, the police searches of homes, and the need to hide any evidence of loyalty to the Dalai Lama, have become part of daily life.

It was a highly frustrating existence for Samphel, who struggled to contain his anger at the imposition of Beijing's rules in the local schools and the monastery. Deeply cynical about the Han, he railed against the way the excruciating, pitted road that runs from Chengdu into Tibet was being turned into a smooth highway. 'The Chinese say they are putting money into the area,' said Samphel, 'but the new road is only being built so Chinese companies can get here more easily to do their mining.'

My irritation with how China's laws were affecting my movements was minor compared to the strictures Samphel faced, but the restrictions were still vexing. Litang was almost the end of the road for me in western Sichuan. I could travel on to the next town of Batang, a mere fifty kilometres from Tibet, but not beyond it because solo foreigners cannot cross Tibet's land borders legally. It is another legacy of the 2008 protests. Just as parts of the borderlands are closed, so now almost all travel inside Tibet by westerners is in groups who arrive by air or train in Lhasa, armed with a folder full of permits that need to be negotiated in advance.

Before 1949, such constraints were unknown. The Tibetan government did not encourage visitors, often banning them outright, but those who wanted to get into Tibet could do so if they were hardy enough to cross the mountains that guarded it from the outside world. Colonel F. M. Bailey entered from Sikkim in India in 1913, five years before his sojourn in Xinjiang, to explore the Yarlung Tsangpo Gorge and procure botanical specimens. He called the book that recounted his adventures *No Passport to Tibet*.

Some intrepid travellers do still try to get in on their own. Occasionally they succeed in visiting certain areas without getting caught, which would entail a fifteen-day prison term, a fine, a return at their own expense to inland China and sometimes deportation. It was difficult but I knew it was possible. I had done it myself, after paying a Han truck driver for a lift into south-eastern Tibet from the far north of Yunnan Province.

We set off early in the morning from the Nujiang Valley, a remote, little-visited region scrunched up against the borders with Myanmar and Tibet. The road was dire, the worst I had travelled in China – a stone and dirt track along which the truck pitched and yawed like a boat riding a heavy swell. There was a vertigo-inducing sheer drop down to the Nujiang River on one side, and I gave up counting how often the truck's wheels spun perilously close to the edge. It took four hours to travel the forty kilometres to the border between Yunnan and Tibet.

The frontier was marked by a dilapidated yellow sign proclaiming, 'Forbid Foreigner Turn into Strictlg' in English and 'Strictly Forbidden for Foreigners to Enter' in Chinese. A few kilometres on, Han workers were tunnelling through the hills, building a new road to tie this part of Tibet closer to the motherland. The truck driver wanted to leave me with them; he was scared of what would happen if we encountered a police or Wujing patrol. Arms are sometimes smuggled across the border from Myanmar, destined for both Yunnan and Tibet, and trucks are routinely searched.

Refusing to get out, I accompanied the driver to a village where he was delivering building supplies. Glimpsed from the road, it looked idyllic compared to many of its Chinese counterparts. Golden barley fields that swayed with the wind and ran flush to the fast-flowing, steel-grey waters of the Nujiang surrounded substantial white-stone, flat-roofed houses with carefully painted, multi-coloured window frames. Overlooking them on a hill above the road, Buddhist prayer flags ringed a makeshift shrine and announced Tibet's fundamental difference from Han China.

Up close, it was less appealing. There was no running water, just a well, and the only lights ran off car batteries. Most of the village turned out to unload the truck, with both men and women slinging the heavy sacks of cement and sand on to their backs and staggering down the steep path that led to their houses. They gazed at me with curiosity and smiled when they discovered where I was from, although few spoke Chinese. But everyone was dirty, their clothes stained and tattered, and they lived off what they grew and their animals. In the winter, when the road became impassable, they were completely cut off.

There was no point in me venturing on from the village. Further up the road was Cawarong, the first settlement of any size in south-eastern Tibet, a former stop on the Tea-Horse Road which once connected Yunnan to Tibet and India. Tea from the plantations in Xishuangbanna in the south of Yunnan travelled north, while prized Tibetan war horses went south, along with missionaries, monks and traders. During the Second World War, parts of the Tea-Horse Road became supply lines for the foreign and Chinese soldiers fighting the Japanese.

Only the odd truck travels the route now. But there is a Wujing base outside Cawarong and checkpoints before then which I would never get through. I was already ducking out of sight whenever I heard a vehicle engine, in case it was the police. After a few hours in the village, I climbed back into the truck and returned, even more slowly in the dying light, to where I had started that morning. I thought of how Heinrich Harrer, the Austrian climber, SS man and unofficial tutor to the Dalai Lama, spent seven years in Tibet. I had managed just one day.

What I wanted to do was travel from Lhasa to the far west of Tibet and Mount Kailash – the seat of gods and their attendants, the holiest mountain in the world for a billion Hindus and Buddhists. Travelling there would take me along 219, the road that connects Xinjiang and Tibet, while running close to the borders with India, Nepal and

Bhutan. Sneaking across the frontier was not going to allow me to accomplish that journey. Travelling in Tibet officially, which meant with a guide, was my only realistic option.

But I was hampered by my journalist's visa, a black spot handed down by Beijing. Tibet is the one part of China where foreign reporters cannot travel, except on trips run by the CCP's propaganda department. The Chinese claim it is for our safety, as if we will be suborned by the natives when they see our notebooks and cameras. As long as my visa scarred my passport, revealing my occupation every time I checked into a hotel, I would never be given the permits to travel in Tibet.

A trump card appeared in the shape of another passport I possessed, one which the Chinese knew nothing about. It offered no clue that I was a China-based journalist, so I took a trip to a Chinese embassy in a neighbouring country and used it to apply for a standard tourist visa. Trusting that the details of my existence in Beijing would be filed away in the netherworld of Chinese cyberspace, I reasoned there was no way, nor any reason, to cross-check a routine visa application with the list of foreign reporters resident in China. I was right. Now it was time for Tibet.

9

Lhasa

The midday flight from Chengdu to Lhasa was delayed, allowing time for contemplation. Other departure gates signalled their less glamorous destinations in red neon dots. I was smug in the knowledge that I was heading somewhere far more exotic. But although my passport and permits had been examined, I was not leaving China, not officially anyway, and I was travelling by air. I felt none of the exhilaration, the spurious sense of achievement, implicit in the crossing of a land border: walking out of a country, the slow march across stateless territory, an abrupt change of language, the dull thud of a new entry stamp.

Tenzin was waiting for me when I emerged from baggage claim. Slim and nervous, short wavy black hair showing flecks of dandruff, he offered a shy smile, hung a *katag*, the white scarf traditionally given by lay people to lamas, around my neck and said, 'Welcome to Tibet.' Moving towards the exit, we sized each other up with swift sideways glances. We would be together for a month – a lifetime in the wrong company.

As my appointed guide, Tenzin was required to accompany me to official tourist sites, such as monasteries and museums, when we travelled between towns, and on the Kora, the three-day pilgrim circuit around Mount Kailash that would be the climax of my trip. The rest of the time, in theory anyway, I could roam alone. Tenzin was Tibetan, and I hoped he would be relaxed about the solo wanderings I had planned. If he was officious or suspicious, he could make it difficult for me to slip away.

Little of the journey into Lhasa has stayed with me: a blurry image of barley fields beyond the car window. Just being here was befuddling. I had skirted the edges of the Tibetan Plateau, but Tibet itself was still an unknown – my first substantial journey into a region that takes up one-quarter of China's landmass. And I couldn't concentrate, not with such a massive sky over me. At 3,650 metres above sea level, Lhasa is actually lower than Litang. But Litang is notorious for its miserable weather and was covered in murky, grey cloud during my stay. Here the sky was a brilliant blue, stretching for ever and rendering everything below it puny in comparison.

Countryside gave way to the outskirts of Lhasa, rousing me from my dream daze. We passed the monolithic train station, opened with much fanfare in 2006, which connects Tibet to Qinghai and the rest of China. It is a source of great pride to the Chinese, who crow about how they laid the highest railway line in the world across the permafrost of the Tibetan Plateau. The locals are more circumspect about the achievement, because the trains bring not only tourists but increasing numbers of Han migrants.

We entered Lhasa at the western, Chinese end of town. Brighter and cleaner than many inland cities, it looked like a place eager to expand, with empty lots of land beckoning to be built on interspersed between the new office and apartment blocks. We drove down Beijing Road, past Han scurrying on their errands, shops and restaurants with Chinese characters dominant over the spidery script the Tibetan language uses. But then, like a hologram of ancient Tibet imposed on a new city, there was the Potala Palace on a small hill above the road, its white and red colours magnificent against the cloudless sky.

Dirty white Tibetan houses, no taller than three or four storeys and separated by tempting narrow streets and alleys, began to appear. Now there were far more Tibetans, some in their traditional garb but most in the same western clothes worn by the Chinese. We negotiated the first Wujing checkpoints and I realised we were in the old town, the Tibetan district of Lhasa.

My hotel was squirreled away in an alley close to the Muslim quarter, home to a small community of Hui, whose forebears began arriving in Tibet in the seventeenth century. Not bothering to unpack, I rushed out to experience Lhasa after being denied the chance for so long. I joined monks, urban Tibetans in jeans and trainers, nomads in long boots and *chubas*, Han and foreign tourists, all moving towards Barkhor Square, the centre of the city.

Within five minutes I ran headlong into crowds of pilgrims travelling in the opposite direction. Oblivious to everyone around them, they spun prayer wheels or fingered beads while chanting incomprehensible incantations. Overwhelmingly country Tibetans, their faces brown and leathery, most were wrapped up in *chubas*, but some men wore the utilitarian blue jackets and trousers ubiquitous across rural China until recently. Many of the women wore the brightly coloured, horizontally striped aprons called *bangden* over long black skirts.

This was the Barkhor Kora, the pilgrim path that runs around the Jokhang Temple, Tibet's most sacred shrine. I was going against the flow; believers circle clockwise and are meant to complete 100 such circuits. The old far outnumbered the young and I marvelled at their energy as they tapped along the uneven streets with walking sticks, gripping over-sized prayer wheels they looked too frail to hold. The most devout prostrated themselves as they went: crawling along the street, with leather aprons, knee pads and wooden blocks on their hands as protection, rising every few feet as part of their prayers, before repeating the process over and over again.

Intermittently, the crowds parted a little and a six-man squad of Wujing moved through. Since the 2008 protests, the Tibetan old town is patrolled twenty-four hours a day by soldiers in helmets and camouflage uniforms, armed with AK47 rifles, shotguns and riot batons. Late at night, they were often the only people walking the streets. Most were teenagers and they appeared more nervous than menacing. But their weapons were real enough, and the Tibetans took care never to acknowledge them, avoiding all eye contact.

Pilgrims, tourists, locals, police and army were massed in Barkhor Square. The crowds were most dense at its southern end, outside the 1,300-year-old Jokhang or the 'House of the Buddha'. It was built on the orders of King Songtsen Gampo, Tibet's most revered monarch and the man who converted the country to Buddhism. Every morning, pilgrims line up five or six deep to prostrate themselves in the dust in front of the surprisingly small Jokhang. Almost as many tourists surround the worshippers, who ignore them as if they are Wujing, but armed with cameras rather than guns.

When the Jokhang was constructed in the mid-seventh century, Tibet enjoyed a prestige it has never managed to regain. Early Tibetan history details a warrior people who functioned less as a nation than as a series of distinct clans. When they did unite, the chainmail-clad Tibetans on their famed chargers were so fearsome they vanquished the armies sent from China to probe their borders.

By the time King Songtsen Gampo was on the throne, Tibet's frontiers stretched east almost as far as the old Chinese capital of Xi'an, as well as extending west, north and south into present-day India, Nepal, Pakistan and Xinjiang. Songsten's status was such that he was able to demand a bride from Emperor Taizhong in Beijing. The emperor sent his niece, Princess Wencheng. Han historians use their wedding as part proof of what they claim is China's longstanding dominion over Tibet, even though the match was tribute paid by Beijing to its powerful neighbour.

Princess Wencheng's arrival did not create or cement a relationship between the Chinese and the Tibetans. On the contrary, the Han had barely any influence or control in Tibet for the next ten centuries. Instead, as the country split into warring states and its borders receded, Lhasa fell under the patronage of the Mongol empire. From the time of Kublai Khan, in the thirteenth century, Tibetan monks were the spiritual advisers to a succession of Mongol emperors. In 1578, one of them, Altan Khan, bestowed the title of 'Dalai', the

Mongolian for 'ocean', on his senior lama, itself a corruption of the Tibetan word *blama*, meaning 'teacher'.

Not till the eighteenth century and the high point of the imperial-minded Qing dynasty did China have a real presence in Tibet. It was still a token one, based on a resident senior official known as the *amban* and a small garrison of soldiers. Beijing, though, had no say in internal affairs – Tibet was a protectorate at best – and Lhasa was a precarious posting; three of the *amban* were assassinated.

After the collapse of the Qing dynasty in 1912 hurled China into chaos, Tibet enjoyed virtual independence until 1950. Crucially, though, no country ever recognised it as a sovereign state. But even when the PLA reached Lhasa in October 1951, the Chinese were at first interested only in controlling Tibet's foreign policy and forging an alliance with the ruling class. Then came the Khampa revolt of 1956, and all pretence of sharing power disappeared. In March 1959, the Dalai Lama left the Potala Palace for the last time and fled over the Himalayas to India.

Wandering through the Potala early one morning, I found it impossible to imagine it as a functioning building, the principal residence of the Dalai Lama and the seat of what passed for the Tibetan government. It was like visiting the Forbidden City in Beijing and trying to summon up the ghosts of the emperors, mandarins, eunuchs and concubines who had conspired in its myriad rooms.

Half disused shrine and half mausoleum, the Potala looms over Lhasa like a phantom from the past: a memorial to Tibet's long-gone glory days. Made up of two separate palaces, known as the white and the red, it is a wooden warren of rickety staircases, tiny rooms with little natural light, a succession of temples and the gold-laden, incredibly ornate tombs of the last nine Dalai Lamas.

Non-resident monks mooch around, as do a number of cats, their presence perhaps required to add some verisimilitude. The living quarters of the current Dalai Lama have been preserved and are on display but there is no picture of him, no mention of his time staying there. He has been expunged from the Potala's history, as all opponents of the CCP are wiped from the official record or ignored, creating a dissonance that only amplifies the building's lifeless feel.

Despair permeates the white-stone walls of Sera Monastery too. One of the big three monasteries of the Gelugpa, or yellow hat, school of Tibetan Buddhism, whose leader is the Dalai Lama, it is stranded on the far northern edge of Lhasa, its 600 monks outnumbered by the tourists who visit daily. They pay a high admission fee to stroll the monastery's paths, while the lamas lurk at the fringes of the complex, marginalised both by the power of the yuan and by the ever-increasing constraints placed upon them.

Until the 1960s, when well over 10 per cent of Tibet's male population were monks, Sera was home to 6,000 monks. Monastic life has always offered Tibetans the chance of a free education in their own language, especially now that all schools in Tibet and the borderlands teach in Mandarin. And like educational establishments everywhere in China, schools in Tibet are not free, which prevents many poor rural locals from attending them.

As a parallel, Tibet-centric school system, the monasteries are not just the messengers of Tibetan Buddhism but highly fertile breeding grounds for dissent. During the 1980s, they emerged as the main centres of resistance to Chinese rule. In October 1987, monks from Sera helped initiate a series of protests in Lhasa that carried on sporadically until March 1989, when the biggest anti-Chinese demonstrations since 1959 ended with Beijing imposing martial law across Tibet.

Trying to curtail the monasteries' power and influence occupies much of the CCP's time. They were a prime target of the Red Guards, Mao's shock troops during the Cultural Revolution. Monasteries were wrecked and monks in dunce hats were paraded through Lhasa's streets – all part of Mao's attempt to reinvigorate China with the revolutionary spirit he felt it had lost, and a typically spiteful way of reasserting his authority.

Lasting from 1966 to 1976, the Cultural Revolution turned China inside out. Every element of traditional Chinese life came under ferocious attack. Children and students were encouraged to attack their parents and teachers, the education and legal systems collapsed and millions were purged, imprisoned and tortured, or 'sent down' to the countryside to work in the fields.

More than anything, the Cultural Revolution gave ordinary people a licence to settle scores, through the simple tactic of denouncing their neighbours as class enemies. In terms of loss of life, it didn't come close to matching the disastrous effects of the Great Leap Forward of the late 1950s. That resulted in between thirty and forty-five million people starving to death in another of Mao's utterly futile and destructive schemes. But the Cultural Revolution was far worse in the way it turned the Chinese on each other, creating huge fault lines in society and morality that remain today.

That inversion of the normal resulted in some Tibetans becoming Red Guards. For them, the sacking of the monasteries was revenge for the inequities of feudal Tibet. With senior monks coming from the aristocracy, the monasteries were seen as part of the system of taxation by bonded labour that left the vast majority of Tibetans living in poverty. It is an uncomfortable fact for pro-Tibet campaigners in the West that the Dalai Lama, like all his predecessors, comes from one of those noble families whose privileged life in old Tibet set them apart from most of their compatriots.

But the Cultural Revolution proved to be a temporary madness, one that soon gave way to the typical Tibetan reverence for monks. Thus Beijing continues to try and curb the monasteries' reach, barring people from joining the monkhood until they are eighteen and requiring them to get permission from their local governments before doing so. Those rules are often flouted, especially in the borderlands. In Litang, Samphel told me he was fifteen when he became a novice.

A police station next to the entrance to Sera is evidence of the authorities' continuing distrust of its residents, and the other 120,000 monks scattered throughout Tibet and the autonomous prefectures. 'It's for the monks' protection,' said Tenzin unconvincingly, when I asked why it was there. After just a few days together, I felt bad about embarrassing him with awkward questions. Sometimes he would respond with only a shrug and a smile, his way of expressing his helplessness at not being able to speak frankly.

I was wary, too, of appearing overly eager to probe the realities of Tibetan life. Tenzin wasn't the distrustful type, but he was already wondering why I spoke better Mandarin than he did. That is not difficult; many Tibetans speak little or no Chinese. I, though, was supposed to be an ordinary tourist and few of them converse in Mandarin. I explained it away by saying I had been an English teacher in Beijing for a couple of years after university.

Sera still bears the scars of the Cultural Revolution in the form of its distressed, crumbling buildings, despite the claim of the local authorities that part of the steep ticket price is going towards its restoration. With its different faculties, including one for the study of Buddhism and one for philosophy, prayer halls and the houses where the monks live dotted around a large area, it resembles a university campus or English boarding school in its layout.

Yet the monasteries' role as educators is less important than it was, despite China's expensive and patchy school system. They remain an option for those who want to study in Tibetan, but the curriculum is a limited one and not very relevant for those eager to make their way in the outside world. Some of the monks' daily rituals too, such as the afternoon debates, appear to be disconnected from their original purposes.

Resembling a challenge between warriors more than a conventional academic argument, the debates are supposed to test a young monk's knowledge of the Buddhist scriptures. One monk sits cross-legged on the ground, while another fires questions at him with a slap of the right hand on the left. A wrong answer is greeted with the outside of the right hand being laid on the left palm. At Sera, it is a performance rather than an exam, the novices leaping high in the air, slapping their hands together like the crack of a whip, playing to the crowd like good showmen.

Reducing an age-old practice to a mere spectacle is part of a wider and ongoing dimunition of the monks' role as the arbiters, the moral authority, of Tibetan society that Beijing's policies are encouraging. The monasteries are treated now as separate entities by the authorities, as opposed to the interconnected network they once were. And with many *tulku*, the most senior lamas, in exile, so that the different schools of Buddhism are now led remotely, monks are no longer as central to Tibetan life as they once were.

The tourists watching the afternoon debates at Sera seemed unconcerned with Tibet's slow slide towards secularism. In part, that is because the vast majority of them were Han. They moved in packs, often behind a young female guide holding a flag, cameras and phones at the ready. Filling out the Chinese restaurants at mealtimes and crowding around the souvenir stalls in the old town's alleys to haggle for Tibetan cowboy hats, amulets and necklaces, their presence is as symbolic of Tibet's conquest as the Wujing patrols through the old town.

Very few people travelled when I first came to China, except for work and study, or to return to their villages and hometowns at Chinese New Year. Now rising incomes have created an urban middle class with cash to spare for luxuries like holidays. The wealthiest travel overseas: to Thailand for the beaches, or Europe and the United States. Everyone else contents themselves with domestic destinations, such as Tibet, Yunnan Province and tropical Hainan Island off China's southern coast.

Most come to Tibet for its sheer exoticism. It is a tacit admission that this land with its extraordinary, unique geography, a people in thrall to Buddhism and a language that has its roots across the borders with Burma and India, is separate from the rest of China. Nothing illustrates the CCP's success in rewriting history more than the irony that all Han will acknowledge how the people and landscapes of Tibet and Xinjiang are so unlike them and anywhere else in China. But they will never admit that those regions have ever been anything but part of the Chinese empire.

Not all Han travel to Tibet because it feels like going on holiday in a foreign country. A small but increasing number visit as part of a gentle spiritual awakening. Tibet may be a less devout place than before, but everyday life remains a world apart from the relentless drive for riches which characterises day-to-day existence for most people in Han China. For a minority of Chinese, it is a place to search for a deeper meaning and understanding. Some seek out monks for guidance; most simply wander Lhasa hoping to absorb an intangible energy, reaching blindly to the gods from the roof of the world.

Repressed during the first forty-odd years of CCP rule, the pent-up entrepreneurial instincts of the Chinese were unleashed in 1992 by Deng Xiaoping, Mao Zedong's successor, with his much quoted, and likely apocryphal, statement that 'to get rich is glorious'. Yet as more people achieve the status symbols desired by all – an apartment and a car, the cash to travel overseas – so a minority are beginning to wonder if there is more to life than what the Chinese press routinely describes as 'money worship'.

Many who don't challenge the prevailing orthodoxy still acknowledge that it is flawed, an unnatural philosophy that is no guarantee of happiness. In Beijing, I liked to tease one particularly avaricious friend by asking her if westerners seemed more content than the Chinese, even though most of us drive cars, fly abroad every year and earn far higher salaries. 'No,' she said, 'but I still want what you have.'

Growing prosperity is now being accompanied by a slow revival of interest in religion, both formal and informal. Accurate statistics are impossible to come by, but it is probable there are more Christians in China than there are members of the CCP. Another 20–25 million people follow Islam. It is Buddhism, though, that remains the most popular faith, with some 400 million Chinese claiming to subscribe to it.

Their interpretation of prayer and meditation lacks the conviction which characterises Tibetan Buddhism, the unshakeable belief that inspires someone to set off on a year-long pilgrimage to Lhasa from a remote village, prostrating every inch of the way. Temples across China are increasingly busy, but the worshippers are nearly always praying for success: for better grades, for more money, or to find a partner.

For the CCP, though, even that mild form of devotion is dubious, a deviation from the credo that the party is as much a faith as any religion. Mao himself was revered almost as a god, just as the Dalai Lama is in Tibet, and was portrayed in official propaganda as a messiah. In his hometown of Changsha in Hunan Province, there is a huge portrait of Mao depicting bolts of light emanating from his head, as if he was responsible for creation itself.

In retrospect, the mere fact that the Dalai Lama is so venerated ensured that Mao would never have allowed him to remain in the Potala Palace, even if the Khampa hadn't rebelled and given the Chinese an excuse to drive him into exile. He was too much competition for the Chairman, a reminder that Mao was just a proletarian version of the emperors who came before him.

Now the Dalai Lama travels the world from his base in Dharamsala. Greeted with sympathy and respect wherever he goes, he is unable to find any government willing to stand up to Beijing and press for his return. He is certainly the last undisputed Dalai Lama. Should he nominate anyone from inside Tibet or the borderlands as his reincarnation, they will suffer the same fate as the six-year-old boy he picked to be the next Panchen Lama and disappear without trace.

Beijing has already said it will be involved in the choice of the next Dalai Lama. That raises the distinctly surreal prospect of the CCP, an avowedly atheist organisation, deciding who will be the spiritual head of Tibetan Buddhism. Meanwhile, the Dalai Lama has hinted that his successor will come from the exile community in India, leaving Tibetans with a foreign-born leader who has never lived in the country he will be expected to guide.

Inevitably, that will reduce the Dalai Lama's standing and push Tibet further into the embrace of Han China. Lhasa is already a city drifting rudderless, caught between its past and present, the stark choice between the emptying monasteries and the enticing new apartment complexes rising towards the vast sky. With no definable border between the old town and the far bigger Chinese city that surrounds it, wandering Lhasa is a schizophrenic experience. Walk too far in any direction from Barkhor Square and you enter a high-plateau imitation of inland China, where karaoke clubs and Sichuan restaurants take the place of temples.

Even much of the old town feels ersatz, despite the numerous pilgrims. It is sanitised and pacified, Tibet transformed into a theme park. It didn't take me long to realise I needed to escape the well-trodden tourist trail if I was to find a more authentic Lhasa, one not mummified like the Potala Palace, or slowly being enveloped by the same materialist vision that governs the rest of China.

10

A Night at the *Nangma*

I started to haunt the teahouses down grubby alleys in the old town, lanes whose entrances were guarded at night by Wujing checking the identity cards of young Tibetan men. Away from Barkhor Square, the old town is a collection of small shops and houses which lack basic amenities. The alleys are strewn with the detritus of day-to-day life: discarded food from the markets, paper and plastic packaging, while the stench of the public toilets, despite the incense sticks planted in them to disguise their odour, hangs in the air.

Exclusively Tibetan, the teahouses are all much the same. Customers sit on long benches covered in cushions compressed nearly flat from long use and drink yak-butter tea, Lhasa beer or *chang*, the cloudy, cider-like alcohol native to Tibet. Local pop videos play in the background, as well as Bollywood movies, in which singers in traditional clothes wander across the grasslands crooning wistful love songs.

Singling out the teahouses was part of my ambitious, perhaps hopelessly optimistic, mission to rummage deeper into Lhasa life. The Tibet I was seeking – a place that is neither the Shangri-La touted by naive foreigners nor the backward region the Chinese stress it was until their arrival – remained elusive. So too did any specific sense of what ordinary Tibetans think about the way their country is changing.

Dispelling a lingering anxiety that my compassion for China's ethnic groups did not extend to the Tibetans was another motivation. Elsewhere in China, I felt a perhaps unjustified sense of solidarity with the minorities, something I put down to my mixed ancestry. As a Londoner with roots in the UK and central Europe, I like to assume that my first-hand knowledge of how ethnicity impinges on our views of nationality has resulted in an empathy with those who live at the edges of countries.

When it came to individual Tibetans, though, I struggled to evoke the sympathy that seemed to come naturally with the other ethnic groups. It was an uncomfortable feeling, one that made me wonder if I had succumbed to the Han virus which differentiates between 'good' minorities and 'bad' ones, the modern-day version of the distinction between cooked and uncooked barbarians.

My fear that I had hit an invisible minority ceiling stemmed back to 1988 and my first, unsatisfactory experiences with Tibetans in the Qinghai borderlands. I remember a mutual incomprehension in the villages I visited that went beyond the language barrier, one that gave way to active dislike as a man in a stinking *chuba* did his best to part me from my watch. I had been expecting to meet people lost in lofty contemplation of spiritual matters, not a black-toothed Amdo bandit.

Subsequent encounters in Beijing and elsewhere were not fruitful either. It was only when I met Samphel in Litang that I found a Tibetan whom I could relax with. Yet even in western Sichuan the strutting nomads had brought back memories of the subdued hostility present in some of the villagers I met in 1988. In the borderlands especially, Tibetans can harbour an aggression that surprises those who believe they really are the Buddhist saints portrayed by pro-Tibet campaigners in the west. And while Tibetans are far more likely to pull knives on each other than on a foreigner, they will turn readily on the Han if they can get away with it.

Separating Tibetans from the propaganda that smothers them, whether western or Chinese, was one of my aspirations. But pushing aside the heavy, patterned blankets decorated with Buddhist symbols that shield the entrances to Lhasa's teahouses did not admit me into a secret world where Tibetans spoke unguardedly. Instead, I was confronted with a passiveness completely at odds with the belligerence of the nomads of Kham and the people of Amdo. Resolving the contradiction between those two extremes was something I never managed to achieve during my time in Tibet.

Conversation in the teahouses would come to an abrupt stop as every person inside turned to look at me. The teenage waitresses would giggle as I attempted to order in Tibetan and then everyone would smile at me. Unnerving as they were, those grins gave me unfulfilled hopes of meaningful contact. It was only later that Tenzin told me some Tibetans have a habit of smiling at random foreigners, and it doesn't indicate a willingness to talk to them. After a few nights of drinking endless toasts of watery beer, I realised I was back where I started – still shut out from the Lhasa of the locals.

Of course, my teahouse jaunts made me no better than the tourists I scorned for arriving in Lhasa with a preconceived picture of holy lamas and unworldly villagers. There is, though, something about Tibet which induces a delirious imagining in visitors; the unfamiliar sensation of living at altitude is perhaps to blame. Certainly, many people subscribe to visions of Tibet which bear little resemblance to the reality.

Those hallucinations take bizarre forms, whether it is movie stars embracing the Dalai Lama as a role model, or the western women who date only Tibetan men. One British woman I knew in Beijing fantasised about sleeping with Tibetan monks, claiming they had both physical and spiritual qualities no other men could match. I used to think of her babbling about something she had never experienced, or was ever likely to, while I was prowling the alleys of Lhasa. It was reassuring; it made my search for the Tibet I thought was out there less fanciful.

Romanticising the Tibetans is an understandable reaction to the colonisation of their country. The empty Potala Palace and the reduction of once great monasteries to simple tourist attractions, along with the Wujing presence in the old town, are just the most obvious signs of Han domination. The real pressure put on the Tibetans is mental: the constant efforts to separate them from their past; the constant reminders of their lack of freedom; the constant striving to impose alien values on a people who have nothing but their ancient beliefs.

It is the monks, the people whose immersion in Buddhism is supposed to have instilled a benign acceptance of fate, who remain the most willing to protest against what is happening in Tibet. From March 2011, lamas, as well as a few nuns and lay people, began setting themselves on fire in public. This desperate expression of dissent started as a rebellion by monks incensed at being confined to their monasteries like prisoners, and by their enforced participation in the 'patriotic re-education' programmes which are aimed at getting them to renounce their allegiance to the Dalai Lama.

Unsurprisingly, the vast majority of these self-immolations take place in Kham – in eastern Tibet and the western Sichuan borderlands – the traditional centres of Tibetan resistance. Unable to demonstrate their discontent publicly and increasingly isolated in a society they once dominated, some monks convey both their anger and sheer lack of hope by turning that rage on themselves – dousing their robes in petrol, clicking a lighter and waiting for the flames to consume them.

Beijing reacted to the fiery suicides in predictable fashion, branding them criminal acts and accusing the Dalai Lama of inciting them. In 1954, he had walked side by side with Mao in Beijing and was treated with, if not deference, then respect. Now, according to CCP propaganda, whose language remains rooted in the Cultural Revolution era when it comes to Tibet, he is a 'jackal in Buddhist monk robes' and responsible for inspiring all opposition to Han rule in Tibet and the autonomous prefectures.

In turn, the Dalai Lama responded by pointing to the repression of the monks. He talked of how virtual martial law in Tibet and the borderlands was pushing some Tibetans to increasingly extreme behaviour. Certainly, the self-immolations pulled me up sharply. If Tibetans are so muted by what is happening in their country that suicide is the only way to make a statement, then it was self-delusion on a grand scale for me to believe I could give them a voice.

All China's minorities lack outlets of expression. Even in the multi-cultural UK, the views of the ethnic British are heard less frequently than everyone else's. In China, it is far worse. The minorities are absent from TV shows, movies, literature, popular discourse and are mostly excluded from politics. Now what little dialogue that takes place in Tibet between the locals and the Han is being replaced by death. And despite my ambivalence towards Tibetans, that left me both depressed and unsure of what I was really doing here.

Yet, not knowing what else to do, I continued my nocturnal rambling through the old town. One evening, I came across a bar called 798, the name of Beijing's hip art district. It was owned by a Tibetan and his girlfriend, a folk singer from Liaoning Province in the north-east. She was quick to tell me she was Manchu, although she didn't look it and I didn't believe her. It was possible she was trying to make life easier for her boyfriend by claiming to be a minority, because mixed Tibetan and Chinese couples are a very rare sight in Lhasa and can provoke a violent reaction from the locals.

Later, I came to think that she was just trying to distinguish herself from the other young, middle-class Han who move to Tibet as supplicants in search of something they struggle to articulate themselves. Known as *zang piao*, literally 'Tibet drifter', they are a vanguard – people who have taken the decision to step off the path that leads from school to university and then on to a high-paying job, the dream all Chinese parents have for their children.

Zang piao can be found running cafés in the old town, buying jewellery to sell in the cities they come from or working as singers and artists; creative Chinese have been travelling to Tibet in search of inspiration since the early 1980s. They are very different from the hundreds of millions of young Han who leave their homes in the countryside for jobs in factories and on building sites, or to work as security guards, waitresses and cleaners. If they come to Tibet, it is to open a tiny restaurant or shop because there is less competition there than in their home provinces.

Their more fortunate counterparts are drawn to Tibet not by economic prospects but by its reputation as an unsullied paradise, one where people don't follow the same tenets as those of the Han, or anyone else. In many ways, the *zang piao* are similar to the westerners who idealise Tibet. Like them, they believe that Tibetans hold the key to a door that is locked for everyone else.

The customers at 798 were much more talkative than the people in the teahouses. 'We don't see many foreigners in here any more,' one said to me. 'There used to be more foreign tourists than Chinese in Lhasa, but in the last few years it's been the other way around.' His name was Pemba, and he was a teacher who had grown up in the old town. Now his parents rented out their house there and the family lived in a modern apartment in the west of Lhasa, a move increasingly made by Tibetans who can afford it.

'Rent for shops and bars in the old town is very high now, because there are so many Han tourists. It's a good thing to own a house here now,' noted Pemba. But although he lived elsewhere, he still socialised in the old town. 'I have to, because all the other parts of Lhasa are like a Chinese city. This is the only place where you'll find Tibetan culture. We say Lhasa is divided into the old town and new town, like two different countries really.'

But 798 could have been a bar in any Chinese city, save for the Tibetan clientele and the prayer flags adorning the walls. And Pemba and his friends were graduates, who had travelled and studied in eastern China. They spoke fluent Mandarin and, for all their talk of the way Lhasa is changing, none appeared particularly upset by the Han influx into their country. Perhaps when they spoke among themselves they got angry, but their fatalism in public reminded me of the passive patrons of the teahouses.

I asked them where ordinary Tibetans went for a night out, apart from backstreet teahouses. 'Well, there's always the *nangma*,' one said with an expression that was half grin and half grimace. They told me *nangma* are nightclubs, named after a classical Tibetan dance. Pemba looked down on them as unworthy. 'I hardly ever go. I feel sad when I do, seeing young Tibetans getting so drunk. You know *nangma* were originally performances for high lamas? They used to be much more traditional. Now it's just about drinking, dancing and sometimes fighting.'

His perception of the *nangma* is typical among educated Tibetans. When I told Tenzin I had visited one, he was shocked and immediately asked me if there had been any trouble. It is as if they have become a codeword for the way Tibetan society is being disconnected from its roots. They sounded less alarming to me, more like an outlet for the general unruliness of country Tibetans.

Pemba wouldn't go with me to a *nangma*, but he did tell me where to find a popular one. It was outside the old town, up a long, steep flight of stairs at the top of which two bouncers in black jackets waited. As a foreigner, I was deemed safe and so not frisked for a knife. Inside, it looked like a scruffier version of a provincial Chinese nightclub, except that there was no dance floor. In its place was a stage lit by coloured neon lights opposite which were tables and behind them more comfortable booths.

A waitress showed me to a table towards the back. I was the oldest person present by some distance and the only one who wasn't Tibetan. Like in any Chinese club, alcohol was ordered in bulk: beers came in groups of six or you could get a bottle of whisky or wine. I was allowed to get away with asking for a single beer. Bottles covered most of the tables and a few people were already slumped head down in their chairs, or sprawled out in a booth. But not everyone was drinking alcohol; cartons of orange juice seemed to be a popular choice as well.

Traditional Tibetan music, with an added electronic backbeat, started pumping out of the speakers and an MC appeared on stage dressed in smart nomad gear – baggy trousers tucked into high leather boots and a fancy *chuba*. He set about cheerleading the audience with a few jokes and songs. Confused, I wondered if I had wandered by mistake into a Tibetan version of the film *Cabaret*, with Lhasa substituting for Weimar-era Berlin.

Nangma were once dances where troupes of beautiful women entertained aristocrats and senior monks, with most Tibetans excluded from viewing them. Here girls in white dresses danced elegantly while waving yellow prayer scarves, but solo female and male singers took to the stage to perform Tibetan folk songs too. Members of the audience could buy a *katag* and drape it around the singer's neck to show their approval. Every so often, the audience was summoned on stage for a collective dance. Led by the MC, they shuffled left and right around the stage in a circle, arms waving, feet stamping.

Compared to what I had witnessed in clubs in Beijing, never mind London, it all seemed very innocent. I couldn't equate what I was seeing with the gloomy view held by Pemba and his friends that the modern-day version of the *nangma* represents the decline and fall of Tibetan culture. Instead, the dances were simply being updated for a new audience. The setting might have been modern, but the songs were the same and the young crowd knew all the lyrics.

Spending their nights listening to such music actually marked them out as rather more conventional than the people in 798. They weren't in a bar named after a Beijing neighbourhood, listening to American rock and talking to *zang piao* and stray westerners. For all their superficial similarities to the nightclubs of inland China, there is nothing remotely Han or foreign about the *nangma*, unless you believe that alcohol abuse is a Chinese or overseas import to Tibet.

Class snobbery inspires much of the disdain for the *nangma*. The aristocracy may have been displaced by the events of the last sixty years, but in Lhasa there is a clear divide between urban Tibetans and those who have migrated from the countryside. In the *nangma*, the clothes of most of the people indicated they were recent arrivals in Lhasa. Their high-crowned baseball caps, mysteriously popular in rural Tibet, fake low-end western labels and no-name jeans gave them away as surely as if they were pilgrims on the Barkhor Kora with braided hair, wearing *chubas* and spinning prayer wheels.

Chinese from the country use the term *chuqu* – 'to go out' – to describe their move to the cities. Often, it is boredom as much as the lack of economic opportunities which inspires them to leave. For young Tibetans, the sheer harshness of life on the grasslands makes the cities of Tibet and the borderlands very attractive. Some are choosing to go further afield; around 50,000 Tibetans are now estimated to live in the Sichuan capital Chengdu.

Many end up unemployed, like the Uighur migrants in Urumqi from southern Xinjiang. For a growing minority, crime is the only way to survive, and conning and robbing tourists is a thriving industry. Lhasa's sex trade, too, is as demarcated as the divide between the Chinese city and the old town, with the Tibetan brothels populated exclusively by teenage girls from the countryside. With prospects like that, a night in the *nangma*, drinking and watching dances their forebears were not considered worthy enough to glimpse seemed to me more like a reaffirmation of their roots than a rejection of them.

11

U-Tsang

Tenzin was singing as his chum Lopa casually steered the land cruiser one-handed out of Lhasa on the first stage of our 1,900-kilometre odyssey to the far west. We were all buoyed up to be leaving, even if we would be crammed together in a white Toyota jeep for much of the time. I hadn't travelled in such close proximity with strangers for so long a journey in years. But Tenzin's high spirits and the bright-blue sky made it easy to relegate any uneasiness to the back of my mind.

Apart from trucks and buses, the traffic was all land cruisers like ours ferrying tourists. Most were bound for Mount Everest, right on the border with Nepal, although the Tibetans and Chinese don't know it by that name and call it Qomolangma. For many visitors to Tibet, a visit to Everest base camp is obligatory and the week-long run there from Lhasa follows a well-worn route that gets crowded in the summer.

Our destination was a very different mountain: Mount Kailash. Known to Tibetans as 'The Precious Jewel of Snows' and standing in majestic isolation in Tibet's western reaches, close to the borders with India and Nepal, Kailash is the centre of the universe for over a billion people, as well as the source of four of Asia's longest rivers. No Buddhist's or Hindu's life can be considered complete until they have made the Kora around Kailash. It is a journey that takes the pilgrims over 5,600 metres, as high as they can go on a mountain so sacred it cannot be climbed by mortals, its summit reserved for gods only.

The idea of a peak so remote yet so venerated and which is also the fount of life for much of the subcontinent, through the mighty rivers that begin at its untouched glaciers, fascinated me. I thought, too, that its significance to both Buddhists and Hindus encapsulates the way cultures and religions take precedence over mere nationality at the far edges of the Chinese empire.

Kailash imposes itself even just outside Lhasa. The road we were on hugs the Yarlung Tsangpo, the highest river in the world. Its source is in the Kailash region. After tumbling off the mountains of the far west, the Yarlung flows through central Tibet. It then turns south and enters north-east India, where it becomes the Brahmaputra River, before crossing Bangladesh and emptying into the Bay of Bengal. Here, far removed from the snow and ice of Kailash, it was sluggish and mud-coloured, its current broken up by mud banks and outcrops of small trees.

Feeding the valleys of U-Tsang, the central province of Tibet we were passing through, the Yarlung's waters render the landscape very different from the bleak high-altitude desert that awaited us further west. This part of U-Tsang is the most fertile area of Tibet, known for the quality of its *tsampa*, and all around were neat barley fields broken up by small settlements of white-stone houses.

An hour and a half from Lhasa we started to climb past grassland away from the Yarlung, before cresting a pass at 4,800 metres. Below us was Yamdrok-Tso, a huge azure salt lake that winds for over seventy kilometres through a valley towards giant peaks that sit off in the far distance. We descended to the lakeshore, where deposits of salt were piled up on its banks, avoiding the piles of rocks that had broken away from the mountainsides and crashed on to the road, and started to circle around it.

For Tenzin, this was the journey home; he was from a village in U-Tsang. Now twenty-nine, he had left at fourteen to walk across the Himalayas to Nepal, and then on to India and Dharamsala. 'I was a pilgrim. I stayed for five years. That's where I got the chance to really study Tibetan, as well as learning English,' he said. Tenzin had also been taught how to paint *thangka*, the scroll paintings of

Buddhist deities and scenes from the life of the Buddha which hang in every Tibetan and Nepalese monastery.

Later, he tried his luck as a *thangka* painter in Kathmandu for a year and a half, before returning to Tibet. For Tibetans of his age, or slightly older, such a journey was not uncommon. In the 1990s, many chose to spend time in India and Nepal, sometimes for religious reasons but often as a way out of farming on the high plateau. It was a chance to experience a different life in countries where Tibetans are not subject to the whims of the Chinese.

Crossing the frontier was still straightforward when Tenzin was a teenager. 'You either went across the mountains or paid the border guards,' he recalled. 'It's much harder now. There are more soldiers and you can't pay to get across any more. You need a passport and they are very hard for young Tibetans to get.' Up to 3,000 Tibetans a year once travelled to Dharamsala. Now, around fifty a month arrive – a similar number reaching Nepal – and the Wujing open fire if they spot them trying to leave Tibet. Only the most religious migrants still aim for India. The less devout are turning towards inland China.

Even without the risk of being shot, Tenzin's journey was a remarkable one for a fourteen-year-old boy to attempt. But he brushed off the difficulties, making crossing the Himalayas sound like a stroll in Barkhor Square, as if traversing 7,000-metre passes, where in the winter you can sink up to your waist in snow, and sleeping on mountainsides for weeks was easy. Maybe it is for Tibetans, because nuns and schoolgirls manage the trip. I read of one crippled monk who crawled most of the way to Dharamsala. Put it down to growing up on the roof of the world, but Tenzin's story was a reminder of just how tough Tibetans are.

Past Yamdrok-Tso, the road rose again and we crossed a 5,000-metre pass, the highest I had ever been. After my time in Litang and Lhasa, I assumed I was more or less acclimatised to the altitude. But we were now 1,300 metres above Lhasa, and a headache made it clear that I was not yet used to being so high. Some people dose themselves with pills to counter the effects of mountain life. I was relying on the time it would take to get to Kailash, during which we would ascend each day, to adapt to the lofty elevations of western Tibet.

Inside the land cruiser, I was insulated against the environment to some extent. But outside it took only moments for the altitude to make its unseen presence known. No matter that it was summer, the wind chilled and chapped me, even as the sun that was closer than ever before turned my skin red in a matter of minutes. Walking up gentle inclines became hard work, as did going up flights of stairs. I got a sore thumb from clicking countless lighters that refused to fire in the thin air.

Throughout this stage of the journey, the road climbed and dipped endlessly as we curled our way through the mountains. Only towards the end, as we dropped down to a plain of barley fields, did we run on the flat before arriving in Gyantse. Like Lhasa, Gyantse is sharply divided between a bigger new town and the Tibetan quarter. But the similarities end there. It is tranquil, a small country town, and I found it hard to believe it was once Tibet's third-largest city.

Gyantse's monastery dominates one end of the Tibetan old town, almost burrowing its way in to the hills behind it. At the other end, a ruined fort, or *dzong*, lies atop a precipitously rocky hill that rises incongruously close to the centre of town. It looms over low-rise Gyantse like a crumbling castle guarding a loch in Scotland. Between those two landmarks, the old town's mostly car-free main street is lined by two- and three-storey white-stone houses. Their window frames and doors were outlined in black, some bearing the *gyung drung*, the Tibetan Buddhist swastika.

Women in long black dresses and *bangden* walked home with baskets of shopping, along with monks and people going to and from the monastery, prayer wheels in hand. A mix of Bollywood tunes, traditional Tibetan music and western pop – the Backstreet Boys – emanated from the shops on the street. There were few tourists here, and after Lhasa's hectic old town it appeared idyllic.

Narrow lanes run parallel to the main street, leading on one side to nearby barley fields. The lanes are like mini-villages transported into the old town, adding to the bucolic feel. Cows were tethered outside almost every house, and there was forage for them along with piles of dung kept as fuel for cooking and heating. The sewage system was primitive, dogs skulked and slumbered everywhere and grimy-faced kids ran up shouting 'Hello' in English and wanting their pictures taken.

On the hillsides near the monastery are the remains of the other monasteries which had made Gyantse a key centre of Buddhist learning, until the Red Guards sacked them during the Cultural Revolution. As many as fifteen monasteries from three different schools of Tibetan Buddhism were located here, attracting monks from all over Tibet, as well as Bhutan and India. Now, only one survives and it is home to just seventy monks.

Bhutan lies eighty kilometres due south of Gyantse across a closed border that has never been fully demarcated. Over the years, the Bhutanese have accused the PLA of extending roads from Tibet into what they regard as their territory. With a similar language and religion, Bhutan and Tibet have long been intertwined, even if for much of their history Tibet, and now China, has done its best to dominate its smaller neighbour.

South-west from Gyantse, and not much further away than Bhutan, is the mountain pass of Nathu La and the frontier with the Indian state of Sikkim. Since 2006, Nathu La has become one of just three points along the 3,400-kilometre-long Chinese–Indian border that is open for traffic. It is for local trade only, like the other two border crossings, with Tibetan and Indian merchants allowed to venture a few kilometres in either direction to sell their goods at designated markets.

More than fifty years after the construction of Highway 219 from Xinjiang to Tibet led to the Sino-Indian War, there is no sign that either Beijing or New Delhi is willing to agree on what constitutes the boundary between China and India. Apart from the disputed territory of Aksai Chin close to Xinjiang, Beijing insists also that the

Tawang region of the Indian state of Arunachal Pradesh, which is sandwiched between Bhutan and Burma, belongs to Tibet.

Inhabited by the Monpa people, who are closely related to both the Tibetans and the Bhutanese and practise Tibetan Buddhism, Tawang was the birthplace of the sixth Dalai Lama. It was the British who ceded Tawang to India, when they imposed the McMahon Line as the frontier between their empire and Tibet in 1914. China has never accepted that definition of the border and continues to refer to Tawang as South Tibet. The 9,000 or so Monpa who live across the border in Tibet are known to the Chinese as the Monba, and are one of the smallest of the country's minorities.

I would have loved to venture into Tawang to explore the Tibetan borderlands in India. But, as with Xinjiang's border with Afghanistan, I was not allowed to get close; the Tibetan side of the frontier with Tawang is barred to foreigners. So is the road south from Gyantse, ruling out a visit to the Nathu La Pass. It was yet another route that Francis Younghusband had travelled. He led his invasion force of British, Indian and Gurkha soldiers through the pass in late 1903.

From the mid-nineteenth century on, as the Qing's hold on power grew progressively weaker, the British were able to sidle into Tibet, motivated by its proximity to India and fears that the Russians might use it as a backdoor route to undermine the British empire. They mapped the country secretly and in 1903 sent Younghusband and his soldiers to force the Dalai Lama to agree to a trade treaty. In March 1904, outside Gyantse, they ran into a 3,000-strong Tibetan force armed with ancient matchlock muskets, weapons over 200 years out of date. The British carried machine guns, and in a matter of minutes they left around 700 Tibetans dead.

Four months later, Gyantse was the site of a more glorious battle. The town's *dzong*, the best-fortified fort in Tibet, guarded the road to Lhasa. Two soldiers won the Victoria Cross for leading the assault up the near-vertical slopes which led to its surrender. An inscription at the bottom of the hill records the event, and condemns

Younghusband and his troops for their colonial arrogance. While I was gazing at it, two young Han tourists asked me why the British had come to Tibet. It was a hard question to answer. 'Because it was next to India,' I said finally. I thought they might understand, now that China is the imperial power in Tibet.

After Gyantse's mellow charms, Shigatse is a harbinger of what all Tibetan towns and cities will look like if Beijing continues to develop Tibet in the image of Han China. Tibet's second city is a sprawling work in progress, its roads and buildings being hastily refashioned in the untidy and anonymous style common to all provincial Chinese cities. Even the tiny Tibetan neighbourhood is modern in comparison to the old towns of Lhasa and Gyantse. It is dwarfed anyway by the Chinese town, and the Han are far more of a presence here than anywhere else in Tibet apart from Lhasa.

They are recent arrivals. Until the CCP took control of Tibet, Chinese settlers rarely ventured any further than Lhasa. In old Tibet, Shigatse was a trading centre and meeting point for Indian and Nepali traders, as well as Mongolians and Uighurs. It was where Tibet encountered the rest of Asia, and far-off China was an irrelevance. Now Shigatse's location on the Friendship Highway, which links Lhasa to Kathmandu, makes it a stop on the tourist route that runs through central Tibet. Apart from small convenience stores and a few restaurants in the Tibetan district, it is Chinese businesses that dominate.

That is partly due to Tibet's rural heritage. 'You have to remember most Tibetans are farmers,' Pemba had told me in Lhasa. 'Only a few do business. So it's mostly the Chinese who run companies, hotels, restaurants. They've taken over nearly all the tourist trade and almost all the money from tourism goes to the Chinese.' But as Shigatse's history indicated, the Tibetans in this part of U-Tsang were once traders. By closing the border with India, the CCP hasn't just sealed off Tibet from foreign influence, it has driven the Tibetans here back to the land.

Shigatse's fifteenth-century *dzong*, supposedly the model for the Potala Palace, was completely destroyed in the Cultural Revolution and has since been rebuilt, using cement rather than Tibetan stone. The Tashilhunpo Monastery, Shigatse's other landmark, is rather more authentic. Like Sera, it is the size of a village and as much a university as a monastery. As the traditional seat of the Panchen Lamas, it is the only place in Tibet and the borderlands where I saw the young, bespectacled face of the present, disputed Panchen Lama on display.

Everywhere else it is the chubby, double-chinned face of his predecessor, with his cropped, receding hair, which stares down at you in restaurants, shops and houses. He is hugely respected by Tibetans for his steadfast opposition to China's presence in Tibet, and probably more deserving than the Dalai Lama of veneration because of his courage in challenging the Chinese and the suffering it caused him.

In 1962, he submitted a damning report to Beijing on life in Tibet. It became known subsequently as the '70,000-character petition', for the number of Chinese characters it took to write it. The Panchen Lama criticised the way the monasteries were being stripped of their traditional roles and sidelined, with monks unable to debate and study and sometimes being sent to work in the fields.

He attacked the CCP's agricultural policies, including the enforced collectivisation of farms, which created chronic food shortages in many areas. He argued that the CCP's reforms to Tibetan society were leading to 'the death of Tibetan nationality' and that traditional Tibetan culture was derided by Han officials as 'backward'. He called for the release of the many innocent Tibetans who had been rounded up and imprisoned during the revolt of 1956–9.

Mao described the Panchen Lama's petition as a 'poisoned arrow', and it was just a question of time before he was purged. In 1964, he was pilloried as an atavistic remnant of feudal Tibet, a 'capitalist serf owner'. For the next fourteen years, he was imprisoned in Beijing. With the Dalai Lama in exile, Tibet had lost its one other leader capable of standing up to the Chinese. It was not until 1982 that the Panchen Lama was allowed to visit Tibet again. But his years of imprisonment had not cowed him. Just five days before his death in

1989, he stated bluntly that the price Tibet had paid for its development under the CCP was greater than the gains.

Like a surprising number of *tulku* throughout Tibetan history, the former Panchen Lama did not conform to the western stereotype of an ascetic monk interested only in arcane spiritual matters. Before his death he got married, to a Han woman, and had a daughter, while his double chin was testament to his reputation as a bon viveur. I wondered where in Shigatse it was possible to party like a Panchen Lama, as Gyantse had been dead at night apart from a few teahouses and Shigatse seemed to be home only to Chinese karaoke bars.

A tip from a Tibetan taxi driver took me one evening to a park on the Han side of town. He pointed into the darkness and told me to start walking. I stumbled around for twenty minutes before I discovered dozens of tents pitched close together. This was Shigatse's Tibetan nightlife district, its temporary status an ominous sign of how Tibet's second city is becoming a Han settlement.

Stepping inside one of the tents was like walking into the sort of remote English country pub where all the drinkers are related to each other and strangers are automatically suspect. One of the waitress's mouths was hanging open as I ordered a beer. But the customers recovered their poise quickly enough and I was invited to join a game of Sho, a Tibetan dice game, the rules of which I failed to grasp on every occasion I played it.

All I could do was the easy bit, which involves slamming two dice down on a pad made of yak leather. I had no idea what that indicated in terms of shuffling around the shells and old Tibetan coins used to play Sho. That was left to my partner, a grinning middle-aged woman. I told her I was on my way to Kailash. She had never been, but then as a gambler and drinker she wasn't an obvious pilgrim. It didn't take me long to realise that the conversation was going to be as unenlightening as it had been in the Lhasa teahouses. I gave in to the flow of the game and carried on downing beers. That was what we were all here for.

12

High Plateau Drifter

The further west we travelled, the more the contrast between the scenery around us and the towns and villages we stopped in became apparent. It is a huge anomaly that western Tibet's mostly untouched landscape of soaring mountains, shimmering lakes and grassland that rolls on and on, all under an immense, mesmerising sky, is broken up by some of the most dismal settlements I have ever visited. Everywhere we went past Shigatse took me back with a shudder to squalid Shimiankuang on the border with Xinjiang and Qinghai, only without the asbestos dust in the air.

Saga was typical. One of only two towns of any size in Ngari, the province that covers western Tibet, its main road was a potholed mudbath along which trucks and land cruisers churned their way further west. It was lined by broken pavements and poorly constructed buildings which housed tiny shops and the odd restaurant. All the locals were covered in dust and dirt. The men pissed outside, rather than braving the pit toilets, with their mini-mountains of human refuse beneath them, which substitute for proper plumbing in Ngari. At night, packs of feral dogs took control of what passed for the streets.

Yet the drive to Saga was sublime – chasing the Yarlung Tsangpo across fields of barley and yellow mustard until we reached Lhatse. There the Friendship Highway forks. We swung right towards Kailash, while most of the convoy of land cruisers we had been part of since Lhasa went the other way towards Everest and Nepal. Now we were on Highway 219, which winds up through Aksai Chin to Xinjiang.

Soon the fertile fields were gone and the hills grew more severe. We drove on over 5,000-metre passes, and the towering mountains in the distance began to draw nearer. Nomad tents dotted the grassland and their occupants could be seen astride horses tending the herds of yaks, rather than the cows I'd seen around Gyantse and Shigatse, grazing near by. Marmots and mountain goats scampered away at the sound of our engine, but for most of the time we had the road to ourselves, passing only a few solitary trucks and tractors towing trailers loaded with passengers swathed in headscarves against the sun and wind.

From here on, we were in the real Wild West. After Lhatse, there are no more conventional hotels, just shared rooms with dirty, damp beds, concrete floors and no heating. The electricity comes and goes and showers are scarce; in most settlements the only way to wash is with a thermos of hot water. During my time in Ngari, I got to shower just once and grew used to matted hair, a week's worth of stubble and clothes stained with mud and dust. Smoking furiously in the pit toilets in an effort to disguise their stink became second nature.

Only the food defeated me. China's cuisines are as diverse as its people and most are superb. Tibet is the exception. *Tsampa*, *thugpa* (a noodle soup) and *momo* (yak-meat dumplings) are the principal national dishes, all accompanied by endless glasses of yak-butter tea. Every morning, Tenzin and the driver Lopa would happily pull out the cloth bags which contained their *tsampa*, before mixing it with butter tea or water and, sometimes, yak cheese. It was a breakfast I tried just once, and the remorseless meals of *momo* and *thugpa* soon began to pall.

I had been spoiled for choice in Lhasa, where there are Nepali places and Tibetan ones that cater to westerners; the finest meal I ate in Tibet was a spicy yak-meat pizza with a yak-cheese base. I was able to vary my diet in Gyantse and Shigatse too, thanks to the restaurants run by migrants from Sichuan. Eating Chinese food induced feelings of guilt, given the way Han culture is encroaching in Tibet, but I blamed Tibetan chefs for their lack of innovation rather than admit my own hypocrisy.

Those meals were a distant memory now. The higher we climbed, the worse the food got. For much of the time, only basic fried rice or *thugpa* was on offer. Fruit became scarcer and much more expensive. Along with vegetables, it has to be transported down 219 from Xinjiang, and it is common in Ngari to see Uighurs selling bruised apples from the back of a truck. Even yak meat is hard to find, as the animals are slaughtered only at a certain time of the year and the meat has to last for months.

One advantage of being so far from Lhasa was that Tenzin was no longer coiled as tight as he had been when we first met. By nature anxious, he began to relax the further we travelled, even offering his opinion on why most Tibetans inside Tibet, as opposed to the still rebellious borderlands, seemed so subdued and inured to the ever-increasing Han presence. He blamed it on the Chinese response to the March 2008 demonstrations. 'Things are much worse in Tibet since then,' he said. 'Many more army and police have come and they are like animals. People are scared of them. That's why there are no protests now. People don't want to go to jail.'

Monks alone retained their pugnacious spirit, as demonstrated by the ongoing self-immolations in eastern Tibet. 'They are the angriest of all. They're not free to celebrate all the festivals or to worship as they want,' said Tenzin. In Dharamsala, he had met the Dalai Lama and he told me he thought he might return to Tibet one day, a statement that could get him locked up if a zealous Han official heard him saying it. 'All Tibetans want the chance to see him here. I hope it will happen and I think it might now that he has resigned from politics. It is his involvement in politics which the Chinese don't like.'

In the summer of 2011, the Dalai Lama stepped down from his role as the head of the Tibetan government-in-exile. I didn't share Tenzin's optimism that giving up political power would alter Beijing's attitude towards him. It is his position as the spiritual leader of the Tibetans that the CCP fears far more. Tibet is a country which has never been especially cohesive and only the Dalai Lama can unite its people. He will retain that authority as long as he lives.

Kailash was slowly drawing us closer as we sped west and always upwards on 219. Saga was over 4,600 metres and from now on we would not descend below that height until we started the trip towards the Nepalese border after the Kailash Kora. We were running parallel to the frontier already. Just forty kilometres away over the mountains on our left was Mustang, a region in Nepal long associated with Tibet.

Jutting into Tibet, so that the borderline is forced to curve around it, Mustang's proximity to Ngari made it the natural base for the armed Tibetan resistance to Chinese rule that carried on after the PLA crushed the 1956–9 uprising. Backed by the CIA, who took some of the Tibetans to train in Colorado's Rocky Mountains, the guerrillas raided across the border, ambushing army convoys travelling 219. Around 2,000 Tibetans, many from Kham, carried on fighting sporadically until the early 1970s, when the Americans stopped funding them after Nixon and Mao met in Beijing in 1972.

Beyond Zhongba, a tiny town dominated by the nearby PLA base, we entered a new, far more otherworldly land. Giant sand dunes appeared, bizarrely sited next to grassland and icy lakes, while serrated peaks sat off on the horizon. This was high-altitude desert, stern yet seductive in the way its extreme contrasts make it so compelling a vista. There were hardly any villages now – only a few nomad settlements surrounded by their animals.

Three hundred-odd kilometres past Saga, we were halted by a Wujing checkpoint. I got twitchy every time I was required to show my permits and passport, wondering if Beijing had perhaps discovered I was in Tibet and had sent through instructions for my arrest. My second passport would be glaring proof that I was not a journalist but some sort of English spy, a throwback to the Indian Raj and the time when the pundits, the British officials who acted as undercover explorers, penetrated into Tibet secretly from India.

This time, my anxiety deepened as it became clear Tenzin had a problem. The first hint came when he called Lopa over, while telling me to stay in the car. As the trucks behind were waved through, I had no idea what was going on. When Tenzin returned, after almost two hours of negotiating, he bore an apologetic smile that I knew could only mean trouble. 'The agency in Lhasa has made a mistake. We haven't got the right stamp on our permits to carry on. I've called them and they'll try and fax the correct ones through. But we'll have to go back to Paryang to do that.'

Paryang was 100 kilometres behind us, a miserable village we had thankfully raced through. Highway 219 was its main street, and off it were unpaved alleys lined with one-storey mudbrick houses behind walls. Everywhere was strewn with rubbish, which the wind blew high into the air as if it was being sucked skyward by heaven's garbage men. I doubted there was a fax machine in Paryang. As we drove through its backstreets, though, I spotted the Chinese characters for an internet café. It was just a shop run by Han migrants, with one computer and a deadly slow internet connection. But they did have a fax.

By now, it was 7 p.m. and I would have to stay the night. Leaving Lopa and Tenzin, who was juggling phone calls to Lhasa and faxes with an increasingly desperate air, I set off for the one hotel I had seen. Named after Shishapangma, the only 8,000-metre mountain solely inside Tibet, it was a series of cramped and dark rooms set around a gravel courtyard, where there were a couple of cold-water taps.

Its owner was a youngish, bearded Han from Guizhou Province in the south-west. 'I moved here because I have bad lungs,' he said, offering me a smoke. 'I've been here five years now.' While haggling over the price of a room, I contemplated the horror of being stuck in Paryang for so long. He wanted far more than his lodgings were worth, claiming that his currently deserted establishment would be teeming with Indian pilgrims returning from Kailash later that night.

After peeking into the kitchen and being offered the inevitable fried rice, I decided to look for a more sophisticated dinner. To my surprise, I found a restaurant run by a genial middle-aged Sichuan couple. It was the most popular place in the village and locals, including a few nomads, were crowded around the tables. The fiery dishes and a succession of beers helped dull the disappointment of the day. When I returned to the Shishapangma, the courtyard was jammed with land cruisers and there was a newly pitched tent in the middle of it. The Indian pilgrims had arrived.

Next morning, there was hardly space to move. Tall, distinguished-looking gents, small and fat Indian matrons and younger men and women who were clearly their sons and daughters bustled between the cold-water taps, the filthy toilets and the tent which was serving breakfast. The fastidious Indians travelled with their own food and cooks. They were a group of 120, all of whom had come to Kailash under the auspices of their guru. His photo adorned the identity cards they wore around their necks and the rear windows of their land cruisers.

The guru had a beatific expression, a beard and a firm hold on his followers, who mostly lived in the States. 'We didn't do the full Kora,' said one young man from California, for whom the pilgrimage was part-celebration of his college graduation. 'We trekked to the north face of Kailash and stayed there. Our guru said there was no need to go further because we wouldn't be able to see the other faces of the mountain clearly.' Before that, they had gone to Lake Manasarovar, the most holy stretch of water in Tibet. 'Our guru said Kailash would be more receptive to us if we went in the lake first.' I asked if it was cold. 'Fucking freezing,' he replied.

While the Indians packed up and prepared to leave, their duty as Hindus done, I hung around waiting for Tenzin. He didn't turn up and called instead. He had been on the road back to Shigatse all night and wouldn't return with the correctly stamped permits until the following morning. I faced another day and night in Paryang. For the first time on the trip I lost my temper, growling futile curses at the walls of my grim room. When I calmed down, I reminded myself of my desire to escape Tibet's tourist trail. Now I had my chance – another twenty-four hours in a place no traveller in their right mind would stay in.

I tried hard to make the most of Paryang. I walked the alleys, passing the dogs fighting over the freshly dumped intestines of some animal and the houses with yak skulls hanging over their doors. I visited the nomads outside town, shouting '*Tashi Delek*' repeatedly as I approached to avoid being savaged by their wild hounds. I found the village temple, a fascinating little shrine with a giant prayer wheel inside and smaller ones around the outside which people circled constantly. I drank butter tea in a tent run by a tall and striking woman with a bronzed face, high cheekbones and braided waist-length hair.

But by the late afternoon I had exhausted Paryang's possibilities. I sat smoking in the once more deserted courtyard of the Shishapangma. It was going to rain. In Tibet's high, empty summer sky, you can see the weather coming hours before it arrives. The approaching clouds were jellyfish-like: dark and bulging, with the rain falling from them in near vertical lines their tendrils. It rained all night, and Paryang looked and felt like the last place on earth.

Early in the morning Tenzin returned, with bags under his eyes and a fistful of permits. 'We can go now,' he smiled. I was already packed; I couldn't wait to leave. An hour later, we were back at the Wujing checkpoint and this time we were allowed to proceed. Lopa stamped on the accelerator and we started to climb up to the 5,200-metre Mayum La Pass. As we descended on the other side, skittish herds of wild antelope raced across the road ahead of us.

Darchen was a few hours on, another one-yak town with worn prayer flags flying over buildings which looked like they were never intended to last longer than a season. This was the starting point for the Kailash Kora, the last place to stock up on whatever the shops could provide before we set off around the mountain. The clouds had followed us from Paryang and hung low and dirty grey over Darchen, shrouding Kailash from view and making me nervous about the weather conditions that awaited us.

More alarming was the sight of the Russian in the room next to me in the hotel, an almost exact copy of the Shishapangma in Paryang. I heard him before I saw him, coughing and gasping for air as his lungs slowly filled with liquid. His name was Mikhail and he was suffering from severe altitude sickness. He had been left behind by his party while they went on the Kora. The Tibetans who ran the hotel told me he needed to descend to a lower height as quickly as possible, the only real cure for his condition.

In a mix of pidgin Russian and English, I passed on their diagnosis. But at first he refused to leave or to take any medication, saying he was determined to survive naturally. Amazingly, he still thought he might attempt the Kora. He changed his story subsequently, saying his friends hadn't left him any cash to buy medicine or the mini oxygen cylinders sold in Darchen. Some Italians staying in the hotel took pity on him and gave him their unused oxygen, but he was still wheezing in bed when I left.

That night, I found a half-decent Tibetan restaurant and gorged myself, not sure what food I would find on the mountain. Later, I drank tea with Sili, a young Tibetan from Lhasa. Her family were Khampa originally and had come to Darchen to sell jewellery to tourists. 'I don't like it here, there's nothing to do, but business is good,' she said. Sili was eighteen but looked older, a result of the cruel effect living at altitude has on the skin. I had given up looking in the rare mirrors I encountered, shocked by my dry, red, wind- and sun-burned face.

Sili was a reverse migrant, the opposite of the Tibetans fleeing the countryside for the cities. There were others like her in Darchen, running restaurants and shops. There are few Han workers in Tibet's far west, just as the region attracts only a handful of Chinese tourists, in part because it is so far from civilisation but mainly because of the altitude. 'The Han don't like being so high, they think it is bad for them,' said Sili.

Many of the senior CCP officials sent to oversee Tibet refuse to live there, citing their susceptibility to altitude sickness as the reason why they have to stay in Chengdu. Hu Jintao, who governed Tibet between 1988 and 1992, and was president of China from 2002 to 2012, went further; he mostly ran Tibet from Beijing. That was almost certainly better for his career than being isolated out west. It was Hu who ordered the violent response to the 1989 protests in Lhasa, when the Wujing opened fire on the demonstrators. That decision established his hardline credentials with the CCP's elders, setting him on the path to the presidency.

Tenzin had a different theory to explain why hardly any Chinese attempt the Kailash Kora. 'The Han are lazy, they like to drive everywhere. You know why so many of them go to Everest base camp? It's because you can drive right up to it,' he said, laughing. But the paucity of Chinese migrants is a blessing because it leaves some space for locals like Sili to profit from the tourist trade, even if they have to go to the ends of Tibet to do so.

Like all the Tibetans in Darchen, Sili was a Kailash Kora veteran. 'I've done it eleven times this year already. We Tibetans do it in just one day. We start at four in the morning and finish at eight in the evening. It takes you westerners three days to do it, but Tibetans are strong,' she said, with a smile that was also a challenge. The Kora is fifty-one kilometres, a negligible distance on the flat but a daunting one at over 5,000 metres unless you have spent your life breathing Tibet's oxygen-depleted air. I had no intention of competing with the locals in a one-day marathon around the mountain.

As I walked back to the hotel, the clouds parted and I got my first glimpse of the strangely elongated summit of Kailash, the snow atop it glinting in the rays of the fading sun. Like everywhere in China Tibet runs on Beijing time, so it stays light till past nine in the evening in the summer. The dying sunset turned the surrounding grassland extraordinary shades of yellow and green, making Kailash's white-coated peak all the more alluring in contrast. I stared at it fascinated until darkness came. It felt as if the mountain was emanating energy, that I was being summoned towards it. I slept restlessly that night, wanting only to set foot on Kailash.

13

The Precious Jewel of the Snows

We set out in a light drizzle as the dark cloak that descends every night on the far west lifted slowly. A pack of amiable, inquisitive dogs escorted us uphill out of Darchen, before we turned left to walk clockwise around Kailash. Every Buddhist site in Tibet has to be circumnavigated in that direction, but I noticed a few people who went the opposite way. Tenzin told me they were followers of the Bon religion, the animist faith which held sway in Tibet until Buddhism began to make inroads in the seventh century. Kailash is a pilgrimage site for them too.

Initially, the going was easy as the stony track wound gently around the south face. Horses moved in packs across the nearby grassland, while berkuts, giant golden eagles, their curved, dark-brown bills clearly visible, circled low for prey above us. Saddled yaks came past, herded by two locals on horseback. 'They're for the Indians. A lot of them ride up to the north face,' said Tenzin. I had refused the offer of a porter, stripping my pack down to the bare essentials: sleeping bag, spare clothes, a toothbrush and some food. But the further we went, the heavier it felt.

There was an encampment of Hindu pilgrims a few kilometres out of Darchen, close to the entrance to a narrow gorge through which the Yarlung flowed. One side of the valley was dominated by the black granite wall of Kailash's west face, a huge, intimidating presence that rose towards the sky as far as I could see. Dank to the touch, it glistened from the waterfalls which had cut shallow channels in the rock, sending streams of water from the glaciers higher up the mountain to feed the Yarlung.

Tenzin pointed to a ledge decked out with a tangled rigging of prayer flags – a sky burial site. For Buddhists, the body is an empty vessel once life has expired, a useless irrelevance. In Tibet, where the ground is often rock hard, a sky burial is an effective means of disposing of it. Bodies are taken to designated locations on mountainsides and quickly chopped and crushed into small pieces, before vultures descend to make off with the remains. I was invited to a sky burial in Litang but had declined, uncomfortable with attending a funeral solely to witness such a shocking spectacle.

The track began to rise gradually as we traversed through the valley. Kailash couldn't have been closer, the west face hanging over us, yet I couldn't focus on it. The clouds were still down, although the rain had stopped, and the brief, tantalising glimpses of the upper slopes didn't clasp hold of my imagination the way the snow-draped summit had the night before. I concentrated on keeping moving as the trail climbed ever more sharply. Soon, I was sucking in air as hard as I could, inching forward in places rather than striding out.

Two nomads I encountered were going more slowly than me; they were prostrating their way around Kailash. 'It will take us fifteen days,' said one as he sat resting on a rock through which seams of rich red copper oxide ran. His scuffed and dirty leather kneepads and the wooden blocks on his hands were his only protection against the sharp rocks littering the track. The Tibetans on foot moved much faster, whether they were old ladies in traditional dress spinning their prayer wheels or young couples in jeans and windbreakers. They would be back in Darchen that night.

Around midday, an apple purchased from Uighurs in Darchen and a cup of black tea laced with salt in a tented teahouse revived me. Other travellers were resting too. One aged man asked me where I was from and when I said 'England' he told me he had once owned an English rifle, a 303 Lee Enfield. 'I used it to fight the Chinese in 1959,' he said, grinning faintly at the distant memory.

It took just over six hours to cover the eighteen kilometres to Dirapuk, where we would stay the first night, and the final stretch was a battle with heaving lungs and tiring legs as I ascended to 4,900 metres. Dirapuk is home only to a small monastery from which it takes its name, a collection of tents and a one-storey, long brick box with broken windows and a few rooms for passing travellers. A few hundred metres below was a newly built, more substantial hotel booked out by Indian pilgrims.

Dirapuk sits right underneath Kailash. As I approached, the clouds miraculously parted, blue sky appeared and suddenly there was the north face above me, a mostly snow-covered slab of malevolent black rock. At just over 6,700 metres, Kailash is not particularly high by Himalayan standards. But with its curved ridges and pyramid-like faces it looks nothing like the jagged peaks around it, or any other mountain. From far off, Kailash appears as a beautiful black and white diamond that has been planted arbitrarily on earth. Close up, it is a brooding, unsettling presence.

For Ippolito Desideri, an Italian Jesuit missionary who in 1715 became the first westerner to visit Kailash, the mountain was 'most horrible, barren, steep, and bitterly cold'. Desideri was no starry-eyed traveller, in part because he was suffering from snow blindness after crossing the Himalayas from India into Tibet. He wrote the first foreign account of the Kailash Kora, detailing how the Tibetan pilgrims 'walk most devoutly round the base of this mountain which takes several days and they believe will procure them great indulgences'.

No one knows how long Tibetans have been making pilgrimages around Kailash, walking for months or longer just to reach the mountain; Kailash's status as a throne of the gods is immemorial. For Buddhists it is the domain of Demchok, the Buddha who represents supreme bliss, and to do one circuit of Kailash will remove the sins of a lifetime. Complete 108 and the transgressions of all your existences are washed away. Sili in Darchen had many more to do before she could be certain of a carefree eternity.

Hindus regard the mountain with even more awe because it is the abode of Shiva, the god who is all things: benefactor, destroyer and transformer. He sits atop Kailash, his presence making it the fulcrum around which the world turns, surrounded by his *ganas*, or attendants, led by the elephant-headed Ganesha, who is both Shiva's son and a significant deity in his own right. Kailash's north face is believed to be etched with the same swastika that is marked on Ganesha's palm, making it the most holy part of the mountain for Hindus.

In the late afternoon, the Indians puffed up past Dirapuk to a location around 5,000 metres high and directly beneath the north face to pray and pose for group photos. Completing the full Kora is not essential for Hindus. Worshipping at Kailash's north face is the most important ritual of all. Nor did most of them even walk to Dirapuk, riding yaks and ponies instead. That they were here at all was enough, because in the recent past Kailash was barred to them. Tensions over the Sino-Indian border resulted in the mountain being closed to Hindu pilgrims between 1954 and 1978, and even now their numbers are limited by Beijing.

I met one of them outside the freezing, tiny room that was my home for the night. Ken was comfortably tubby, middle-aged and originally from Mill Hill in north London, but now resident in Germany. He had walked away from his group for a sly cigarette. 'I don't want the others to see me smoking,' he said. Not even Tibet's oxygen-light air can stop a dedicated smoker.

Ken told me he had been in 'unit trusts' in London, before giving it up to become a homeopath. Now he ran a company selling electronic medical devices. One of his products was strapped to his left arm. It looked like an over-sized watch and he claimed it increased the amount of oxygen carried in red blood cells through electrical pulses. Ken was a fount of dubious health tips and a natural salesman, and kindly offered me a balm which he said would cure my aching calves.

He was part of a group of seventy pilgrims and was frank about how he was here more for the experience than for religious reasons, admitting he had failed to make out the swastika on the north face that is supposed to be the representation of Ganesha. He was scathing about the motivation of the other Indian pilgrims too. 'Most of the people who come to Kailash are rich Hindus, many who live abroad,' he said. 'Real devotees can't afford to make this trip.' Nor was he in thrall to their swami. 'The best gurus are storytellers really. They can recite the scriptures in such a way that they enrapture the people listening.'

His concern about maintaining his strength at altitude was being sorely tested by what passed for bathroom facilities in Tibet's far west. 'I can't go here, can you?' he asked me. 'I try but I just can't. Once I see the toilets, it's enough to block me up.' I sympathised with him. A Tibetan pit lavatory can induce constipation in someone suffering from dysentery. On Kailash, where the temperature dropped significantly when the sun went down, crouching over them at night with a cold wind blowing brought the added risk of a frozen arse.

Tibet, and China, was of little interest to Ken and the other Indians. Kailash was the sole purpose of their trip. With so many foreigners in the area, and no Han present, the mountain was like its own little country, one which just happened to be on territory claimed by Beijing. I thought of Vatican City in the heart of Rome, yet a separate state from Italy. But the comparison is too simplistic and narrow because Kailash is claimed not just by one faith but by four. As well as adherents of Buddhism, Hinduism and Bon, the followers of Jainism, another religion whose origins lie across the Indian border, regard Kailash as sacred.

Once dominant in southern India, Jainism is now a minority faith which preaches pacifism and strict vegetarianism. Like Bon worshippers, Jainists do the Kora anti-clockwise, and both religions believe Kailash is where their founders had their spiritual awakening. And just as many elements of Bon ritual were incorporated into Tibetan Buddhism, so Jainism influenced Hinduism. Kailash is a catalyst, a place where religions meet and merge and spiritual precepts can be adapted while the fundamental holy nature of the mountain stays the same.

Just about the only locals Ken had met were the guides steering his group. He asked me if mine spoke English and I told him Tenzin had spent five years in Dharamsala. 'So many Tibetans go there. I don't know why they come back,' he said. Ken was another exile floating around China's borders. His parents had left India for east Africa before coming to the UK and now he was in Germany. When I asked him if he missed London, he shook his head. 'I don't care where I live.'

That night, I huddled close to the yak-dung stove in Dirapuk's one teahouse, delaying the moment when I would climb fully clothed into my sleeping bag to try and sleep. A husband-and-wife team ran the place, which was a prefab structure tacked on to the block I was staying in. Their newly born child was tucked tight in a fur-lined bag, his cheeks already spotted red. 'We stay here during the summer when the pilgrims come,' the wife told me. 'We go down to Darchen for the winter.' From October to April, with deep snow blocking the Kora route, Kailash is mostly deserted, home only to a few monks and the deities.

A boisterous crew of Tibetans sat drinking beer and *baijiu*. They weren't pilgrims, but a road crew slowly expanding the track leading back to Darchen. One day in the future the Indians will be able to drive all the way to Dirapuk and, if Tenzin's theory on how the Han like to ride rather than walk was true, they might be joined by a few Chinese. But somehow I doubted it, because there is nothing for the Han here. I couldn't imagine even the *zang piao* abandoning their Lhasa cafés for a mountain so alien to their culture. In a land the Chinese have occupied so comprehensively, perhaps Kailash alone remains truly independent.

Next morning, it was cold and wet again as I shouldered my pack for what would be the hardest leg of the Kora. There were more than twenty kilometres to cover, and most of them would be above 5,000 metres. Straightaway, I began ascending on a narrow track made slippery by the rain, stumbling and taking far shorter steps than I would lower down, my breathing shallow and quick. The first hour was agonising, as I struggled to get my protesting legs moving after a night of inactivity.

At 5,200 metres, we reached the snowline and the rain was replaced by a sky of high clouds broken up by patches of blue. For a brief, glorious period we trudged along on the flat, winding slowly right as Kailash's north face began to give way to the east, through a plain of rocks covered in ice and snow and interspersed with countless little streams running down from the summit of the mountain.

Those insignificant brooks are the source of four of Asia's major rivers. The Indus, Sutlej, Brahmaputra and Karnali, the largest tributary of the Ganges, begin on or near Kailash, feeding vast swathes of the subcontinent. The Indus crosses into India, before running the full length of Pakistan and into the Arabian Sea. Its easternmost tributary is the Sutlej, which flows into the Punjab in northern India and Pakistan. Nepal is watered by the Karnali, before it enters Bangladesh and India, as does the Brahmaputra, and becomes the Ganges, the lifeblood for the 400 million people who live in the surrounding river basin.

Perhaps it was some unconscious realisation that Kailash was giving them life that made Hindus and Buddhists, as well as the Bon adherents and Jainists before them, pinpoint the mountain as the heart of the world millennia prior to the region being identified as the source of the four rivers. By the nineteenth century, Europeans were vying to discover where they started from but it took them another 100 years actually to do so.

Sven Hedin, a dogged, driven Swedish explorer who criss-crossed central Asia, Xinjiang and Tibet repeatedly, is credited with discovering the origins of the Indus, Sutlej, Karnali and Brahmaputra on his 1905–8 expedition to the area. But it was the Englishman Bailey, during his unauthorised 1913 foray into southern Tibet, who confirmed that the Yarlung Tsangpo turns into the Brahmaputra.

Harnessing the hydroelectric potential of the rivers that flow from Kailash is a long-held dream of Beijing's, as is diverting them to help water inland China's increasingly parched landscape. In the 1990s, there was talk of building a dam in the Yarlung Tsangpo Gorge, the deepest canyon in the world, which would have dwarfed the giant Three Gorges Dam on the Yangtze River. Soon after I visited Kailash, Beijing was forced to abandon plans to re-route water from the gorge north to Xinjiang, after vehement protests from New Delhi over the impact it might have on the people living downstream in India and Bangladesh.

China is going ahead with building a smaller dam on the Yarlung Tsangpo, one of twenty-eight proposed hydroelectric projects on the river, despite India's opposition and fears of the effect it will have on the rare and fragile ecosystems dependent on it. With water an increasingly scarce and valuable commodity, the prospect of an environmental war between India and China is rather more likely than future clashes over their unresolved frontier.

Musing over geopolitics, as well as raising my eyes from the treacherous track occasionally to glimpse the snow and rock of the east face, helped distract me from thinking about the pain I knew was about to come. A second wind was pushing me across the all too short flat plain, but ahead I could see the start of the final climb up to the Dolma La Pass, the highest point of the Kora. The path rose dramatically, a near-vertical series of what were almost ledges cut into the rock. It was steep enough to make even the Tibetans slow down and the trail was choked with pilgrims bunched close together.

Walk, stop, go became my mantra as I hauled myself step by twisting step up to the pass, gulping air greedily. I could manage only twenty to thirty metres at a time, before being forced to pause, both leg-weary and short of breath. A yak train came through, pushing everyone to the side of the track. The shaggy-haired beasts were loaded with boxes and stumbling for grip as their handlers drove them upwards. Despite their size and horns, they were alarmed at being near so many humans, their eyes startled and wide open, and they veered hurriedly away from anyone who got too close.

Finally, after what seemed like an age but was actually about an hour, I was standing on the Dolma La at the heady height of 5,650 metres. Draped in prayer flags, so many I had to lift up the ropes they flew from to get to a position where I could take a photo of the mountain, it was narrow and crowded with pilgrims praying and resting. There were whole families up here, including grandparents and children – three generations united on the Kora.

Staying long was not an option. Close up, Kailash's east face is less impressive and sinister than its counterpart to the north. It looks more like a conventional peak from this angle, lacking the elemental magnetism that had made it so hard to tear my eyes away from the north face. The Dolma La was exposed too, windswept and cold, and although Tenzin muttered an incantation under his breath, I wasn't here to make merit like the pilgrims. We headed down, with deep snow on either side of the track, already more than halfway back to Darchen.

Any exultation in knowing that the climbing part of the Kora was over didn't last long. A fifteen-minute scramble at speed down a near-sheer slope of shifting rock, which Tenzin said would be quicker than following the path hugging the contours of the east face, proved fatal for my left boot. The outer sole was almost completely ripped off by the descent and soon I was walking on just the inner sole. Having thought I could be at our destination for the day in a couple of hours, I realised I would have to go slowly to ensure I didn't end up walking in my sock alone.

While Tenzin moved ahead, I limped along putting my weight on my right boot and constantly scanning the track for the water I thought would seep into my left boot. It was a dull ten kilometres to Zutrulphuk, a Dirapuk-like hamlet with a monastery and a few brick houses. Kailash was mostly hidden from view and the hike was enlivened only by the marmots popping their heads up from behind rocks to look at the people passing by, before swiftly ducking out of sight again. By the time I got to Zutrulphuk, I had blisters on both my big toes, and my right boot was showing signs of distress too.

Trekking slowly back on the final day, dipping down the track in bright sunshine, until finally rounding the east face to meet the southern side of Kailash, gave me time to contemplate the meaning of the journey I was about to complete. I struggled, though, to comprehend the true significance of the mountain for those who treat the Kora as a spiritual rite of passage, rather than a mere physical challenge in one of the world's remotest spots.

But as I walked the final few metres down Darchen's main street, while a convoy of land cruisers loaded with Indian pilgrims drove past, I thought at least I had done the Kora the way it has been done for thousands of years. More than that, I had come to the one part of Tibet still free of real Chinese influence. Kailash stands as an unchanging testament not only to the power of belief but to its supremacy over the diktats of the CCP – just another of the dynasties that have risen and fallen throughout Chinese history.

14

Going Down

There is a unique intensity to travelling in Tibet, at odds with the empty landscape and a people who subscribe to the fatalism inherent in Buddhism. Just being on the move all the time, shifting huge distances between towns that appear far more significant on the map than they are in reality, is wearing. And every day of the journey seemed to bring some new drama, whether it was incorrect permits, misunderstandings or an incident as insignificant yet vital as the disintegration of my walking boots. After almost a month in Tibet, I needed a holiday.

Tenzin suggested a rest cure of sorts: a drive further west along 219, where few travellers venture. It would take me as close to the Indian frontier as I could get, and there was the tantalising prospect of visiting a rare Bon monastery. After a hot shower in a public bathhouse, my first since Shigatse, and with the sky a commanding blue I felt more relaxed as we set off down the deserted 219, accompanied by herds of antelope running parallel to us on either side of the road.

To the right, there were tremendous views of Kailash's south face, its ridges so extreme that I doubted any climber could make it across them. Then, on the left, the western Himalayas appeared, dominated by the unmistakable, double-peaked Nanda Devi, the highest mountain in India. Despite being so visible, Nanda Devi is also sufficiently secluded that it took decades before a route through the valleys on the Indian–Tibet border to the starting point for its ascent was discovered. The men who achieved that feat were the intrepid explorers H. W. Tilman and Eric Shipton, long before their adventures in Xinjiang.

Speeding on, the land cruiser savouring the smooth tarmac of 219, the only properly paved road in western Tibet, we reached the hamlet of Tirthapuri. Wujing jeeps were parked up, checking trucks coming in the opposite direction from Xinjiang. A local bus sat waiting for passengers. I asked where it was going. 'Ali,' replied the driver, the last town of any size before the disputed region of Aksai Chin. He gestured at me to get aboard. I smiled and shook my head, tempted as I was by the prospect of travelling on.

Turning off 219, a rutted track took us into the Garuda Valley, once the capital of the ancient Bon kingdom of Shang Shung which ruled western Tibet – with Kailash at its heart – more than 2,000 years ago. A solitary village marked by a cairn of white stones and yak horns and surrounded by barley fields, irrigated by the Sutlej flowing down from Kailash towards India, occupied the valley plain. But the hills overlooking it were austere and lunar-like, a hint of the extreme landscape that lies further north in Aksai Chin. Shaded a dirty yellow, they were pockmarked with caves and strewn with stray rocks, many of them pure quartz.

High up on the far hillsides, ruined monasteries were visible, a reminder that much of what is now Tibetan Buddhist culture originated in Shang Shung. Stretching north towards Xinjiang and west into Nepal, it was so powerful a state that even King Songtsen Gampo, who united Tibet briefly in the seventh century, had been obliged to offer his sister as a bride to the kingdom's then monarch.

A sole Bon monastery survives still in Shang Shung. It is one of the few functioning ones left in Tibet, although there are others in western Nepal and Bhutan. Fewer than 10 per cent of Tibetans have stayed loyal to the Bon religion, most of them Ngari people. But, initially, nothing distinguished the monastery from its Buddhist counterparts. Prayer wheels ran around the exterior, a giant spider's web of prayer flags covered the hill behind it and a swastika adorned the entrance to the prayer hall – all symbols appropriated by Tibetan

Buddhism after King Songtsen Gampo imposed it as the country's primary faith.

Inside, though, the prayer hall was far less ornate than its Buddhist equivalents with fewer statues and *thangka*, or paintings, of deities. The skins of a leopard and wolf hung prominently, a legacy of the animist origins of Bon. Early Tibetan Buddhists traduced Bon adherents as members of a wrathful cult, known for bloody rituals and sacrifices, despite it also being a faith ultimately centred on the search for enlightenment.

Those distinctions made no difference to the Han, who sacked both Buddhist and Bon monasteries during the Cultural Revolution, according to the middle-aged monk, his close-cropped scalp bare in places from alopecia, guiding us around. 'I think the Chinese see Buddhists and Bon as the same essentially, except that they sometimes refer to our religion as "primitive". They don't understand us,' he said.

The second stage of Tenzin's post-Kora relaxation plan was still to come. A few days at Lake Manasarovar – the opportunity for a break from both trekking and the interminable hours we spent in the land cruiser. Two hours east of Darchen, Manasarovar is one of the highest freshwater lakes in the world, a body of water ninety kilometres round sitting just above 4,500 metres. As we descended towards it, the lake was cobalt blue in the sunshine, its shores gently sloping grassland. Behind us, the distinctive diamond shape of Kailash stood out like a beacon amid the mountains ranged around it.

Manasarovar is almost as sacred a spot as Kailash and is linked inextricably to it. Buddhists identify it as Lake Anotatta, where Maya, the mother of Buddha, was brought by the spirits to bathe in its waters before giving birth. Along with Kailash, Manasarovar is the only place in Tibet the Buddha is said to have visited. Some of Gandhi's ashes were scattered here, and for Hindus the lake signifies ultimate purity. Bathing in it to cleanse themselves of sin, as well as sometimes drinking its waters, is an essential part of their Kailash journey.

Indian pilgrims were walking back from the lakeshore as we arrived in Chiu, Manasarovar's main settlement, a line of low white-stone houses sited right by the lake and overlooked by a small monastery on a craggy hill. A tall man with a ponytail, moustache and dark-brown face emerged from one of them and shook Tenzin's hand. Tashi was a former monk from a nomad family. After the death of his parents, he sold their herd of yaks and settled by Manasarovar to run a guesthouse with his wife, who looked almost Native American with her broad, high-cheekboned face, pulled-back hair and fingers covered in silver rings.

An erudite man, Tashi spent much of the day in his study where the walls were lined with the *thangka* he painted. He liked to tell stories of his time as a monk, picking precise holes in the arguments the CCP employ to justify their role in selecting the most senior *tulku*. In addition, he was a welcoming host who brewed the finest *chang* I drank in Tibet. His wife, too, still had some yak meat left to liven up the fried rice I ate twice a day. My room was the usual concrete box, but I could reach the shores of Manasarovar from it in less than a minute.

I enjoyed the peaceful existence by the lake. Each morning, I climbed up to Chiu's monastery under the near-perfect blue skies that now appeared every day. Perched precariously on top of a prayer-flag-covered hill that offered spectacular views over Manasarovar and towards Kailash, it was home to six ancient monks. Hundreds of similar monasteries – tiny and isolated – are scattered across Tibet, manned by skeleton crews of lamas determinedly maintaining them despite the CCP's constraints on their numbers and practices.

Before the Cultural Revolution, there were eight monasteries sited around Manasarovar. Now, the five left are mere shadows of what they once were, even if Tibetan pilgrims still circumnavigate the lake on a Kora route that hasn't changed for thousands of years. But Chiu's temple was a superb vantage point, and luxuriating in the sunshine and looking down on the lake was an easy way to pass a few hours. In the harsh light of the midday sun, it appeared almost anaemic. By the late afternoon, though, the lake turned a rich blue again that made me long to jump in it for a swim, although I knew I wouldn't last long in its icy waters.

Killing animals, except for food, is prohibited in Buddhism. Nor do Tibetans eat fish; at least, I never met one who did. Manasarovar, like all Tibet's lakes, teems with life, its clear waters making the fish easily visible. When I waded in to see just how cold the water was, I was soon surrounded by fish of different sizes and colours, brushing and nibbling my legs and pulling at the hairs on them. It was an unusual but not unpleasant sensation.

Buddhism's strictures on the taking of life mean also that stray dogs far outnumber humans at Manasarovar, like everywhere outside Lhasa. But not even their random howling could disturb the supreme serenity of the lake. It is especially magical at night. Chiu is far smaller than Darchen or Saga and not on the electricity grid. The only lights at Tashi's place ran off car batteries and, once the sky had turned a black so inky and dense that it redefined the colour, we might have been invisible. I would step outside and listen to the water lapping against the lakeshore, while gazing up at more stars than I had imagined it was possible to see.

Elsewhere in Tibet, clouds had cloaked the constellations, or I had been in places lit up enough to dilute the effect of a star-filled sky. At Manasarovar, the nights were clear and the view was a canopy of stars that stretched for ever. I gaped at what appeared to be the entire Milky Way, thousands of little white dots so close together they seemed to merge into one colossal star glowing intensely bright. Just as I never got bored of looking at Tibet's never-ending sky during the day, I ended every night at Manasarovar staring upwards.

Climbing back into the land cruiser and departing from the lake felt like the end of my Tibet adventure; with the Kailash Kora completed, the only remaining task was to leave without being rumbled as a fake tourist by the authorities. But there was still time for more excitement. Soon after departing from Manasarovar, Tenzin, Lopa and I were standing by the car on a forsaken stretch of 219, peering at the engine and trying to figure out why it wasn't working any more. Lopa diagnosed a problem with the distributor. He called a friend in Darchen and asked him to come out with the part to rectify it.

Waiting for hours by the roadside didn't appeal. Having expected to spend the day inside the car, and lacking even vaguely clean socks, I was in bare feet and flip-flops, not the most suitable footwear when you are exposed to the wind at 4,800 metres. I decided to hitch a ride to Saga, leaving Tenzin with Lopa, counting on my Mandarin to explain why I was without my guide when I reached the Wujing checkpoint I would have to pass through before Paryang.

Hitching on a mostly traffic-free Tibetan highway is easy: the moment a vehicle approaches you rush out into the middle of the road and make it stop. That was my tactic anyway and it worked. A land cruiser full of rare Han tourists returning from Kailash, probably intrigued by the bare-footed foreigner, kindly offered me a cramped space alongside their luggage in the boot.

Their Tibetan driver fuelled himself with cans of energy drinks, lurching around corners so fast I thought we would turn over. But seven uncomfortable hours later I was back in Saga, the Wujing having given my passport and permit only the most cursory glance. Squelching through the familiar mud of the main street in my flip-flops, trainers in hand, I found a shop selling socks, which I put on straight away to the amusement of its owner.

One final stretch on 219 awaited us after a night in Saga, before Lopa's revitalised land cruiser turned south on an unsealed road leading to Nepal. It ran through a lonely valley of grassland, interspersed with exquisite, turquoise-coloured lakes, heading towards a long, unbroken line of splendid peaks: the spine of the Himalayas. I glimpsed Shishapangma, towering over the mountains around it, before we entered the western end of the Everest National Park.

We were still over 4,500 metres, and rose for one last time above 5,000 metres to cross the Tong La Pass. Everest was to the left, disappointingly obscured by clouds. But I jumped out of the car for a final look at the mountains that could be seen. The wind howled across the pass, busy with tourists in land cruisers coming from Nepal. This was their first proper stop on the high plateau, and they snapped pictures eagerly while talking excitedly about the altitude.

Going down was far quicker than driving up. In less than an hour, we were below 4,000 metres and the barley and mustard fields we had driven through in U-Tsang reappeared. We stopped for lunch in Nyalam, where Indians on their way to Kailash perused shops run by Nepali migrants selling the widest range of merchandise I'd seen since Shigatse. It was a shock to find places that didn't just offer instant noodles, water, beer and cigarettes. Nyalam is far cleaner than the towns of the far west, and I became conscious of how dirty and dishevelled I was in comparison to the people just arriving in Tibet.

It was thirty-two kilometres on to Zhangmu, the border town, zigzagging down a dizzying road which followed the contours of the deep gorge leading to Nepal and the Kathmandu Valley. In the time it took to get there, we dropped to 2,350 metres, the lowest altitude I had been at for a month. The air was suddenly heavier and stickier, the sides of the gorge covered in pine trees and lush green vegetation, among which purple and yellow flowers stood out – a delight after the high-altitude desert of western Tibet.

Zhangmu has by far the most spectacular setting of any border town in China I have visited. Spread out along the sides of a narrow road sloping sharply downhill towards Nepal and running along the left-hand side of the giant gorge, with the houses and shops rising up the hillside behind it, it was crowded with Chinese and Nepalese trucks waiting to cross the frontier. The spices of the subcontinent floated in the air, and Han and Nepali traders outnumbered Tibetans.

Being so low was invigorating. I charged up Zhangmu's steep street like an athlete who has been training at high altitude before descending to race at sea level. Sadly, the effect wore off after a couple of days. And for the first time in weeks, I was in a genuine hotel room with both a shower and a sit-down toilet. Lying on a bed with clean sheets and a real mattress felt as good as staying at the Ritz.

Demob happy at the prospect of leaving, I was taken aback the next morning when the Wujing soldier inspecting my passport at the frontier handed it to an officer who then disappeared. I had never seriously considered that, after the deceptions involved in reaching Tibet, I might have a problem getting out. I tried to convince myself that this was just a routine extra check, while doing my best to appear relaxed yet also a little annoyed at being held up – the natural reaction of any traveller anxious to move through a busy border as quickly as possible.

Ten nervous minutes later, my passport was returned with an exit stamp and I walked across the bridge that leads to the other side of the gorge and Nepal. I found a shared taxi and for five hours wound lower and lower through the Kathmandu Valley, with the temperature and humidity rising all the time, until we reached the frantic streets of Nepal's capital, where cars, bikes and pedestrians jostled for space. Tibet was already a memory, the mountains far behind me.

Part III

YUNNAN – TROUBLE IN PARADISE

The term savages, used by so many authors to denote all hill tribes of Indo-China, is very inaccurate and misleading, as many of these tribes are more civilised and humane than the tax-ridden inhabitants of the plain country and indeed merely the remains of once mighty empires.

Archibald Ross Colquhoun, *Amongst the Shans* (1895)

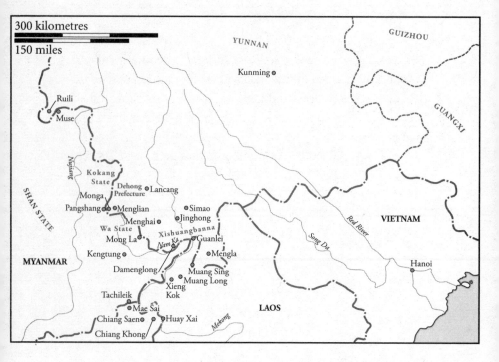

15

Shiny Happy Minorities

Early evening in Jinghong and the tour buses arrive in clusters at the town's theatre. They disgorge group after group of Han visitors, who are shepherded inside by their guides for the daily performance. To the accompaniment of music with only a tenuous link to the old songs of the region, young and attractive ethnic-minority women sashay across the stage in body-hugging dresses, performing fake versions of their traditional folk dances.

The dance show is the single most popular part of any trip by Chinese tourists to Jinghong, the capital of the Xishuangbanna region, deep in the south of Yunnan Province. With Laos and Myanmar a few hours' drive away, this is where China meets Southeast Asia. People from across the country are drawn here by a combination of the tropical climate and the perceived exoticism of the local minorities.

An unspoken but intrinsic aspect of Xishuangbanna's appeal for the Chinese is the reputation those ethnic groups have for being free and easy in their attitudes to sexuality, a vivid contrast with Han China where even talking publicly about sex remains something of a taboo. Alongside pictures of palm trees and elephants, the advertising used by the tour companies invariably includes tantalising photos of scantily clad, long-haired women bathing in the local rivers, or dancing gracefully in idyllic outdoor settings.

At one of Jinghong's most popular restaurants, visitors can listen to a band while teenage girls in traditional costume showing off their bare midriffs go from table to table singing. Then they sit on the laps of the male customers and make them drink a glass of beer over their shoulder. It is a ritual from the wedding ceremony of the Akha people, appropriated now by the tourist trade to cater to Han fantasies of licentious minorities living in paradise.

Those dreams are rooted in what the CCP regards as fact. Until the communists seized power in 1949, the Han knew little about the borderlands of Yunnan except that they were home to numerous peoples whom they regarded as barbarians. When the CCP started to classify them in 1953, no fewer than 260 different groups came forward asking to be registered as ethnic minorities. That was far too many for the Beijing bureaucrats, who swiftly lumped many of them together into larger, more manageable units.

Even so, almost half of China's fifty-five official minorities come from Yunnan, making it the most ethnically diverse region of China. It is also the most varied part of the country geographically. Taking up a large chunk of the south-west, Yunnan sprawls from the mountainous border with Tibet in the north, via temperate plains dotted with the remains of ancient kingdoms, south to the jungles of Xishuangbanna and the frontiers with Laos, Vietnam and Myanmar, which also borders Yunnan in the west.

Chinese anthropologists spent much of the 1950s investigating the minorities of Yunnan. Their approach was coloured by an inevitable assumption of Han superiority and their conclusions reveal an almost wilful misunderstanding of the local cultures and traditions. They pander both to every cliché about tribal peoples imaginable and to the demands of the CCP's propaganda department.

Thus the age-old animist beliefs of the minorities were categorised as 'primitive spirit worship', while the local landlords were slave-owners operating a 'feudal' system. The propensity of the minorities for singing and dancing was noted, as was their practice of what the Beijing academics described as 'free love', even though no evidence was offered to support that. As nonsensical as those reports are, they have been quoted in countless Chinese books since. That leads many

Han to associate Xishuangbanna with carefree savages who spend their time sleeping around and celebrating endless festivals.

Like the Han tourists, I was in search of tropical China when I first visited Xishuangbanna, which the locals abbreviate simply to 'Banna'. It was just after Christmas in 2008 and I was escaping the glacial embrace of Beijing's winter. As I travelled around, though, I was intrigued not by dance shows but by how different ethnicities and cultures exist in a space which mirrors other similarly diverse regions across the nearby borders.

Officially, Jinghong is the capital of the Xishuangbanna Dai Autonomous Prefecture, because around a third of its million-odd people are members of the Dai ethnic minority. But Banna is also home to at least twelve other ethnic groups. And what the anthropologists in the 1950s chose to ignore is that most of Banna's minorities can also be found living in other parts of South-east Asia.

The Dai are spread across the heart of the Golden Triangle, the notoriously anarchic enclave where the borders of Thailand, Myanmar, Laos and Xishuangbanna meet, and are especially numerous in Shan State in the far east of Myanmar and in the north-west of Laos. Also present in large numbers in eastern Myanmar are the Wa and Bulang, while the Akha, who the Chinese group with the Hani people, occupy hill regions across Laos, Myanmar, Thailand and Vietnam. They are joined there by the Lahu and Miao, who are known outside China as the Hmong.

Their languages, cultures, traditions and religions overrule the frontiers which were imposed on South-east Asia in the near past. The individual minorities feel a far greater sense of kinship with their cousins across the borders than they do with the Han, or the other ethnic groups who live alongside them. For the many different peoples of Banna, nationality is far less important than ethnicity, and the fact that they are technically Chinese citizens is almost an irrelevance.

Adding to the sense that Banna is a zone where the state is sidelined is the supremely porous nature of the frontiers here. Compared to Xinjiang and Tibet, where the natives are penned in by either the Wujing or the landscape itself, Yunnan's 4,000-kilometre-long boundary with South-east Asia is a mere line on a map. The largely unsecured borders are demarcated by narrow rivers, or run through rainforest, making moving between Banna, Myanmar, Laos and Vietnam easy. In some places, it is possible to drift across the frontiers without knowing you have done so.

While it is impossible for an army even the size of China's to monitor Yunnan's frontiers, Banna's near-open borders are in part due to Beijing's belief that the minorities here pose no threat to its hegemony. Unlike the Uighurs with their stealthy separatist groups, there is no Dai or Akha nationalist movement. And while the Dalai Lama sits across the border from Tibet, along with tens of thousands of exiles, mobilising international support for the Tibetan cause, no single leader could ever unify Banna's numerous minorities.

So apparently placid and genial are the local ethnic groups that some are held up as so-called 'model minorities'. They are ideal junior comrades, happy to sing and dance in their colourful costumes for Chinese tourists while Han officials get on with running the show. There is no overbearing security presence anywhere in Banna. On the contrary, when I moved to Jinghong for a few months I visited a succession of empty police stations while vainly trying to register my presence in the city.

Being stateless, though, is a way of life for Banna's minorities, who for centuries have defied frontiers and moved between countries at will. The name Xishuangbanna itself reveals the Dai's presence throughout the Golden Triangle. It is the Chinese version of the original Dai name 'Sipsongpanna', which translates as 'twelve rice-growing districts'. Those twelve different areas made up a former Dai kingdom, which ranged across what are now Banna, northern Laos and eastern Myanmar's Shan State.

No matter how apparently amiable the minorities appear to be, the pan-border ties they maintain have a dark side. With the CCP believing Banna's ethnic groups to be no challenge to their authority, the combination of those multi-national links and a lack of state supervision render the Yunnan borderlands the most lawless in all China. Beneath the swaying palm trees, drug smuggling, people trafficking, environmental crimes and illicit gambling are rife. More than anywhere else in the country, Yunnan's frontiers truly are places where the emperor is far away.

On its own that was enough to entice me to the region. But I didn't want just to investigate Yunnan's hidden smuggling routes and crime networks. I had a nagging urge to find out whether the accepted view of Banna's minorities as happy baby brothers to the Han was true. In a land where the concept of Han dominance is such a fundamental element of the Chinese state, I wanted to see if Yunnan is really a place free of ethnic tension.

To do that, I decided to base myself in Jinghong. Once more, I fled the snow and smog of the Beijing winter for Banna, only this time not for a holiday. I have been to countless provincial Chinese towns and cities over the years, but never lived in one. Jinghong, the capital of a frontier region where the Han are outnumbered two to one by other ethnic groups, was to be my introduction to small-town life in China.

A few hours south of Kunming, the capital of Yunnan, and I squirmed out of my coat for the last time for months to come. The closer the bus got to Jinghong, the easier it became to forget the winter I was leaving behind. Outside, the air was gloriously warm, sticky with moisture and the fragrant scents of South-east Asia. In Banna, the temperature never dips below 20 degrees Centigrade, and that is considered cold by the locals.

We raced along a fine highway, past tea, banana and rubber plantations. Ahead on the far horizon were the jungle-covered hills through which the frontiers with Laos and Myanmar run. Until the early 1960s, most of Banna was rainforest where tigers roamed and cobras and pythons awaited the unwary. People never worked in the fields alone, lest they encountered wild bears or rogue elephants.

Now, just 12 per cent of Banna is jungle, despite it being the last significant area of tropical rainforest in China. Much of it has been cleared for the rubber plantations that drive the local economy. They are pushing into the upland areas where the hill tribes practise shifting cultivation: moving from plot to plot to preserve the land. The rubber farms are Han-owned and leave a dwindling amount of space for peoples like the Akha, Bulang and Lahu, forcing more and more of them to descend to the towns they have spent their entire history avoiding.

Deforestation has also resulted in the Chinese turning to Myanmar and Laos to supply their timber needs in the south-west. In Myanmar especially much of the logging is unauthorised, done in collusion between Han-run companies and the Myanmar army with the local ethnic groups providing cheap labour. The mines that plunder jade, rubies and sapphires, as well as minerals like bauxite and copper, from Myanmar's borderlands operate in similar fashion.

But compared to the devastation wrought on much of inland China by unfettered industrialisation, Xishuangbanna still looks like the Promised Land. Shaded in multiple hues of green and irrigated by the Mekong River (which the Chinese call the Lancang) and its tributaries, tropical fruits grow in abundance here, while rice terraces rise up the hillsides in giant fertile steps. Yunnan is the most bio-diverse province in China, home to 150,000 different plant species alone. Banna's rainforests house many of them, as well as rare animals, even if the encroaching rubber plantations increasingly threaten their existence.

Jinghong was much as I remembered it – an overgrown village cut in half by the Mekong, so laid back it appears to be masquerading as Banna's capital. In the early 1980s, there were only 30,000 people living here, mostly in the wooden houses on stilts traditionally favoured by the Dai. Jinghong has expanded since then, as the jungle around it has receded. Now the town sprawls down both sides of the Mekong, linked by a couple of bridges, and the wooden homes have been replaced by uniform white buildings with sloping yellow roofs in the South-east Asian style.

Nevertheless, it still takes little more than ten minutes to drive across town, while the names of some of Jinghong's palm tree-lined streets are those of the villages it has absorbed in recent years. After frenetic Beijing, adapting to Banna's sluggish pace was a challenge. Jinghong doesn't really wake up till the late morning, a distinct contrast to the rest of China where the noodle and dumpling shops get going by dawn. And rather than manning their emporiums, many of the store owners sit in chairs on the pavement gossiping with their neighbours.

Only in the evening does Jinghong truly come alive, when the heat of the day diminishes and street-side barbecue stalls appear and stay busy until the early hours. I arrived in Banna's peak season, the time when Han tour groups visit for the balmy weather. From the Dai New Year in April onwards, the temperature and humidity rise remorselessly, and outbursts of torrential rain punctuate the muggy days. During the summer the locals retreat inside for much of the day, waiting for the sun to go down before emerging.

Increasing numbers of Han have bought holiday homes in Jinghong. New apartment blocks are mushrooming by the banks of the Mekong to house rich retirees from the east and north of China eager to see blue sky and feel a warm sun. China's colder cities get grimmer by the year when winter arrives, the skies a rancid mix of yellow and grey, as rising numbers of cars vie with coal-fired heating systems to send pollutant-rich smoke and fumes into the air.

Han immigration has caused both house prices and rents to spiral in Jinghong. I was taken around a number of uninspiring apartments by local estate agents, none able to comprehend that my idea of a shower didn't involve a rusty pipe. Then a friend suggested I try asking her landlady, a woman named Xiao Yu. I was still thinking like a Beijinger. In Jinghong, as in all small Chinese towns, almost everything is achieved through personal connections.

Xiao Yu, 'Little Yu', was a pretty, plump thirty-year-old Bulang woman with a squeaky voice. Later, I discovered that all Dai and Bulang women have the character for jade, or 'Yu', as a surname. Xiao Yu had grown up a couple of hours from Jinghong in one of the hill villages near the Myanmar border populated by the 90,000 or so Bulang in Yunnan. More of them live across the frontier, or work as migrant labour in northern Thailand.

In the 1950s classification of Banna's ethnic groups, the Bulang came out badly. Their isolated existence in the hills and belief in polytheism led to them being categorised as 'aborigines' and so ranked near the bottom of the Han hierarchy of minorities. Not only that, but the different Bulang clans were all grouped together as one minority, despite the fact that they regard themselves as individual entities and sometimes speak a completely separate dialect.

They are easy to spot in Jinghong, being darker-skinned and shorter than the Dai, and remain one of the poorest of China's ethnic groups. Xiao Yu's early life had not promised much. Married at fifteen to an older Han man, she gave birth to a daughter a year later but that didn't stop her husband from bringing his girlfriends home. Xiao Yu divorced him, before finding a much more suitable spouse: a French designer holidaying in Jinghong. Now she owned three apartments, one of which she agreed to rent to me, and commuted between Banna and Paris.

Other minority women in Jinghong, and some Chinese, were keen to follow Xiao Yu's example and land themselves a western man. In 2008, there were just a handful of foreign residents in Jinghong, all old China hands burned out by big-city life. Now the expatriate community in Jinghong has grown, in part because the reputation the local ladies have for being beautiful and accommodating has spread beyond the Han.

Around thirty or forty westerners were living in Jinghong when I arrived and they were mostly middle-aged men. All of them claimed it was the weather which had brought them to Banna. Sometimes, they said it was the last undiscovered corner of South-east Asia, a refuge from the masses that rampage through Thailand's islands each winter. But they were all single. Most spent their evenings flirting with the waitresses in the couple of restaurants that cater to foreign tourists, or visiting the karaoke bars and nightclubs in search of female company.

It is all very tame compared to the industrial nature of sex tourism in Thailand, and few of Jinghong's women were fooled. Most were like Xiao Yu, sweet and sensible people looking for proper relationships, as opposed to being the plaything of a fat European for the winter months. I did wonder, though, if the presence of libidinous foreigners was an omen of the future, like the golf courses and five-star hotels being constructed on the outskirts of town. Almost everyone in Jinghong believes it is on the verge of a boom, that the Han tour groups are just the advance party of the holiday hordes set to descend on sleepy Banna.

Western lotharios are still far outnumbered by the Burmese in Jinghong. On almost every street there is at least one Burmese-run jade or teak shop selling jewellery and elaborate wooden statues. There are so many that they defy economics: there simply aren't enough passing tourists to support them. Most of the time they are empty, apart from the staff lounging around in their *longyi*, Myanmar's version of the sarong, watching TV.

Locals whisper that the shops exist only to launder the proceeds of the various smuggling operations between Banna and Myanmar. There is a lot of idle chitchat in Jinghong, much of it malicious. It is a small enough place for people to know your business, or to speculate about it. Coming from Beijing, it was a shock to pass the same people in the street all the time and to realise they knew who I was without us ever having spoken.

Despite the gossips, Jinghong is a far more friendly and open place than Xinjiang and Tibet, where the overwhelming presence of China's security apparatus means the natives are often too scared to speak frankly to westerners, if at all. It was easy to get to know people and they were nearly always from the minorities. Within weeks, I had undergone a crash course in the different ethnic groups and began to gauge something of their different personalities and lifestyles.

Few people stayed in at night and my fondest memories of Jinghong are of the evenings spent eating delicious sour and spicy Dai food in open-air restaurants on the banks of the Mekong. We would sit for hours on low stools talking and toasting each other with rice wine. Each glass would be prefaced with everyone shouting 'Shuay! Shuay!', the Dai equivalent of 'cheers', a toast which has been adopted by the other minorities too. Compared to the often insular Han, spending time with Banna's ethnic groups is refreshing because they are both more outgoing and more inclusive.

As time passed, though, I started to suspect I was being told only so much and that what I was seeing and hearing was somehow censored for foreigners. I wondered at first if I was just being paranoid. But as I widened my social circle, I began to realise that acting one way in public and another in private is second nature for Banna's minorities. There are invisible barriers erected between the different ethnic groups and the Han and other outsiders. It was as if the hundreds of Burmese jade shops were a metaphor for Jinghong, that everyone here was hiding behind a false front.

16

Dailand

O f all Jinghong's different ethnic groups, it is the Dai who are the most impenetrable. Alone of Banna's major minorities, they are not a hill people. The Dai are historically sedentary farmers, valley dwellers who cultivate rice, pineapples and other tropical fruits. And unlike the hill tribes, the Dai did once have their own state, Sipsongpanna, although it spread beyond borders and has left them dispersed on either side of the frontiers between Banna, Myanmar and Laos, as well as northern Thailand.

But Banna remains the heartland of the Tai Lue, the name the Dai from here are known by outside China. From at least the twelfth century until 1953, Sipsongpanna was ruled from Jinghong by a monarch known as the Chao Fa, or the 'Prince of the Heavens'. He abdicated under pressure from the CCP and lived out his days in Kunming, while many of his relatives moved to Thailand. His wooden palace above the Mekong was torn down during the Cultural Revolution and replaced with a rubber farm.

Rubber, and before that tea, first brought the Han to Banna in significant numbers. In the 1950s, the government started taking over the long-established tea plantations around Simao, a town a couple hours north of Jinghong sometimes called Pu'er after the famous brand of tea grown there. The following decade saw the beginning of the deforestation of Xishuangbanna, as land was cleared for the first rubber farms. They were overwhelmingly staffed by Han migrants from Hunan Province in the south of China.

Many of the Chinese in Jinghong are their descendants and it is they who are behind most of the changes to the city. Until a decade or so ago, Manting Lu in the centre of Jinghong was lined with the same wooden Dai houses which had been there when the street was a village called Ban Tin. 'In 2008, we were forced to leave Manting Lu,' a Dai woman named Li Qingmei told me. 'Our house was demolished and replaced by a hotel run by Hunanese people. It was the last traditional Dai house left on Manting Lu.'

Li Qingmei was actually half Dai: her father was Han. But she had been raised by her mother and considered herself Dai, always dressing in the sarong-like patterned long skirt and embroidered top Dai women wear on formal occasions or holidays. Along with her husband, she ran a restaurant and bar. Shy initially, over time she revealed a teasing smile and personality.

At first, Li Qingmei seemed resigned to the loss of her home and the fact the Hunanese in Jinghong run virtually all the hotels and karaoke bars. Later, she voiced her true thoughts. 'The local people aren't happy with all the Han coming here. It's more competition, so it's harder for Dai people to start businesses now. And the Han tend to rent land and houses from other Han,' she told me one evening. 'You know, Dai people are Buddhist and easy-going and more concerned about their quality of life than the Han are. Han people are more aggressive and more focused on getting rich.'

In turn, the Chinese of Jinghong regard the Dai as indolent, a common criticism of minorities everywhere in China. And it is partly true. Banna's fecund landscape ensures that farming remains profitable and the Dai have also benefited by renting or selling some of their land to the rubber companies. Their lives are generally far easier than those of Banna's hill tribes and the minorities elsewhere in Yunnan, as well as most rural residents of inland China.

Few Dai are willing to admit they enjoy a comfortable lifestyle, but Banna's less fortunate peoples are happy to say so. The 300,000 Dai are the largest ethnic group in Banna and that complicates their relationship with the other minorities, who are jealous of their status as the leading minority. Animosity between the Dai and the hill tribes is longstanding anyway, stemming from the Dai being ruthless about pushing some of them, such as the Akha, Lahu and Wa, to the upland fringes of Sipsongpanna when they ruled it.

'For the Dai, the big money comes from the selling of their land to the rubber and tea plantations, as well as all kinds of illegal enterprises,' one Hani woman told me. 'Jinghong will always be sleepy and laid back because it is sub-tropical, but I think it is more sleepy than before. Easy money makes people lazy. I don't think there's ever been as much gambling in Jinghong as there is now.'

Gambling cuts across ethnic boundaries in China. Han high-rollers have made the casinos of the former Portuguese colony of Macau more profitable than those of Las Vegas. In Jinghong, regular cock fights take place on the less salubrious eastern side of town. But the serious betting occurs during mahjong and card games held in private apartments, like elsewhere in China.

More than anything, the Dai are less malleable than Banna's other minorities because their ownership of valuable land gives them economic power. Local Han officials and companies used to getting their own way with minorities who have nothing to bargain with, like the hill tribes, resent that. And unlike Xinjiang and Tibet, the Chinese cannot impose their will at the point of a gun. In Banna, Beijing is careful to maintain friendly relations with all the minorities, but especially the Dai. The last thing the CCP wants in Yunnan is a repeat of the tension which has polarised the Han from the Tibetans and Uighurs.

Keeping their relationship with the Han outwardly cordial is important for the Dai too. In public, they appear as the cute sidekicks of the Chinese. They smile at the tourists and speak Mandarin, while offering them a diluted, utterly unthreatening glimpse of their traditional lifestyle. Like animals in the wild using camouflage as protection from predators, the Dai have learned to present themselves in a way which is guaranteed to charm the Chinese. It is as if they instinctively know how the Han want the minorities to behave and flatter them accordingly.

That leaves the Han with little alternative but to be bowled over by the hospitality and the alluring women and to accept the Dai as wholly benign. In the unconscious orientalism which informs the Han vision of China's minorities, the Dai are like a dream of how a subservient ethnic group should act. Many Chinese coming to Banna for the first time wonder why those ungrateful Uighurs and Tibetans can't accept Han dominion as gracefully as the Dai have.

Out of the gaze of the tour groups, though, the Dai behave very differently. It is as if an unseen veil segregates them from the Chinese. Behind it, they preserve the most valuable aspects of their identity – language and a culture and religion that transcend borders – which would likely antagonise the CCP if put on show. To reveal them could result in officialdom taking a more quizzical view of their ties outside China, or adopting a more forceful attitude towards the acquisition of Dai land.

Their Janus-like approach to dealing with the Han reminded me of their close relatives the Thais, another pragmatic people adept at presenting a smiling face to visitors and quite another one in private. Over time, I came to believe the Dai to be the most Machiavellian of all China's ethnic groups. By acquiescing in the Chinese appropriation of the most superficial aspects of their culture for the tourist trade, they have created some room in which to preserve their fundamental uniqueness in the face of the increasing Han presence in Banna.

Penetrating the hidden layers of the Dai existence is difficult, because they are so accustomed to hiding much of their lives from view. In public, they speak Mandarin but privately many dislike the way it is slowly replacing the Dai language in Jinghong and Banna's towns especially. 'A lot of people in Jinghong don't speak Dai now. It has a big effect on our culture if no one speaks the language, or they don't wear our traditional clothes,' said Yu Shumei, one of my Dai friends. 'None of the schools teach Dai now, so kids can only pick it up at home, like my son. They can understand what we are saying, but they can't really speak Dai.'

A smartly dressed divorcee in her mid-thirties, Yu Shumei ran a jewellery shop. Like Li Qingmei, she was cautious and more than a little suspicious of me when we first met. But after I started helping her nine-year-old son with his English homework, she relaxed and began to show me the Dai side of Jinghong. She was from a well-off family, and I knew I had her seal of approval when I was introduced to her mother, a tiny, elegant woman who always wore Dai garb. I bumped into her often as she trotted around Jinghong collecting rent from the properties they owned.

Shumei invited me to celebrate the Dai New Year with her friends and family. It is a very different festival to the Chinese New Year, which falls in January or February and is known in Mandarin as Chun Jie. Outside the borderlands it is celebrated with a cacophony of fireworks. Chinese New Year in Jinghong, though, was the quietest I had ever experienced. Han restaurant owners set off firecrackers strung together like machine-gun belts outside their premises. But for everyone else it was just a normal day. 'We're OK to skip Chun Jie,' Shumei told me. 'It's the Dai New Year that is important for us.'

Following the traditions of the Thai New Year, which both the Dai and Thai call Songkran, the Dai New Year is a three-day celebration in the middle of April. It starts soberly with the statues in Buddhist temples being washed, before ending with a chaotic street party on the final day in which water is hurled around and everyone gets soaked – a symbolic way of rinsing away the old year and its sins and starting afresh.

Celebrating New Year at the same time as much of the rest of South-east Asia offers the Dai another chance to affirm their essential separateness from the Han, as well as revealing how they continue to regard ethnicity as more important than the state. To reject the most significant Chinese festival, the Han version of Christmas and New Year rolled into one, is some statement. But the Dai New Year illustrates also the way less crucial elements of Dai culture have been handed over for public consumption, leaving the essence uncontaminated by Han hands.

Nothing appeared to be happening for the first two days of Songkran, as the locals worshipped at their temples out of sight of the tourists. Only the presence of Dai women walking around in their Sunday best of bright long skirts and tunic-like blouses, with their hair coiled in buns and carefully made-up faces shielded from the sun by umbrellas, gave the clue that something out of the ordinary was taking place.

To the Han, the religious aspect of the Dai New Year is unimportant and largely unknown. They call it the water-splashing festival, a reference to the events of the final day and a way of avoiding having to acknowledge that the Dai choose to celebrate a different New Year to them. The chance to throw water around all day is the appeal for the Chinese. Many buy powerful water pistols and guns, with attached water containers which they wear on their backs like a scuba diver's air tank.

Emerging from my apartment on the morning of the third day of Songkran, I found the water war in full flow. The Han ran around firing their guns and squealing when they were hit themselves. Women on the streets sold plastic buckets and bowls for those who lacked their own weapons. Groups of Dai drove down the main streets in pick-up trucks, their flat beds lined with plastic sheets and filled with water. They threw it over passing pedestrians, or hurled it through the windows of any car whose occupants were foolish enough to be driving with them open.

By the time Shumei arrived, I was drenched. Foreigners are a particular target, so almost everyone who passed either sprayed me, or sneaked up behind and tipped water over my head. My phone was wrapped in a plastic bag to preserve it – the watching police did the same with their radios – and in the fierce sun the impromptu showers were rather pleasant. I was happy too in the knowledge that the wetter you get at Dai New Year, the luckier you will be over the next twelve months.

I jumped in the car quickly, to spare the other occupants from getting soaked through the open door. We headed out of Jinghong to Man Sha, a village that was home to one of Shumei's childhood friends. Young Dai lined the road chucking water at the cars driving past. 'I used to go out and splash water, but I'm older now and don't want to go to all that trouble,' said Shumei. 'Going to the temple to wash the statues and pray for a good year is more important for me. But the kids love it.'

Our destination was a substantial Dai wooden house, raised up almost level with the surrounding trees by its stilts. A concrete wall guarded it and a terrace had been tacked on, where card games were already under way. Inside, the two floors of the house were crowded with people sitting on stools around low tables laden with Dai delicacies. We ate tangy beef that had been hung and dried and cut into long strips, sour bamboo shoots, fish from the Mekong covered in herbs, chicken on the bone and sticky rice which we scooped out of bowls with our hands.

There must have been over fifty people in the house, ranging in age from toddlers to eighty-year-olds. Everyone moved from group to group constantly, toasting each other with beer or rice wine and the inevitable shout of '*Shuay! Shuay!*' In one corner upstairs, where the family slept on mats on the floor, was a makeshift shrine decorated with money and offerings of food and alcohol.

What was going on in Man Sha and in Jinghong at the same time reveals how the Dai are so adroit at maintaining the division between their public and private personas. In Jinghong, the Dai shared the streets with the visiting Han, who were allowed to participate in the water-splashing and made to feel welcome. But the celebration in Man Sha was specifically Dai and took place out of sight of the Han, like their visits to the Buddhist temples on the previous two days. It was far more relaxed too than Chinese New Year, which is principally an event reserved for close family only.

Songkran has a very different purpose. It is an excuse to gather together as many friends and family as possible for a party, a philosophy embodied in the Thai concept of *sanuk*. Literally meaning 'to have fun', *sanuk* is about milking any event for as much enjoyment as possible and always with a big group of friends. Sitting with your family watching the Chinese New Year Gala on TV, as much of a ritual for the Han as viewing the Queen's Christmas Message is for the British on Christmas Day, is the opposite of *sanuk*. For the Dai, celebrating that way is as alien an idea as Chun Jie itself.

Fresh dishes were still arriving on the tables and boxes of beer were stacked up waiting to be drunk when I left. Back in Jinghong, the water battles were still going on, with people opening up the pipes on the streets to find fresh fluids or running into shops to use their taps. As I made my way home, there were shouts of '*laowai*', one of the Mandarin words that means 'foreigner', and I was doused almost every step of the way. Everyone grinned at me and I smiled back; it was *sanuk* in action.

If Songkran reveals the duality of the Dai personality, then so does almost everything they do. Dai teenagers listen to the same Taiwanese pop as their Han contemporaries, but they also attend concerts where Dai bands from Banna, and sometimes Myanmar, sing and play in Dai. Some head to Kunming to work; others slip off to northern Thailand where the dialect spoken is almost the same as the Dai language. Most Dai dress like the Han in public, yet the women revert to their traditional dress for family events, festivals and private parties.

Especially essential for the Dai is the need to protect their religious lives from the Han, a vital part of their cross-border identity. The Dai follow the same tradition of Theravada Buddhism as most of the rest of South-east Asia does. Banna's other minorities are Buddhists as well, apart from some of the hill tribes who have abandoned their animist beliefs and converted to Christianity, a result of extensive missionary activity in the Yunnan borderlands before 1949.

Monks in their bright-orange robes are a familiar sight in Jinghong. A first-time visitor might regard their presence as evidence of the CCP's tolerance of the Dai's Buddhist practices. Backing that theory up is the monastery perched on a hillside on the southern outskirts of town overlooked by a giant golden statue forty-five metres high of the Buddha Sakyamuni. It is a reasonable assumption to make, because it is by far Jinghong's most distinctive landmark and visible for miles around.

Like Jinghong's jade shops, though, the monastery is just another front. It is a functioning temple, but one that is a Chinese creation, designed as a commercial enterprise to take advantage of Han visitors and populated by a crew of mutinous monks. Even the giant Buddha isn't what it seems, being made of mundane steel covered in gold leaf rather than solid gold.

Although it is the largest Theravada Buddhist temple in China, the Dai have boycotted it since it opened in late 2007. They continue to attend Wat Pajay, Banna's most historic and important monastery. Close to the centre of Jinghong, Wat Pajay is known as Zong Fosi, or 'middle temple', to the Chinese. But it gets only a passing mention in the Han guides to Jinghong. They direct everyone to the newer monastery, which they call Da Fosi, 'big temple', in an attempt to establish its credentials as the principal place of worship in the area.

When I visited Da Fosi, I was stunned by the extortionate entrance fee: double the price of a ticket to the Forbidden City in Beijing. But there were plenty of Chinese tourists milling around the entrance, perusing the Han-run stalls selling incense, jade and Buddhist icons while they waited to go in. 'The most expensive incense is 300 yuan [£30]. 300 yuan! But the Chinese will pay, they have money,' a monk named Zhang Wei told me.

Zhang Wei got me in for free. A mutual friend had arranged for us to meet. He turned up in a new Honda, shaven-headed and incongruous in his robes behind the steering wheel. 'We need the car so we can visit all the villages,' he said. 'Every village has its own temple now.' Out in rural Dailand, well away from Chinese eyes, there has been a quiet revival in Buddhism over the last thirty years. Fewer than 150 temples in Banna survived the Cultural Revolution. Now, there are close to 600, all administered from Wat Pajay.

We drove up a side road until we reached the four-storey building that houses the monks of Da Fosi. There was a small covered terrace outside, where we sat alongside a couple of novices flirting gently in Dai with two teenage girls. 'We all speak Dai here. A lot of the young monks are from the countryside and their Chinese is not very good,' said Zhang Wei. Small and slight, he looked no older than twenty himself, fingering his iPhone like any fidgety teenager enduring an unwelcome chat with a boring adult.

With his latest-model phone, a computer in his room, a car to get him around and, as I learned from subsequent meetings, a taste for coffee and western food, Zhang Wei was considerably more sophisticated than the monks I met in Tibet. But like most of his Tibetan and Dai contemporaries, he was a country boy. The son of farmers from Damenlong, a village on the border with Myanmar, Zhang Wei had joined his local temple aged nine before graduating to Wat Pajay at sixteen.

Now he was twenty-five and a veteran monk. He was more assertive than he appeared to be at first and didn't pull his punches as he described the dispute between the monks and the company who built and run Da Fosi. 'We don't like them and we're always arguing with them. But they don't listen to us and they are very close to the local government,' he explained. 'We'd all rather be at Wat Pajay instead. We're trying to expand it so we can move back.' Banna's Buddhist resurgence has left Wat Pajay unable to accommodate the growing number of monks, and Zhang Wei was bitter at the way he and others had been duped into moving to Da Fosi.

'Originally, the company told us they were going to build a new temple and would we like to come and live there. Wat Pajay was already too small for us so we said yes. Then we moved in and they started to charge 120 yuan [£12] for tourists to come here and it became clear it was just about making money for them. We don't agree with such a high price, or all the stalls that cheat people by over-charging. That's not the Buddhist way.'

The move to Da Fosi provoked a schism in Jinghong's monastic community. Around twenty-five of the oldest and most senior monks flatly refused to leave Wat Pajay and still live there, including the Abbot. Zhang Wei showed me the house built for him at Da Fosi, which the Chinese call the 'Grandmaster Residence' as if he was a chess superstar. It has never been occupied. But around 100 monks are resident at Da Fosi, including the novices whom Zhang Wei taught Dai to.

'Many young Dai can't read our language and don't really under-stand our culture or Buddhism. A lot of Dai people can speak Dai, but they don't teach it in normal school any more so you have to become a monk to learn how to read and write it,' said Zhang Wei. As in Tibet, the monasteries have become the only place in Banna where locals can get an education in their native language. But unlike Tibet, and in another sign of the Dai's success in convincing the CCP of their essential affability, novices in Banna are allowed to partici-pate in the regular school system as well.

'You can study Dai here in the morning and go to normal school in the afternoon,' said Zhang Wei. He believed that was behind the recent rise in the number of monks. 'A lot of young Dai were put off becoming monks because they thought it was a hard life and what they learned wasn't useful in the outside world,' he told me. 'Now it's not as strict a life as before. When I was a young novice, the teachers would beat you if you disobeyed them. But we're not allowed to do that any more.'

Less welcome has been the diminishing of Banna's role as a key centre of Buddhist learning for Dai people across South-east Asia, a result of the devastation wrought on Banna's monasteries during the

Cultural Revolution. Large numbers of monks fled across the frontiers, while villagers buried scriptures and icons in the jungle so the Red Guards couldn't destroy them. Many of the temples have since been restored, but Wat Pajay's status as a spiritual university has been superseded by monasteries outside Banna.

'Before the Cultural Revolution, Thai and Burmese and Lao monks came to Wat Pajay to study. Now, we go to Thailand and other places. It's a complete change,' said Zhang Wei. Fluid borders mean Banna's monks can visit monasteries in Myanmar and Laos unofficially. But the Dai's position as a model minority makes getting permission to go abroad far easier than it is for Tibetans or Uighurs. Zhang Wei had already spent a year in Yangon, as well as three in Singapore.

Wat Pajay's links with overseas monasteries are a crucial element of the cultural and religious networks that tie the Dai of different countries to each other. Da Fosi is an irrelevance in that scheme; its imposition on Jinghong just another instance of Dai culture being appropriated by the Han for the purposes of tourism. And, inevitably, pretty Dai women act as the guides there. But out in greater Dailand, in Banna's villages and across the borders, the Dai are quietly getting on with worshipping their way, while keeping their language and traditions alive.

17

Down the Mekong

South of Jinghong, Banna's hills grow steeper as they roll towards Laos and Myanmar. Although the rubber plantations are increasingly infiltrating here, much of the area is still thick jungle. A highway runs to the frontier with Laos, but otherwise just a few roads cut through the rainforest. Parts of it bear the telltale signs of the slash-and-burn agriculture practised by the hill tribes – blackened land where the trees and vegetation have been burned off so the ash will fertilise the soil. Hidden tracks known only to the locals lead across the borders.

Beijing has grandiose plans to link Banna with the rest of South-east Asia via high-speed trains which will depart Kunming, reach Jinghong in an hour and then speed on to Singapore via Vientiane, Bangkok and Kuala Lumpur. Other branches will reach into Myanmar, Vietnam and Cambodia. It is not a new notion; both the British and French proposed a Kunming–Singapore line as far back as 1900. Yet only Laos's leaders, the Lao People's Revolutionary Party – an organisation even more opaque than the CCP and less tolerant of dissent – have truly embraced the idea.

Rather than roads or railways, the Mekong remains South-east Asia's main transport artery for now. Rising in Tibet, the Mekong runs south for 4,300 kilometres, first through Yunnan and then acting as the border between Myanmar's Shan State and Laos, before it arrives at a junction where the frontiers of Thailand, Laos and Myanmar meet. From there, it changes course, veering east and then south again to flow through Laos and into Cambodia and Vietnam, where it empties into the South China Sea.

Long before there were roads in Banna, the Mekong was the means by which its peoples moved around; travelling by water was easier than hacking your way through the jungle. The Mekong was the lifeblood for the minorities. It was both a source of food and the means by which they traded with the rest of South-east Asia, exchanging cotton, tea, salt and opium for betel nut, silver and pepper. Above all, it was the Mekong which facilitated the cross-border ties that link Banna's ethnic groups to the rest of the region.

Even now, the Mekong remains vital to trade between Yunnan and the neighbouring countries. Around 300,000 tonnes of cargo moves to and from China along the Mekong each year, and that is just the legal shipments. Utilising the river was the logical way for me to explore greater Dailand. I wanted to travel south down the Mekong to Thailand and then venture north to Kengtung in Shan State, before crossing the Mekong to Laos and returning to Banna by land.

It would be a journey through the heart of the Golden Triangle, one of the world's most lawless zones and the last great gathering place for the minorities of South-east Asia who still resist the concept of statehood. Technically, the Golden Triangle refers to the junction on the Mekong where the borders of Laos, Myanmar and Thailand converge. In reality, it spreads much further. Greater Dailand stretches deep into the Golden Triangle and it has always been a place of refuge for those who have rejected Chinese rule.

To travel the Mekong, I needed to find a ride on a cargo boat. In the past, Jinghong was the starting point for the maritime traders going south. The city is divided by the river and it took only a walk to its banks to find transport. Now the river has been dammed upstream. The Mekong's muddy waters still run wide and slow through Jinghong, but much of the time it is far too shallow for anything more than a small craft to navigate it.

Instead, I arranged to join a boat which made regular runs from Guanlei, a town a few hours south-east of Jinghong, to Chiang Saen, a port in northern Thailand just south of where Myanmar, Laos and Thailand meet. But after arriving in Guanlei at midday, blinking in the blinding sunlight, I wondered if I was in the right place because I could see no river or anything resembling a port.

A phone call prompted the arrival of one of the boat's crew on a motorbike. We raced through Guanlei's streets, before the road started curving downhill and the Mekong appeared below, glistening green in the sun, the palm trees on its far bank leaning out over the water like natural derricks. At the port, cargo boats were moored three deep and I was directed to the vessel that would be taking me to Thailand.

Like the boats around it, the *Pao Shou Ba* would never win any prizes for its graceful lines. It was essentially a long, flat-bottomed barge, most of it taken up by an open hold, of the type that still haul garbage down the Thames in London. Attached at its stern was a rickety, two-deck superstructure, which housed the engine room, bridge, galley and cabins for the crew. A large Chinese flag fluttered above the bridge. In a pleasing nod to the trans-national nature of the Mekong, the flags of Laos, Myanmar and Thailand flew either side of it.

Our cargo was sunflower seeds, 500 sacks of them, and for the next couple of hours, wiry, dark-skinned Dai men hauled the bags off a truck on their backs before tipping them into the hold. 'We normally carry food, fuel, cement and other building supplies, tyres, construction machinery – anything made in China they need in Thailand really,' said Cao Mei, the boat's owner.

Cao Mei was pudgy and cheerful, a thirtysomething Han woman originally from Kunming. All the boats that ply the Mekong from Banna are Chinese owned. Their crews, though, are mostly minorities and live on board full time. The *Pao Shou Ba*'s captain was Yi, one of the largest of China's ethnic groups with over eight million people spread across the south-west but originally from central Yunnan. Two friendly Dai men, their arms covered in Dai-script tattoos, assisted him, while a grumpy Hani man looked after the engines. A taciturn Han woman was responsible for cooking and washing.

I was assigned a bunk in the engineer's disgusting cabin, which was possibly why he was so bad tempered. Or it could have been the infernal noise of the engine, which was located next door and made the whole boat vibrate. I spent most of the journey on the cramped bridge, where the skipper steered with an old-fashioned wooden wheel, or perched on the bow of the boat watching the Mekong glide by beneath me.

Later, I trooped up to passport control to get stamped out of China. The actual frontier is three hours south and unmarked, making Guanlei the last place where there is an official Chinese presence. It was the sleepiest border post I'd been to in China. Empty when I got there, I hung around until a flustered female Wujing officer appeared and swiftly scanned my passport.

Just before we left, a couple of Wujing boarded the boat but only to check we weren't carrying anyone they didn't know about. Even in laidback Banna, the lax security surprised me. We were going to be sailing through the Golden Triangle, infamous for once being the capital of the global heroin trade. The region still accounts for around 10 per cent of all the opium grown in the world, as well as being home to jungle labs that manufacture huge quantities of *yaba*, an amphetamine pill popular across Asia, and ice, an even more potent stimulant. We could have been carrying the precursor chemicals needed to make them, yet no one bothered to inspect our cargo.

My trip down the Mekong came before thirteen Chinese sailors were found murdered on two vessels sailing out of Guanlei. They had been blindfolded, handcuffed and shot in the head. According to the subsequent investigation by the Chinese, Burmese and Thai authorities, their boats had been hijacked by pirates based in Shan State and used to transport almost one million *yaba* pills.

Few people who know the Golden Triangle believed the official story. Infuriated by the killings, Beijing had demanded a swift response from its far less powerful neighbours. The leader of the pirates, a Shan man named Naw Kham, was subsequently caught in Laos and immediately sent north to Yunnan without anything as formal as an extradition request, despite technically being a citizen of Myanmar, to be executed in Kunming.

Naw Kham was certainly a pirate, and familiar to all who sail this stretch of the Mekong regularly. 'I never encountered him but I know people who did,' one Lao boat skipper subsequently told me. 'They were an extended gang really. There were Chinese, Lao and Thai people in it too. They would come from the Shan State side of the river in fast longtail boats and pull up alongside with guns. Then they'd jump on board and raid the cargo, or demand money.'

Whether he was responsible for the murder of the Chinese sailors is less certain. Some locals regarded him as a convenient scapegoat. Others said he had become too greedy and wasn't sharing enough of the profits from his stand-and-deliver trade and so had been given up to the Chinese as punishment. What is definite is that Naw Kham could not have operated independently of the ethnic minority armies who control much of Shan State, while overseeing the heroin and methamphetamine business in the Golden Triangle in close co-operation with their Wa and Dai cousins in Banna.

River traffic from Yunnan was temporarily halted after the murders and Guanlei's somnolent Wujing garrison was reinforced. Some soldiers took to boats to patrol the Mekong beyond China's borders, another display of Beijing's might in a region where Chinese companies are increasingly active in their search for new economic opportunities. The militias in Shan State responded by starting to take pot shots at passing vessels. I was lucky to have travelled when I did; the days of foreigners hitching rides down the Mekong from China are gone for now.

At four in the afternoon, the boats hemming us in moved away and the skipper backed the *Pao Shou Ba* away from the dock. Mid-river, he spun the wheel and we swung slowly around until the bow was pointing south. A long string of firecrackers was set off, to mark the fact that this was the boat's first voyage after Chinese New Year, and then we were pulling away from Guanlei, accelerating surprisingly quickly as we headed downriver.

Almost immediately, it became apparent how treacherous this stretch of the Mekong is. Far narrower than in Jinghong – less than twenty metres wide in places – the water eddied around partially submerged rocks, while sand banks waited to wreck the unwary. We progressed not in a straight line but by weaving in wide arcs from side to side. The water level, too, was low even here thanks to the dams upstream.

Occasional strips of white sand made sections of the river banks look like untouched beaches. Odd areas had been cleared for farming and we passed a few tiny hamlets of wooden huts. Mostly, though, there was no sign of life. The jungle started where the water stopped, rising up the hills beyond the banks, and it was impossible to see anything through the green barricade of tall, tangled trees. Only glimpses of smoke curling up above them revealed that people were living close by.

After a few hours, my phone lost its signal. 'We've left China,' the skipper said. Now we were floating stateless between countries. The Mekong here divides Laos on the left-hand bank from Myanmar on the right. Thailand was due south and Banna behind us, but out on the river we were nowhere except greater Dailand. In the time before South-east Asia's frontiers were fixed, this stretch of water was part of Sipsongpanna, the old Dai kingdom which reached from Banna into the far east of Myanmar and north-west Laos, its twelve rice-growing districts divided on either side of the Mekong.

Sipsongpanna was already a thriving state by the time the Han started to show a real interest in Yunnan. In common with all Chinese versions of the history of the borderlands, which aim to prove Beijing's incontestable right to rule the furthest-flung parts of its empire, official accounts emphasise the sheer antiquity of the

Chinese presence in Yunnan. They date it back to the second century BC and the Han dynasty. But at that time the Han were confined only to the area around what is now Kunming, while the rest of the region was divided into mini-states governed by Yunnan's different minorities.

Not until the late fourteenth century did the then ruling Ming dynasty start formally to incorporate those statelets into China. They showed scant respect for the different ethnic groups living in them, categorising the minorities as 'wily and deceitful, barbarous, rebellious and perverse'. The Ming emperor Jiajing thought Yunnan's peoples no better 'than the birds and the beasts' and 'without human morality'. Jiajing was not exactly the humane type himself. He had all his concubines sliced to death in 1542 after they conspired to strangle him in his sleep – their reaction to his ill-treatment of them.

During this period, the Dai, far from being a model minority, were regarded as uncooked savages like the hill tribes. By resisting incorporation into the Chinese empire, they revealed their atavistic tendencies. But ultimately Banna's remoteness ensured it could not be conquered by the Ming, who settled instead for a fragile alliance with Sipsongpanna while leaving it largely alone. Banna had similar slippery treaties with neighbouring Dai kingdoms, such as Kengtung in present-day Shan State, sometimes fighting on their side, sometimes against them.

Centuries of cutting deals with both the Chinese and rival Dai states, playing one side off against the other, perhaps explains why the Dai are still so skilled at keeping the Han at arm's length. But the hill tribes, then as now, were less lucky. As the Chinese moved inexorably south, the Akha, Lahu, Miao, Wa and others fled ahead of them, marking the beginning of their dispersal across the Golden Triangle. In a neat irony, they were joined in the mid-seventeenth century by Han refugees, Ming loyalists who refused to accept the authority of the Qing dynasty and chose exile in what is now the Kokang region of Shan State.

Of all China's dynasties, the Qing were the most fervent colonisers and in their early pomp they pushed the boundaries of China further than ever before. By the eighteenth century, Chinese merchants were trading in Pu'er tea from Simao, just north of Banna. That, though, was as far as they went. The Qing officials nominally in charge of Banna were based in Simao and ventured south just once a year. Only in 1899 was Sipsongpanna formally annexed by Beijing, although by then the French and British empires had already absorbed its southern and western fringes into Laos and what was then Burma.

Banna was granted autonomous status within the Chinese realm and its Dai king continued to rule until 1953. But if the kingdom of Sipsongpanna disappeared when he was forced to abdicate by the CCP, the Dai still remember the state they had for at least eight centuries and how far it spread. 'There are many Dai people here,' said Hai Yan, one of the Dai crewmen, pointing to both the left- and right-hand side of the Mekong's banks. He was envious I was travelling to Kengtung. 'It's an important place for us – there are many monks there.'

We anchored for the night close to the Lao side of the river. Apart from our lights, the moon and stars provided the only illumination amid the pitch black of the jungle. Hai Yan and the rest of the crew went fishing after supper, standing up to their waists in the water, armed with nets and torches strapped to their heads. They returned with a bucket full of small fish, which they tipped on to the deck and immediately began gutting. Once they were finished, it was time for bed. There was a prolonged round of coughing and spitting and then the boat fell silent, waiting like the jungle around us for daylight to bring it to life again.

The roar of the engine starting woke me up. It was seven in the morning, cold and damp. A dense fog hung low over the boat, partially masking the trees on the banks and turning them a sinister grey-green. The captain wouldn't move in such bad visibility, so we waited for the fog to lift over a breakfast of *miantiao*: thin noodles sprinkled with *suancai*, the pickled vegetables that accompany many Yunnan dishes, chopped spring onion and chilli.

Less than an hour later we were under way, moving slowly at first and then gathering speed as the morning sun emerged to burn off the mist. As we drew closer to Thailand, more settlements started to appear on the Lao side. Women in sarongs washed clothes by the bank, while men prepared to go fishing. Wooden, longtail speedboats flying the Laos flag zipped past to the left, scudding over the wake of our boat and travelling at up to 40 knots careless of the dangers of the river.

There was little activity on the Myanmar side. But wooden jetties jutted out from the banks at a few points, and at one a Guanlei vessel was unloading three brand-new Japanese pick-up trucks. It was a bizarre sight – the latest model Toyotas arriving by boat in the middle of the jungle. I wondered who in Shan State could afford vehicles like that and why they were being imported at such an obscure location, rather than being driven across the land border.

More and more Chinese boats began to pass us, heading upriver to Guanlei, and the Mekong grew wider and wider until the banks were over a hundred metres apart. The jungle became less impenetrable, with ever-bigger gaps in it where trees had been felled for farmland. There was one more stop, after lunch, to wait for another boat travelling behind us. We were about to go through a particularly dangerous, shallow stretch of water and the skipper didn't want to do it alone. When we did move forward Hai Yan stood at the bow with a bamboo pole, using it to check the depth of the water every few metres.

Pagodas were stationed like lighthouses on the Lao bank of the river as we sailed the final few kilometres to Chiang Saen. A giant Golden Buddha on the Thai side announced our arrival at the junction where the borders of Laos, Myanmar and Thailand meet: the official Golden Triangle. The Mekong was now the busiest it had been all voyage, with cargo boats from four countries heading in both directions and numerous smaller craft crossing between Thailand and Laos.

Han-owned casinos operate just inside Laos here, catering for Chinese and Thai gamblers. The twin golden domes of the newest were visible from the river, looming over the basic concrete low-rise buildings typical of provincial Laos. It is overseen by a Han man with close links to the ethnic armies of Shan State. The militias run casinos on their side of the border as well – a convenient way to launder some of the proceeds of the drug trade.

Chiang Saen was another twenty minutes away, its small port dominated by Guanlei boats, and the *Pao Shou Ba*'s crew hailed their friends as they docked. It had taken twenty-four hours to reach Thailand, about the same amount of time it would take me to travel on by land to Kengtung. Banna's minorities can get there much faster. They can either slip across the land frontier or take a boat down the Mekong, jumping off at one of the isolated little jetties we had passed. But I was confined by borders and they were not.

18

The Dai Diaspora

Eastern Shan State remains isolated even now and the few foreigners who venture there are regarded with distrust by the Burmese authorities. That became apparent at the border post at Tachileik, as I watched the travel permit I needed to get to Kengtung being photocopied no fewer than thirty times. 'We have to give one copy to each checkpoint we go through,' explained Kyio, the guide assigned to me. As Kengtung is only 160 kilometres north of Tachileik, I asked if there was a checkpoint every few kilometres. 'Oh no, there aren't that many. But you need to do the same coming back.'

He had already relieved me of my passport, now tucked away in a drawer, an effective means of ensuring I wasn't tempted to abandon him. 'You'll get it back when you leave,' he said. Without Kyio, I could not proceed. Much of Shan State is barred to visitors – the Burmese do not like westerners wandering through the Golden Triangle – and the areas close to the Chinese border are especially sensitive. Just as in Tibet, I had to employ a guide.

Bordering Yunnan in the east and Thailand to the south, Shan State takes up most of eastern Myanmar. I had visited the north of Shan before, travelling to Hsipaw and Lashio from Mandalay. The old Burma Road, one of the routes by which the British and Americans supplied the Chinese nationalists fighting the Japanese in the Second World War, started in Lashio. From there it is a short journey to the border with Yunnan and Dehong Prefecture, the heartland of the Tai Neua, another branch of the Dai family, in China.

Myanmar is gradually opening its land frontiers to westerners. But when I travelled through Tachileik it was no ordinary border crossing, as the removal of my passport indicated. People entering Myanmar here are permitted to visit only Kengtung and Mong La, a town on the border with Yunnan, and a few points in between before either flying to Yangon or returning to Tachileik and exiting the country.

But I failed to get Mong La included on my permit. 'It's closed now,' said the Burmese official. I asked why. 'It's closed now,' he repeated, his very dark skin revealing him as coming from inland Myanmar rather than Shan State. It was a blow. Mong La is one of Shan State's gambling and crime capitals, a rackety mix of minorities, Burmese and Han, and I wanted to see it. I told the official I would just go to Kengtung, while silently determining to try and reach Mong La anyway.

I suspected I was being kept away from Mong La because of fighting between the Tatmadaw, Myanmar's army, and the ethnic minorities in the area. Like China, Myanmar's far edges are populated by a medley of peoples. There are 135 officially recognised ethnic groups in the country and many inhabit Shan State and Kachin State further north. In Shan State, the Dai are the dominant minority. The majority are Tai Yai, sometimes called Tai Long, while others are Tai Lue like the Dai in Banna, Tai Khun or Tai Neua. But throughout Myanmar all Dai are known generically as the 'Shan'.

Also present in Shan State are large numbers of Wa, as well as Akha, Bulang and Lahu. But, unlike their peaceful relatives in Banna, some of the minorities in Shan and Kachin States are restive. They want their own sovereign nations, or at the very least autonomy, and have been agitating for that ever since the then Burma gained its independence from Britain in 1948. A few – the Kachin, Karen, Shan and Wa – have their own armies, funded by their control of drug trafficking in the Golden Triangle, smuggling operations along the Yunnan and Thai borders and the shadowy trade in precious gems and jade.

So powerful are those forces that parts of Shan State are designated as 'Special Regions', a euphemism that enables the Myanmar government to avoid admitting that its remit doesn't extend to the country's extremities. Mong La lies in Special Region 4. It is controlled by the National Democratic Alliance Army, a militia originally formed by the descendants of the Ming loyalists who fled to the Kokang region of Shan State in the seventeenth century to escape Qing rule.

Beijing funded and armed the ethnic armies for many years, even if it is now more and more concerned by the ever-increasing flow of heroin into China from the Burmese borderlands. The CCP was the biggest supporter of the Communist Party of Burma (CPB) in the 1960s and 1970s, as it attempted to overthrow the military junta then ruling Myanmar. The minorities in Shan and Kachin States sided with the CPB and China supplied them with weapons and cash.

They were also allowed to use Yunnan as both a hideout and a training area, a logical step given that the soldiers of the rebel armies shared the same ethnicity – Dai, Wa and Kachin mainly – as the minorities in Banna and Dehong Prefecture. Indeed, some of the leaders of the militias were technically Chinese citizens, or had parents who were. It was a rare, if unstated, acknowledgment by Beijing of the ties that bind the minorities of Yunnan to their cousins across the frontiers.

Adding to what was an already impossibly tangled web of ethnic allegiances and political loyalties, Shan State and the hills just across the border in Thailand were the base for the last remnants of the Kuomintang (KMT) forces, the Chinese nationalists defeated by the CCP after the Second World War. Just as some Han chose to live in Kokang rather than accept a Qing emperor, so elements of the KMT refused to submit to Mao and sought sanctuary in the Golden Triangle after 1949 – one more army in a region of many. Like the Tibetan guerrillas based in Mustang in Nepal, the KMT diehards were backed by the CIA and mounted raids into Yunnan until the late 1970s.

By then, Beijing had cut off its support for Burma's ethnic armies. But the minorities had already realised they could fund their struggle with the opium growing in the hills around them. The Shan and Wa generals turned the Golden Triangle into the world's heroin hub, while signing subsequent ceasefire deals, often broken, with the Myanmar government which enabled them to run the special regions of Shan State as effectively separate countries.

Tachileik itself had been the stronghold of Khun Sa, the most notorious of all the Golden Triangle's warlords cum drug barons. The son of a Chinese father and a Shan mother, Khun Sa's real name was Zhang Qifu and in the early 1960s he trained with the KMT rebels. Soon afterwards, he set up his own army and began to take control of much of the opium business. For the next two decades, he flooded American cities in particular with the purest heroin around. Despite the best efforts of the US Drug Enforcement Administration, he was still a free, and extremely rich, man when he died peacefully in Yangon, Myanmar's former capital, in 2007.

Outside Tachileik, in the hills that run along the border with Thailand, are the camps where the 8,000-strong Shan State Army (SSA) is based. Other splinter factions of the SSA operate elsewhere in the region. The checkpoints I would go through on the way to Kengtung and the refusal to let me travel to Mong La were a reminder that one of the longest-running conflicts of recent times is still going on in this part of Shan State.

Once Kyio's satchel was stuffed full of permits, I was allowed to leave the border post and go in search of a moneychanger. I handed over a small pile of Thai baht and in return got a doorstep-sized wedge of kyat, the Burmese currency, which was far too big for my wallet or pockets. The notes were filthy almost beyond recognition. Chinese money is frequently grubby but compared to Myanmar's it looks like freshly minted notes from the Bank of England.

Using some of my kyat to pay for water and cigarettes brought a disapproving shake of the head from the shopkeeper. Tachileik is a popular day trip for Thais, who come to gamble and buy the cheap rubies and sapphires mined on the Shan Plateau, and the Thai baht is the preferred local currency. Tachileik's proximity to Thailand makes it one of Myanmar's few thriving towns. Its streets are much dustier and shabbier than the neighbouring Thai border town of Mae Sai, but the new cars on the roads and the foreign goods for sale are a measure of a prosperity that is rare in Myanmar.

At the bus station, the crowds of Shan returning to their homes in the country with their latest purchases were another sign of Tachileik's importance as a regional retail centre. They squatted out of the sun in their *longyi*, chewing betel nut and depositing red spit on to the floor, while guarding boxes of Thai coconuts and pineapples, sacks of rice, TVs and DVD players. 'Everything in Shan State comes from Thailand,' said Kyio, 'apart from the things that come from China.'

Kyio was twenty-one and, I thought, harmless. A lank mop of black hair obscured his forehead and straggled over his dark eyes. He wore skinny jeans, flip-flops and a red-and-white-striped shirt for all the time we were together. Kengtung was his hometown and he was Tai Yai, although one of his grandmothers was a Tai Lue from Banna. A physics student, his fluent English enabled him to work part-time as a tourist guide. But what Kyio really wanted to do was move to Bangkok, where his mother ran a hairdressing salon.

Public transport in Myanmar is rarely reliable. As we waited for the bus to leave, we got to know each other. In Tibet, I had been tight-lipped from the moment I arrived, fearing what would happen if anyone found out I was a journalist. I felt more secure in Myanmar, a country I knew, and some of my questions to Kyio were injudicious, his youth making me more garrulous than I would have been with someone older. But he was far sharper than Tenzin, my guide in Tibet, and soon began punctuating our conversation with outbursts of 'You know about that?'

Asking about the possibility of getting to Mong La, despite the ban on foreigners going there, was especially foolish. By the time we left Tachileik, I had the uncomfortable feeling that Kyio was already suspicious of my reasons for visiting Kengtung. I said I was a history teacher with an interest in Buddhism, but I noticed him trying to read the notes I occasionally scribbled. I claimed it was a diary and knew he wouldn't be able to decipher my handwriting, but I wished I had kept my mouth shut. Kyio was less naive than he looked.

On the outskirts of Tachileik, we stopped at the first checkpoint. Kyio told me to stay on the bus and not to take any photos, while he and the rest of the passengers got off to have their identity cards scrutinised. I watched Kyio hand over one of the photocopies of my permit, a sight that would become wearyingly familiar. But before long we were on our way again, the decrepit bus climbing slowly upwards towards the Shan Plateau and Kengtung.

As we travelled higher, the villages grew more primitive: no more than roughly assembled wooden huts perched precariously by the road, with not even the corrugated iron favoured across Myanmar as roofing to protect them. They were Akha homes, their rice terraces cut into the hillsides above them. Most of the farming, though, was going on below us in the valleys and flatlands, where the Shan villages are. Lining the road were bamboo poles supporting electricity lines and I knew that, like elsewhere in rural Myanmar, the power would be on for only a few hours a day, if at all.

Shan music videos played throughout the journey. One of the singers was Sai Mao, the most famous of the Dai musicians whose songs inspired many young Dai imitators in Banna in the 1980s and 1990s, a musical movement that was the heir to Changkhap, the oral poetry and folk music the Dai have always used to transmit their culture through the generations. Sai Mao is Tai Yai and his lyrics stress pan-Dai identity. In the late 1970s, he was imprisoned for two years after writing a song calling for an independent Shan State.

Five hours out of Tachileik, we began a steep descent into a valley where rice paddies shone bright green in the sun. The hills of the Shan Plateau rose all around, their red earth visible from many kilometres away, as the forests that cover them are increasingly chopped down to supply China's voracious need for timber. It was a spectacular approach to Kengtung, which appeared suddenly like an oasis in the desert, the first settlement of any size in eastern Shan State.

Kengtung, pronounced 'Chiang Tong', is the unofficial capital of the Golden Triangle and is proud of that status, despite the region's dubious reputation elsewhere in the world. You can smoke locally produced Golden Triangle cigarettes – opium-free of course – or play a round at the Golden Triangle Golf Club, mostly patronised by officers from the nearby army base. And there are many substantial houses sprouting satellite dishes and with new land cruisers parked inside their high gates – the homes of those who have prospered from selling the area's most famous product.

Long before heroin started spreading worldwide from here, Kengtung was a Tai Khun kingdom that rivalled Sipsongpanna. It remains a gathering point for Dai people from across greater Dailand, as well as for the hill tribes in the nearby mountains. Set on a series of short, steep hills, Kengtung reminded me of Chiang Mai in Thailand because of the sheer number of monasteries and pagodas scattered around town. Monks were everywhere, either in the blood-red robes worn by the Burmese or in the bright-orange ones seen in Banna and Thailand.

Naung Tung, a small lake ringed by open-air restaurants and a few grand residences from the colonial era, dominates the centre of town. Kengtung was one of the places from where the British had governed Burma's borderlands as the Federated Shan States – recognition of their essential separateness from the rest of the country. But the former palace of the princes who ruled the old Dai kingdom of Kengtung is no more, demolished by the Myanmar government in 1991 as revenge for the Shan's quest for independence. It was a petty move, akin to the destruction of the Chao Fa's palace in Jinghong during the Cultural Revolution.

After arriving at my guesthouse, I told Kyio I didn't need him for the rest of the day and hired a bike. I knew a guide was required only in Kengtung itself and didn't want Kyio dogging my footsteps. With the still fierce late-afternoon sun on my back, I pedalled off up the bumpy and potholed streets in search of Naung Tung. Saying its Burmese name brought only puzzled expressions. Then I tried asking a man in Chinese and he immediately pointed the way.

Subsequently, I discovered that every second or third person in Kengtung spoke or could at least understand basic Mandarin. The trick was not to ask the darker-skinned residents, who were generally migrants from inland Myanmar, but to talk to the lighter-complexioned Shan. With Mong La and the border with Yunnan a mere eighty kilometres north of Kengtung, many of the locals are regular visitors to the villages in Banna their families are originally from, or are involved in nefarious smuggling schemes with relatives and friends in China.

The Dai diaspora from Banna into Shan State and the north-west of Laos, which borders both Shan and Banna, dates back centuries. Sipsongpanna stretched into what is now Myanmar and Laos, and the Dai have always moved beyond borders to different areas of their old kingdom. But it was the CCP's takeover of China and the subsequent chaos of the Cultural Revolution especially which prompted the last great mass migration of the Dai and the other ethnic groups of Banna into the Golden Triangle.

Not even the remote rainforests of Yunnan's borderlands were spared the Red Guards. As monasteries were raided and wrecked, monks took sanctuary in the temples of Kengtung and Muang Sing in north-west Laos. With schools closed for years in the turmoil, many Dai sent their children to stay with relatives over the borders, or went with them to escape being punished for adhering to their traditional lifestyle.

Their descendants make up many of the Tai Lue who live in Kengtung. Nang was one of them. She ran a tea shop with her husband, serving up Chinese green tea or the sweet, milky Burmese version in the day and beers and whisky after dark. Nang was short, skinny and serious in glasses. Her husband was darker, heavy-set and tattooed and always dressed in a *longyi*. Both their families were from Banna.

'My grandparents came to Kengtung in the 1960s, in the early days of the Cultural Revolution. My dad was a small child and they didn't want him to be in the village then. They didn't know what would happen in the future,' Nang told me. They stayed for over twenty years. Nang's father had met her mother, who was also the child of Tai Lue refugees, in Kengtung and both Nang and her sister were born there. But as conditions in China improved dramatically in the 1980s, while the security situation in Shan State deteriorated, her parents and sister had returned to Banna, which Nang still referred to as Sipsongpanna.

Nang remained in Kengtung with other relatives. Now she saw her family in Banna a couple of times a year, making sure she celebrated Songkran, the Dai New Year, with them in their home village near Menghai, a couple of hours from Jinghong. As the minorities have always done, Nang didn't bother with a passport or designated border crossings when she visited. 'I get the bus to Mong La and then I take a small road to Banna,' she said. It was a euphemism for slipping across the frontier unofficially. 'It's no problem for us. Many Tai Lue living in Kengtung go to Banna and lots of Dai from Banna come here.'

She had no desire to follow her parents' and younger sister's example and live in Banna. 'This is my home. I was born here and my business is here. I don't speak very good Chinese, so I wouldn't get a decent job in Sipsongpanna. It's easier for me here.' Her husband's parents were also migrants from Banna. Along with their daughter, they are now citizens of greater Dailand, speaking the Dai dialect of Banna among themselves and the Tai Khun language spoken in Kengtung to their customers.

It was Nang who finally dashed my hopes of reaching Mong La. 'They have been fighting there for the last three months. There are many checkpoints and you'll get caught if you go.' I resigned myself to staying in Kengtung for a few more days. It wasn't a hardship because I was already fond of the place and found its peaceful rhythm soothing, even with a guerrilla war between the Tatmadaw and Shan going on around it.

Soon I established a simple routine. Every morning, I woke up to find Kyio outside my door waiting to ask me what I planned to do today. I would tell him that I was just going to cycle around Kengtung and so didn't need him, a reply he found increasingly disturbing and which he clearly didn't believe. 'You can't leave Kengtung on your own,' he warned me each time we met. I assured him I wouldn't, a promise I kept.

Most days I ended up in the main market, a fascinating maze of shops and stalls offering everything from Chinese cosmetics and clothes to Indian chewing tobacco, Lao Beer and out-of-date medicines from Thailand. Early in the morning, Akha women arrived to sell what they grew in the hills. They squatted in long lines according to which village they were from, their produce piled in front of them, dressed in *longyi* and black tops whose edges were lined with different colours. Some wore sun hats, others their traditional headdress decorated with silver discs and jewellery.

Every night, I went to Naung Tung. It was Kengtung's most lively area. The open-air restaurants were always busy with people eating grilled fish or skewers of chicken and horse meat, a popular snack in Kengtung. They drank Myanmar lager and the rotgut local whisky, while watching the English Premier League football games screened most nights. English football is a passion in Myanmar, in part because it was one of the few foreign imports shown on Burmese TV when the military junta ran the country.

Eating, drinking and talking with the Shan, under the big yellow moon that hung over the pagodas atop Kengtung's hills, made for pleasant and enlightening evenings. Almost everyone was friendly and frank about their desire for independence and contempt for the Tatmadaw. The longer I stayed in Kengtung, the more I noticed the military presence. Most of the soldiers were from inland Myanmar. They have an unsavoury reputation among the Shan for beating and raping the locals, while coercing bribes from them at every opportunity.

Yet I was aware that I was probably being closely watched. I reasoned that Kyio must have to report to someone, and I knew that was why he was growing more and more unhappy with my refusal to use his services. Even if I wasn't actually being tailed, it wouldn't be hard to find out where I went or who I was speaking to because, as far as I knew, I was the only westerner in Kengtung at the time.

One morning, I got confirmation of how people were noticing what I did. I opened the door bleary-eyed and with a whisky head to find a stern-faced Kyio pointing an accusing finger at me. 'You were in the nightclub last night,' he said. It was true; I had been. The club was by the lake, located in the ground floor of an empty hotel, and was Kengtung's only such establishment.

I paid 1,000 kyat to get in, or about 70p – the equivalent of a day's wages for many people in Shan State. But after some enthusiastic dancing to western techno imported from Thailand, spun by a surprisingly competent DJ, and a few too many drinks, my evening was cut short when a fight kicked off between rivals for a girl. It sucked in their friends and everyone around them. The bouncers reacted by ejecting everyone and shutting the club, leaving me to cycle home unsteadily through the dark streets while dogs growled at me.

Neither Kyio nor the owner of the guesthouse was impressed. I was told I was staying out too late, although I had been back by midnight, and that they were going to impose a curfew on me. From now on, the gates to the guesthouse would be locked at nine. Unwilling to be confined like a prisoner in the dark, as the guesthouse generator shut down at 9.30 leaving me unable to read or write, I decided it was time to leave Kengtung.

Returning to Tachileik, with Kyio silent in the seat next to me, was an anti-climax, made more so by the knowledge that I was running more or less parallel to the Mekong, somewhere out of sight to my left. On the other side of the river was Xieng Kok, a port in north-west Laos that was once a key transit point for the opium grown in the nearby hills. That area was my next destination and I reckoned I was about 150 kilometres away from it. But foreigners cannot take the direct route across the Mekong. I would have to return to Thailand to travel on to Laos.

With the local border crossings barred to me, it took two frustrating days to reach north-west Laos. I travelled by bus and then in a *songthaew*, a pick-up truck with benches in the back and a roof, to Chiang Khong where I caught a boat across the Mekong to Huay Xai, the port in Laos where Naw Kham the pirate had been captured. After that, it was another day's ride on two buses before I reached Muang Sing, a town ten kilometres south of China and less than eighty kilometres from Xieng Kok and the banks of the Mekong.

Muang Sing has long been synonymous with the poppy trade. When the French were still running Laos, it was the largest opium market in the Golden Triangle. The Akha would bring their sacks of the sticky black resin down from the surrounding hills and sell it, before it was taken west to Xieng Kok and shipped off. Aged Akha women still patrol the main street offering small packets of fresh opium to any foreigner they encounter, but the hill villages around Muang Sing are now mostly free of poppy fields.

Instead, they can be found further west. Laos remains the world's fourth-largest supplier of opium, although it produces far less than Afghanistan and Myanmar, and much of the annual crop is grown in the remote villages high in the hills above the small town of Muang Long, close to Xieng Kok. They are all but inaccessible, and reaching them involves hours of bouncing down rutted dirt and stone tracks that become mudbaths in the rainy season and then walking.

'The people who live there have no choice but to grow opium. They either do that or starve,' said an Akha man named Ber Ko I met in Muang Long. 'Where they live is so isolated that they can't grow rubber or bananas because they can't get to Muang Long to buy the stuff they need to grow those crops. Even if they could, they wouldn't be able to sell it because they can't reach town. They can grow enough rice and maize to feed themselves and that's it.'

Ber Ko was a loquacious, youthful-looking thirty-five-year-old with a prized pick-up truck. He described himself as a 'transporter of goods', without specifying exactly what he carried. One day, I became the cargo and we headed into the hills to a village where opium is grown. Low down, much of the rainforest that once covered the area has gone, replaced by rice paddies and corn fields, or just stripped bare of its precious wood. But the higher we climbed, the more jungle appeared.

Our destination was a collection of wooden shacks, more desperate even than the Akha villages I'd seen in Shan State. Naked, filthy children played, while women of all ages wandered around barechested, a peculiarity of Akha settlements in Laos. I received a cautious welcome, but was soon invited into a house where the celebration of a boy's coming of age was taking place. We drank lao-lao, the local version of *baijiu*, and took turns to tie money to the boy's wrist with coloured threads while offering him a blessing for the future.

No one admitted to cultivating opium in any quantity. 'The old people still smoke it, so they grow a personal crop but that's it,' one farmer named La Te told me. And I had arrived at the wrong time of year to see any poppy fields. 'There's only one crop a year and it's planted after the maize has been cut down in October. They use the same fields and the opium is ready for harvest in February. Then the people transport it on foot to either the Mekong or the Chinese border where Tai Lue people collect it,' said Ber Ko.

Just as they do in Banna, the Tai Lue control both the drug trade and the lowland towns of the area. Muang Sing, Muang Long and Xieng Kok are all Dai strongholds, while the Akha can only gaze down on them from the little-developed hills. 'The Akha are at the bottom of the chain,' said Ber Ko with a resigned shrug. 'It's the Shan people and the Tai Lue who turn the opium into heroin and sell it on.'

Centuries ago, this area of north-west Laos had been part of Sipsongpanna with Muang Sing then, as now, its largest town. Later it came under the protection of the Dai kingdom of Kengtung. But when the British and French decided the borders of Burma and Laos at the beginning of the twentieth century, Muang Sing and the surrounding area was allocated neither to China nor to Burma, but to Laos.

China's influence looms large here now, though. Much of the land has been sold to the same Chinese companies that run Banna's rubber farms, while the bananas grown locally are packed into boxes marked 'Produce of China' and sent north by foremen from far-off Sichuan Province. And unlike their cousins in Banna, the Tai Lue of north-west Laos are not prospering from the rubber boom. The Chinese trucks kick up clouds of dust as they rumble to and from the border along Muang Sing's long, barely sealed main street, while the buildings are a mix of decrepit white-stone French colonial structures and hybrid wood and brick houses.

Despite the pervasive Chinese presence, this corner of north-west Laos continues to preserve aspects of Dai culture no longer present anywhere else in greater Dailand. Two aged ladies at the restaurant in Muang Sing I ate at reminded me of that daily. 'This is the only place you will find proper Tai Lue food,' they said, serving up dishes such as a tangy paste of chilli, garlic and cilantro eaten with sticky rice. Muang Sing's pagodas, too, were pure Tai Lue. Wat Pajay in Jinghong reveals the influence of Thai, Burmese and even Sri Lankan temple architecture. But in Muang Sing strange vertical prayer flags flew above spartan, less decorative monasteries.

A relic of a long-distant Dailand, Muang Sing's uniqueness is perhaps due to it having been on the fringes of two Dai kingdoms, Sipsongpanna and Kengtung, rather than at the heart of either of them. Its survival is all the more remarkable given the upheaval and violence Laos has endured since it gained independence in 1953. But Dai identity is as hardy as the opium poppies that grow in the hills around Muang Long and the vagaries of national politics have never been able to diminish it, whether in China, Laos or Myanmar.

19

With the Wa

I was tired of being restricted by borders and rules which the minorities blithely ignored. My failure to reach Mong La and the wasted days spent getting to north-west Laos were unwelcome reminders of how conventional my journeys in the Golden Triangle had been. Being forced to employ Kyio was the final insult. It was annoying enough using a guide in Tibet. Having to do so in a region of fluid frontiers was an affront, a challenge to my abilities as a traveller. To do as the minorities do, moving between countries without the trappings of passports and visas, became an obsession.

With Myanmar's army pushing further into eastern Shan State, as well as into Kachin State in the north, there was only one place I could go without being caught by the Burmese authorities and that was the homeland of the Wa people. To Myanmar's leaders it is Special Region 2. But in the Yunnan and Burmese borderlands it is known simply by its Mandarin name of Wabang, or Wa State. An unofficial country within Shan State, it is sandwiched between Kokang in the north and Mong La to the south with Yunnan to the east.

Wa State is the most lawless and least visited part of the Golden Triangle. Even among the combative minorities of north and east Myanmar, the Wa have a fearsome reputation. Until fifty years ago, and more recently in the most remote hills, the Wa were headhunters. They took the heads of their enemies, or any unfortunate traveller in their territory, and hung them in their fields so that the decomposing skin and brains fertilised their crops, a brutal, if organic, way of ensuring a bountiful harvest.

Avoiding being governed by anyone is the guiding principle behind everything the Wa do. They sided with the British, who called them the 'Wild Wa', against the Japanese in the Second World War, but since then have fought with great success to create their own homeland. The Wa in China are not much different. There are 400,000 Wa in Yunnan, spread across two autonomous counties. But there were far more until 1958 when around one-third of them packed up and marched into Shan State, their way of giving a resounding thumbs-down to being part of Mao's China.

Like the other hill tribes in Yunnan, the Wa were classified as savages by the Chinese because of their existence beyond the state, their animist beliefs and their lack of any formal writing system. But while the Akha, Bulang, Lahu and others have submitted to Han authority, even if they are inextricably linked to their cousins across the frontiers, the very existence of Wa State ensures that the Wa in China are to a large extent beyond Beijing's control.

Across the narrow river that separates Yunnan from Wa State, the United Wa State Army (UWSA) is 20,000 strong and able to call on another 30,000 reserve soldiers in times of war. Even China has to accept that, with a force almost as big as the Australian military, the Wa are not to be tamed. They move at will between Wa State and Yunnan, and Beijing does not try to stop them doing so.

Having rejected both the Burmese and Chinese states, the Wa are barbarians by choice: the only truly independent, self-governing minority left in the region. They owe their allegiance to a country not formally recognised anywhere in the world, whether they live there or in Yunnan. And if the Wa have given up headhunting, they have taken up another activity that still places them beyond the pale. Washington cites the UWSA as South-east Asia's biggest drug-trafficking gang, and there are multi-million-dollar rewards on offer for the capture of some of its generals.

Much of the narcotics business in the Golden Triangle is controlled by the UWSA. Myanmar supplies 10 per cent of the world's opium annually and most of it is grown in Wa State, as well as in nearby parts of southern Shan State that are under Wa supervision. It is refined into heroin there too, as well as increasingly in Yunnan. The UWSA is also believed to be behind the manufacture of *yaba*, the amphetamine pills that have become an epidemic across Asia. It is the profits from the drug trade that have enabled the Wa to carve out a country for themselves, one complete with its own flag, government, banks and tax system.

Few outsiders penetrate into Wabang. Myanmar bars all foreigners from travelling there. But alone out of the special regions, Wa State is the sole place in the country where the government has no official presence. There are no Tatmadaw checkpoints to pass through, no police to arrest a stray westerner. That made Wa State the place for me, if only I could establish the contacts to get across the border. I had no wish to arouse the ire of the Wa by turning up uninvited.

Fate was kind. A friend introduced me to Justin, a lanky New Yorker in his early thirties who, in one of his many previous jobs, had taught English to the daughter of a UWSA general. He had stayed with her family in Pangshang, the capital of Wa State, and had an open invitation to return. We met late one afternoon in Kunming and bonded over a few beers, drawn together by our similar histories. Our fathers were both Jewish and engineers, we were the children of divorced parents and had spent much of our lives outside our home countries.

Justin promised to find out if we could visit. A couple of weeks later, he called to say the trip was on. We arranged a rendezvous in Lancang, the nondescript capital of Yunnan's Lahu Autonomous County in the south-west of Banna. I arrived to find him slurping noodles with Piero, a Venetian photographer whose lugubrious demeanour concealed a warm heart and utterly sound personality.

They made a fine double act, with Piero the gloomy straight man and Justin the wisecracking, outgoing one. Justin has a knack of winning people over. He speaks fast and fluent Mandarin, his enthusiasm overriding its lack of grammatical accuracy, and combined with his broad smile it makes the locals warm to him in a way they do with few foreigners. Justin was always the centre of attention, while Piero and I lurked on the fringes, surfing the waves of goodwill he generated.

From Lancang, we moved south-west into Chinese Wa territory: first by bus to Menglian and from there by taxi through a landscape of banana and rubber plantations to Monga, a tiny village on the border. The driver knew our ultimate destination and called ahead so that three motorbikes were waiting to take us to the Nam Ka River, which divides Yunnan here from Myanmar and Wa State.

Then it was a scramble down the banks and a swift ride on a shaky raft made of six bamboo poles lashed together, squatting on our haunches as the boatman punted us across the river, and we were in Wabang. After waiting so long to take advantage of Banna's wide-open frontiers, the ease of the journey was something of a letdown. I had imagined a march through thick jungle to reach an isolated point of the Nam Ka, but we crossed into Wa State by what seemed like a very public route.

Groups of Wa were waiting for a ride to Yunnan as we disembarked. Climbing up the banks, we were greeted with amusement by a dark-skinned woman selling cold drinks and a group of young lads whose motorbikes acted as transport into Pangshang. There was no linguistic divide here. Mandarin is the local language, along with the various Wa dialects, just as Chinese money is the currency.

A-sui, one of the general's three daughters, picked us up in a land cruiser covered in the sticky yellow dust that envelops all of Wa State and bearing licence plates that said 'Wa' in capital letters. Slim and pretty, she knew Justin from his previous visit. A teenage girl sat in the front clutching a baby, the youngest of A-sui's three children. A-sui had been married at sixteen and was still only twenty-three.

We accelerated up a track to a checkpoint where two boys and a girl, none older than sixteen, were lolling in chairs in the shade, an

AK47 rifle near to hand. They wore olive-green uniforms, those of the boys bearing the patch of the UWSA and its distinctive logo: a shining red star surrounded by yellow shafts of light above green hills and set against a blue background representing the sky. The design dates back to the 1960s and 1970s, when the UWSA was allied with the Communist Party of Burma in its fight against the generals who then ran the country.

Checking our passports was the girl's responsibility. She wore a badge identifying her as police, but she also sported a furry hairgrip that only reinforced how young she was. She was clearly nonplussed by the sight of three foreigners. I was equally startled at seeing teenage soldiers. But the Wa recruit children as young as ten into the UWSA. In Pangshang especially, it is commonplace to see boys and girls who are scarcely in their teens armed and in uniform. The adult soldiers are needed to guard the 'borders' with Myanmar further west, north and south, to repel any possible invasion by government troops.

No record was made of our names or nationalities; A-sui's presence vouched for us. It was another few kilometres to Pangshang itself, a route which took us on to sealed roads and past the official border crossing, a bridge over the Nam Ka River. Wa State may not be a formal country but China still maintains a frontier and customs post manned by the Wujing, like it does with all the other states it borders.

Pangshang, sometimes spelled Panghsang, is a jungle town, set in a shallow depression beneath hills covered in thick green foliage which look down on the other side of the Nam Ka and Yunnan. Home to around 50,000 people, it is rather more impressive than most Chinese cities of an equivalent size and some thought has gone into its design. When I climbed up to the vast all-metal memorial to the Wa war dead atop the hills, I found it surrounded by neatly landscaped flowerbeds.

Soldiers were everywhere, mostly male teenagers but some girls, in forage caps with their AK47s slung over their backs and holstered pistols dangling from leather belts. They gazed at us curiously, sometimes offering a smile, but no one ever asked what we were doing in Pangshang. That we were here at all meant we were guests; we would never have made it past the checkpoint otherwise.

Gaudy, newly built three- and four-storey houses line the more salubrious streets leading up the hillsides. They are a mix of Burmese and Chinese contemporary styles: all white and blue tiles with balconies supported by grandiose columns. High walls topped with coiled barbed wire and metal gates guard them. They were the first sign of how the profits from the heroin and *yaba* trade have turned Pangshang into one of the most unlikely, and least known, boomtowns in Asia. It is the jungle equivalent of an offshore tax haven, where no questions are asked providing you have cash and connections.

Equally incongruous in this remote enclave was the parade of new cars roaring up and down the streets, sending up huge clouds of dust that hung in the air, interspersed by the elongated golf carts that act as buses in Pangshang. 'There are more cars than people in Pangshang,' A-sui told me. I remembered the Toyota pick-up trucks I saw being unloaded at a remote jetty in Shan State when I sailed down the Mekong. Now I knew where they had been headed.

More evidence of how vehicles outnumber people in Pangshang was on show at the general's home. It was really two houses, the smaller of which was for the family's servants and bodyguards, behind the inevitable gates which opened to reveal a concrete forecourt the size of a car park. Seven land cruisers and pick-up trucks were lined up, all Japanese and American brands. Such vehicles sell for £40,000 each in Pangshang, a result of them having to be imported illegally from China or Thailand.

Jutting into the forecourt was a covered terrace as big as a small apartment leading to the entrance to the family home. The floor was polished marble, with a star etched in it, and the tables and chairs strewn across it were all fine teak. Two Chinese-style vases, as big as grandfather clocks, sat either side of the double doors leading into the house. A table-tennis table was an unlikely addition. Above it was an ornate chandelier which wouldn't have looked out of place in a nineteenth-century ballroom.

Waiting on the terrace was Yilan, the general's daughter Justin had taught English to. A plain, smart and lively twenty-four-year-old, Yilan was quick to joke with Justin but rather more reserved with Piero and myself. Plying us with delicious cherries, she relayed the news that she was to be married at the end of the year and that we would get to meet her fiancé the next day. She wanted Justin to come to the wedding and he promised to attend.

This was just the family's Pangshang residence. The general and his wife were at their country house, in their home village three hours north. 'We have houses in Tachileik and Yangon too,' said Yilan. There was also property elsewhere in Pangshang, as well as in Thailand and Yunnan. Yilan told us excitedly that she and A-sui were overseeing the decoration of a new hotel the family were opening in Simao, a town in southern Yunnan with a large Wa population.

I never asked Yilan what exactly the general's role in the UWSA was and Justin hadn't talked to her about it either. I felt it was desperately inappropriate to ask my hostess if her father was a drug lord. But with vehicles worth close on half a million dollars parked in front of the house and a property portfolio spread across four countries, if you count Wa State as a nation, it was clear the general wasn't just involved in overseeing military strategy.

Adding to the impression that the general was no conventional soldier was the appearance of James, his son-in-law and the husband of A-sui. He was a bear of a man, small in height but built like a rugby prop forward, his sleeveless vest revealing powerful shoulders covered in tattoos. Aged twenty-three, like A-sui, and from a prominent Wa family, James was already a major in the UWSA. The whole dynamic of the evening shifted with his arrival, the girls becoming less effusive and fading into the background, as James directed his conversation to Justin, Piero and me.

James was the original alpha-male and trailed supporters in his wake – a few of the family bodyguards. Dressed in a mix of UWSA uniforms and civvies, they were exceedingly polite and friendly to us but it was obvious that crossing them would be extremely unwise. They were taller than most Wa men, who don't normally get above 5 foot 8, and, so Justin said, martial arts experts. With their easy, muscled manner of moving, I believed him.

Yilan and A-sui drifted off, saying they would see us tomorrow, and it became clear why there was a table-tennis table on the terrace. James was an avid fan and we had to take turns to play him. I disgraced myself, hardly able to get the ball over the net, but Justin was good enough to win a few games while Piero lost in style, playing his shots with the panache of a Latin tennis player.

It was a surreal scene. Like everywhere in South-east Asia, night descended swiftly, shutting out the sun as if someone had flicked a light switch, leaving the ridiculously grand chandelier to illuminate the games. The bodyguards acted as ball boys, chasing across the terrace after errant shots, while young servant girls padded around silently in bare feet, replenishing glasses, supplying cold towels at the end of each game and emptying ashtrays as soon as a cigarette was stubbed out in one.

Ping-pong was just the start of the evening's entertainment. Around nine, James laid down his bat and summoned us to a room at the back of the house. Unlike the rest of the home, it was a spartan space with bare walls, decorated only with a few chairs, a table, cupboard and large TV. Next door was another room with a couple of beds in it, where the bodyguards could rest when they weren't needed. 'This is my office. I come here to get away from my wife and kids,' said James, speaking in the English he had learned in Yangon.

Despite the Wa's animosity towards the state of Myanmar, there have always been close contacts between the UWSA and the government. The heroin and *yaba* produced in Wa-controlled terri-tory could not be smuggled out of the country without the collusion of senior officials. That makes it necessary for the Wa chiefs to speak Burmese. As the UWSA is very much a family business, their male children, like James, spend time at school in Yangon to learn the language. In contrast, Yilan and A-sui could barely speak Burmese; they had mostly been educated in Kunming.

Friends of James arrived and the room grew crowded. The body-guards hustled around collecting half-empty plastic bottles of water, tin foil and straws from the cupboard, which they started to join together expertly. '*Yaba*,' mouthed Piero. Sure enough, a tin full of small, bright-red pills emerged on the table. The water bottles, tin foil and straws were the paraphernalia needed to smoke them.

Yaba is a Thai word, meaning 'crazy medicine'. It is a highly addictive form of speed, a mix of methamphetamine and caffeine that was once legal in Thailand but is now proscribed there and every-where else in Asia. Far cheaper than cocaine or ecstasy, it is the drug of factory workers and farmers and is popular everywhere in South-east Asia. But it can also be found in southern China and across India and Bangladesh, Japan and even North Korea.

Some time in the early 1990s, the UWSA began to diversify into the production of *yaba*. Opium requires land and labour. But to make *yaba* all you need to do is kit out a shack in the hills with some rudimentary equipment and a supply of chemicals. There are now so many jungle labs in Wa State that the United Nations Office on Drugs and Crime estimates that the traffic in little red pills and other methamphetamines like ice is worth $15 billion a year, making it by far Myanmar's most lucrative industry.

Although it comes in pill form, *yaba* is usually smoked in the same way a heroin user chases the dragon. The pill is placed on a piece of tin foil, a lighter flame is played underneath it until the pill starts smoking and then the fumes are inhaled. James and his friends, though, smoked *yaba* the sophisticated way. The bottle, straw and tin foil combination constructed by the bodyguards acts to burn off some of the pills' impurities, while cooling the smoke by passing it through the water in the bottom of the bottle.

Before long, it became clear that the *yaba* was for us. While James was indulging in his own personal supply of ice, he insisted Justin, Piero and I start smoking the *yaba* along with his chums. Just as playing table tennis was compulsory, so was amphetamine abuse. The bodyguards, like good soldiers, followed his orders rigorously, not letting more than a few minutes go by between each pill being smoked before another bottle was held up for us and straws placed in our mouths.

Soon the room was filled with the distinctive, chocolate-sweet smell of *yaba* smoke. We were all suddenly more alert and talkative, full of energy despite a day spent travelling, yet also both hyper and confused from the drug. As the bodyguards started to double the hit by loading two pills instead of one on to the tin foil, I began to wonder where my *yaba* initiation was going to end.

Next to me, one of James's friends was smoking a water pipe. A common sight in rural Yunnan, they are long cylinders with a little water in the bottom and a steel funnel sticking out of one side where tobacco is placed, the liquid acting to cool the rough smoke produced by the locally grown weed. But the sickly smell emanating from the water pipe of James's friend indicated he was using opium instead of tobacco. He offered the pipe around and we started to smoke that too, thinking it might counteract the *yaba*, which was already toying with our nervous systems, tensing our muscles and jerking us up in our chairs.

A DVD started playing. It was hardcore European porn, featuring large blonde women with over-sized fake breasts moaning loudly in German. 'I like western women,' said James, smiling broadly. 'They have big asses and tits.' He had a beautiful Wa wife next door, but European blondes were as exotic to James as A-sui was to me and he wanted what he couldn't have. I taught him the meaning of the word 'curvy', my main contribution to the evening, while James peppered Justin with questions about life in New York, talking wistfully of his desire to visit America.

He was drug-dreaming; senior UWSA figures are wanted criminals in the US. In Wabang, James was a god: an untouchable scion of its ruling class with unlimited resources to do what he liked. But Pangshang is a gilded cage, a place the Wa elite cannot escape from. Even though James had a Chinese passport, like many Wa State residents, Yunnan and Thailand were as far as he could go before questions would be asked about what exactly he did in his pseudo-country.

Time seemed to have stopped. But after midnight we all staggered out and piled into James's pick-up truck, the back of which was emblazoned with a bumper sticker proclaiming, 'Motherfucker Wants To Kill You That's Right'. With hip-hop blaring and James's friends and bodyguards following us, we drove in a convoy to the centre of Pangshang, passing the main Wa government building with its teenage sentries and the twenty-four-hour casino, where equally youthful prostitutes waited outside for customers.

Arriving at a nightclub, we were greeted with deference and ushered into a large private room, its windowless walls decorated in black and silver and lined with plush leather sofas which we sank into. The bodyguards were even more solicitous and protective here, making sure we always had a fresh beer to hand, while escorting us when we visited the dance floor or the toilet. We were temporary members of James's gang now and so their responsibility.

Ten young women lined up in front of us, eyes demurely down to the floor. They were hostesses, whose job is to take care of the club's high-paying customers and sometimes to go home with them. As the guests of honour, Justin, Piero and I were instructed to pick one each. The rest dispersed to James and his friends. All were from Yunnan and were mostly Han. My companion was a nineteen-year-old from Lancang. She had been lured to Pangshang by its reputation as a town where people have more money than they know what to do with, and the chance of earning far more than she could as a migrant worker elsewhere.

For the next five hours we sat in the room drinking, playing liar's dice with the girls, where the object is to fool the other person into thinking you have higher dice than they do and the loser has to drink, and singing karaoke. Every so often, more *yaba*, which the girls refused to touch, would materialise in front of us. Before long, the walls felt like they were closing in on me. The smoke from the *yaba* and hundreds of cigarettes was stifling. As the night went on and on I was rendered barely capable of speech, although I felt no urge to sleep.

Only at dawn were we able to escape, driven back to James's office where some of the group carried on drinking and smoking opium. I tried to sleep. After a couple of hours of lying on my bed wide awake, I went to find Justin and Piero. They hadn't slept either and we decided to go into town. We walked uncertainly, like passengers at a distant airport just off a long flight. It was *yaba*-lag; we had skipped a night to emerge in a strange new country where the rules were very different.

Even in the morning sun, Pangshang defied any sense of normality. The casino was still crowded with punters, and soldiers with their guns were striding around. Two teenagers were carrying a tiger's claw. They told us they had killed the animal in the hills and were going to sell the claw to a purveyor of traditional Chinese medicine. Using the body parts of rare animals in herbal remedies is now illegal in China, but demand for those medicines and aphrodisiacs remains high. Pangshang is full of dispensaries displaying leopard skulls, bear bladders and the remains of other animals I couldn't identify.

At the main market, the local Wa women down from the hills in their traditional dress – black, bonnet-like hats and striped long skirts – were far outnumbered by Chinese Wa in western clothes.

They commute daily from Yunnan to work. 'Pangshang is better for business than Menglian,' one woman told me. 'It's bigger and there's more money here.' There were also Han from further afield. 'I came ten years ago because I had a friend doing business here and it sounded so mysterious,' said a man from Hunan Province who was selling jeans.

Along with the other Chinese, he was unconcerned about living in a city controlled by drug traffickers and where children carry automatic weapons. 'Pangshang is much safer than China. There's no petty crime here. I don't have to worry about people stealing from my stall, or business rivals trying to do bad things to me,' he said. His only gripe was culinary. 'I like the Wa but I can't eat their food. If there wasn't any Chinese food here, I'd starve.'

There was no danger of that, not with so many restaurants run by Han migrants, as well as an unlicensed outlet of Kentucky Fried Chicken. Its owners had brazenly copied the Colonel Sanders logo, packaging and recipes. They were safe. I thought it unlikely that any KFC executives would pass through Pangshang. There were western restaurants too, alongside Japanese and Korean ones. At lunchtime, we met Yilan in a café offering pasta, cakes and coffee, as well as Cuban cigars and single malt whiskies. It wouldn't have been out of place in Beijing or Shanghai.

Yilan's fiancé Ngo joined us. A year older than her, skinny and mild-mannered with a thick head of black hair and the beginnings of a moustache, Ngo was also the son of a general but a very different character to James. He was a rich kid with a social conscience. 'Some of my family live in Thailand now. I could leave too, but I want to stay and help my people, so I give money to villages so they can build houses and buy food,' he said.

Ngo was keen to show us the work he was doing. After lunch, we climbed into his three-litre pick-up truck. 'I'm famous for how fast I drive,' he said, grinning. 'But don't worry. I've been driving since I was ten.' Piero and I hung on tight in the back as Ngo sped uphill through Pangshang's northern suburbs. The houses here were the biggest I had seen yet. One was like a fortress, set behind high walls of grey stone and surrounded by a dry moat – a Wa version of a medieval castle. Ngo knew the owners. 'It cost 20 million yuan [£2 million] to build.'

Without warning, the outskirts of Pangshang gave way to the countryside. One moment we were on a paved street going past mansions, the next the road had become a winding, deeply rutted track flanked by trees. Ngo raced along it, so giant clouds of dust billowed behind us while Piero and I bounced high off our seats. 'The Wa government keeps the roads outside Pangshang bad deliberately. If the Burmese come, it'll make it difficult for their tanks and armoured personnel carriers to get to Pangshang,' Ngo explained.

Ascending to a ridge which curved sharply ahead for as far as I could see, I spotted an open-cast mine far below us. 'For rubies,' said Ngo. Further out to the west, jungle-covered hills rolled towards Shan State proper. This was the real Wabang, where the vast majority of Wa State's estimated 600,000 people live, although accurate population figures in Myanmar are impossible to come by and there are likely many more.

Another thirty-odd kilometres on and Ngo swerved left down a steep track that led to one of his villages. We stepped out on to yellow earth that exploded in puffs of dust with every pace we took. It clung to our clothes, while creating a haze that made everything appear to be hidden behind a thin layer of gauze. The village was as poor as the Akha homes I'd seen in the hills of north-west Laos – miserable one-room houses with thatched straw roofs, the people dirty and dispirited. There was no electricity or running water. 'The people here are mostly Wa, but there are a few Lahu too. They earn about £6 a month,' said Ngo.

As well as Lahu, there are also Akha, Dai and Burmese in Wa State. Many of the migrants from inland Myanmar run shops in Pangshang, or are monks. 'We Wa don't have a problem with ordinary Burmese and a lot come to Wabang,' said Ngo. 'This is the most free part of Myanmar and if you need to hide from the government, this is the best place to do it.' But Ngo, like all the Wa I met, was vehement in his dislike of the regimes which have run Myanmar since independence. 'We don't want to be ruled by people like them. It doesn't matter if it is the generals or Aung San Suu Kyi, we will never accept that.'

In Pangshang there are monasteries and churches, but many rural Wa are still animists, or follow a hybrid religion which blends elements of Buddhism with their ancient beliefs. There was a strange, spooky shrine in the village, decorated with figures cut out of white paper. They were sinister double-headed icons, barely resembling humans. Inside one of the houses, I saw a table loaded with incense sticks, offerings of food and a Japanese sword captured in the Second World War. The same white-paper icons hung from the ceiling above it. Ngo wasn't sure of their significance, saying only that they were to keep evil spirits away.

Beyond the village was a hill where rubber plants stood in neat lines. 'This was all opium until five years ago,' said Ngo. 'A Chinese rubber company rents the land now. The government doesn't give the villagers any choice over renting their land out. They need the money the Chinese pay. They think only about fighting and the army. They're too preoccupied with that to do anything to help the ordinary people.'

Rubber and opium are two of the few profitable crops that can be grown in Wa State. Even in the nineteenth century, the region was known for opium because its arid soil is unable to support much else. With poppy production in this area stopped and their land in the hands of a Chinese firm, the villagers were helpless and fortunate to have Ngo taking an interest in them. He distributed sacks of rice and handed out small amounts of cash, but I suspected that not many members of the Wa elite were similarly generous.

Workers from Lincang, a town in southern Yunnan, were building a new accommodation block for the rubber farm's employees, who were all Chinese too. Their overseer joined us, a pistol strapped to his waist. I asked him why he was armed. 'There are tigers in the valley and snakes as thick as this,' he said, holding his hands wide apart. I didn't believe a handgun would be much defence against an onrushing tiger, or if he stepped on a deadly reptile. He was more likely worried about the locals turning nasty.

Renting out land for rubber farms has pushed the opium fields deep into the hinterland, while raising additional cash for the UWSA and enabling it to claim it is preventing people from producing poppy. The reality is that opium cultivation is rising in Wa State, and the rest of Shan, just as it is in Laos. Most of the heroin refined from it is destined for the unknown millions of addicts in China. *Yaba* production continues to increase too, an adept shift of strategy by the Wa as it is not a drug exported to the US and so is of little concern to Washington.

Lines of water buffalo were being herded down the track by farmers as we drove further into the hills, before reaching another settlement named Cawng. The houses were more substantial here, the residents better dressed, and there was even a concrete path running through the village. 'The people here are Wa and Dai. The headman used to be in the UWSA, so he has good connections in Pangshang and the village gets some help from the government,' said Ngo.

Scruffy children crowded around, shouting at the sight of strange men, while their parents peered at us from the houses. At the end of the village, perched on the crest of a ridge overlooking the deep valley below, was a small monastery. The younger monks were playing football in bare feet, their robes tucked up around their waists. 'We always have a game at the end of the day,' said one with a grin. It was a Dai monastery and the scriptures the monks studied were in the Tai Lue language. A few of them had been to Wat Pajay in Jinghong and they told us monks from there sometimes visited.

Watching the novices kick the ball around in the shade of giant, gnarled trees, with a spectacular view across the valley to the thickly forested hills rising and falling out to the west, it was hard to believe that twelve hours before I had been trapped with James in the Pangshang nightclub. Cawng was by far the most peaceful and pleasant place I visited in Wa State. But as we walked back to the truck, past the Dai-style houses on stilts, I could smell the unmistakable sweet odour of *yaba* smoke. Even in the shadow of a monastery, Wa State's principal product was present.

Back in Pangshang, over a late dinner in a Wa restaurant, Yilan was less impressed by Ngo's philanthropy than I was. 'He needs to sort his own life out and decide what he is going to do before he helps other people,' she said. It was typically pragmatic of Yilan who, like A-sui, was much more aware of the oddity of life in Wa State than any of the men I met there. The women of the Wa elite don't spend their time fighting on the front line or trading narcotics. In the traditional, macho world of Wa State, they raise families, and that gives them far more perspective than can be gained from the extreme existence James led.

When I said to Yilan that I was surprised by how developed Pangshang was, she looked at me quizzically. 'You think Pangshang is a nice city? I think it is a frightening place because of all the drugs.' Yilan must have known where the family money came from but that didn't mean she had to like it, or wasn't aware of its consequences. It was obvious that both she and A-sui would rather be living on the other side of the border in Yunnan.

Nights out with Yilan and A-sui were very different from an evening with James. They moved in a mob too, always accompanied by some of the girls who worked for the family, as well as the inevitable bodyguards, but the atmosphere was far more relaxed. They told jokes for a start, albeit Wa-style ones. One of the girls had a crush on Piero, and Yilan teased him, saying the young woman had never had a boyfriend but that he should be careful because she came from a 'scary' village where people still took heads. When we returned with them to the same nightclub we had gone to with James, we stayed sober and sang Chinese pop songs.

Once, though, we were driving through Pangshang when Yilan pointed to a woman emerging from a shop. 'She just sold her baby to a Chinese couple.' Yilan said many childless couples from Yunnan come to Pangshang to buy infants. 'It happens more with the country people. They'll sell their babies for as little as 2,000 yuan [£200].' Such things happen in rural China too, but I was still shocked at how stoically Yilan accepted the market for children as just another fact of life in Wa State.

Maybe it is a consequence of living in a jungle city where the streets are safe to walk, but the laws regarded as important almost everywhere else in the world are broken daily. Even during my short spell in Wa State, I grew used to the child soldiers and teenage hookers, the precious gems sold next to vegetables and the huge contrast between the palatial houses of the wealthy and the huts in the countryside where people merely subsisted. Above all was the unspoken understanding that all this is happening because of the *yaba* and opium being produced in the hills beyond Pangshang.

One day, it was time to leave. We returned to the banks of the Nam Ka and joined the queue of people waiting to cross to Yunnan. On the other side, we were picked up by two Chinese Wa friends of Yilan's family who had driven down from Simao for a visit and offered us a ride back. Everyone was silent, preparing to adjust to life back in China. 'I always like going to Wabang,' one of the men said after a while. 'But I wouldn't want to live there.'

20

Women for Sale

Aba looked like an ordinary fifteen-year-old girl, her face still showing signs of puppy fat, dressed in jeans and a T-shirt and clutching a prized mobile phone. She was more nervous than most teenagers, with a shy smile and a voice that rarely rose above a whisper. But I assumed that was the natural reaction of a Kachin girl confronted with the first westerner she had ever encountered. It was only later, after she had told me her terrible story, that I understood why Aba had every reason to be timid and uncertain around strangers.

We met in Ruili, a border city notorious across China as one of the nation's crime capitals. Part of the Dehong Dai and Jingpo Autonomous Prefecture in the far west of Yunnan, Ruili is indelibly associated with smuggling and women-trafficking – a consequence of its proximity to Shan and Kachin States. It is separated from the town of Muse in Myanmar by an ancient metal fence. Aba, who had lived all her life in Muse, had climbed through one of the many holes in the fence for the first time when she was just twelve. A female neighbour of her family had persuaded her to visit Ruili, promising to take her home the same night.

It was a dreadful lie. Aba didn't see her parents again for three years. Like thousands of other girls and women, she had been duped into coming to China so that she could be sold as a bride to one of the increasing number of Chinese men who cannot find a wife any other way. Soon after Aba had crossed into Ruili, she was taken on a three-day journey across China and deposited with a Han family on a farm in a place she still does not know the name of. She endured routine beatings during her enforced stay there, while never being allowed to communicate with her family or even go outside on her own.

Worst of all, Aba was destined to be married to the son of the family who had bought her as if she was one of the chickens which ran around their farm. 'I was sold for 20,000 yuan [£2,000],' Aba said. 'I was too young to get married when they bought me. It was later they told me I had to get married to their son. I was lucky in a way. If I had been two or three years older when I was taken, I would be married to him now.'

At first, I thought it odd that she considered herself fortunate to have been kidnapped so young. I know I wouldn't have done if I had been stolen as a child and sold into virtual slavery. Later, though, I realised Aba was right. Most of the Kachin and Shan women tricked into coming to China to be unwilling wives are not rescued, nor do they manage to escape. They never get to see their families and homes again.

Just as in Banna, the minorities in Ruili and Dehong Prefecture are tied to their cousins across the frontier by a shared ethnicity and culture. But the Dai here are Tai Neua and have far more in common with their relatives in Shan State than they do with the Dai in Banna, who are Tai Lue and speak a different language. The 130,000 Jingpo in Dehong are the same ethnic group as the Kachin people in Myanmar. Also present in the region are the Lisu, found all over Kachin State, and the De'ang, known as the Palaung in northern Shan State where they are far more numerous.

Being Kachin and coming from Muse dramatically increased Aba's chances of becoming a victim of the gangs who trade in women. As well as bordering China, Muse sits almost on the boundary between Shan and Kachin States, the two places where the majority of the women trafficked into China now come from. Vietnamese and North Korean women are also sold as wives, or as sex workers, but in recent years it is Myanmar which has been the main source of forced brides, a consequence of the wide-open frontier between Muse and Ruili.

So ineffective a barrier is the fence which separates the two towns that some people cross over from Muse in the morning to go to work, return home for lunch and then travel back to China in the afternoon. A couple of hundred metres away from the official border post, gaps have been prised open in the rusty railings and at all hours there is a constant parade of people going through them. During the day it is migrant workers from Muse coming to Ruili to work on construction sites or as domestic servants. In the evening prostitutes arrive, while Chinese gamblers head to Myanmar and the casinos in nearby Maijayang.

All manner of contraband moves through the fence each night from the Ruili side: chickens, pigs, sacks of rice, phones, computers and even light machinery. Under-developed, cash-strapped Myanmar can't offer much in return. But there is a big market for three of the things it does have plenty of: drugs, jade and women for the ever-growing army of single Han men in search of wives.

Bachelors in China are known as *guang guan*, literally 'bare branches', and not to be married is a significant stigma. But despite the country's massive, and probably much under-estimated, population of 1.3 billion people, there is now a severe shortage of females of a marriageable age. Over thirty years of the one-child policy, which restricts most Han families to having just a single child, has combined with the traditional Chinese preference for boys to create a devastating gender imbalance. Official statistics indicate that 120 male babies are now born for every 100 females, a ratio that is higher in some provinces.

Selective abortions are technically illegal, but many parents-to-be bribe their doctors to tell them the sex of their babies and terminate them if they are female. In rural China especially, boys have always been valued above girls. Not only are men seen as more capable of doing farm work, but they continue the family name and, crucially, are tasked with looking after their parents when they are old.

With no social security system to speak of in China, caring for the aged is the job of individual families. Even in the big cities, it is common for three generations to live together and grandparents often assume the role of principal guardians for children while their parents work. But in the country it is always the son's responsibility to provide a home for his mother and father, because when a daughter marries she becomes part of her husband's family and so has to care for his parents.

Exacerbating the demographic divide is the increasing tendency of young women to leave the countryside for the cities. In the past, village girls were often not sent to school because it was seen as a waste of money as they would only end up living with another family after they married. Now more widespread education opportunities, as well as the desire to escape the tedium of rural life, mean many are moving away to find better-paid work. Few return to their villages, and there are plenty of settlements in China where the only females are old women.

Increasing numbers of men in farming areas are now faced with a harsh choice: stay single or buy a bride from somewhere else. An underground industry has grown up to meet the demand for wives, and Myanmar is the perfect place to find them. In Kachin and north-ern Shan State, where the average salary in rural areas is the equivalent of £1 a day, it is easy for traffickers to persuade women to leave for China and jobs that don't exist. By the time they are through the border fence in Ruili and discover they have been lied to, it is too late to return and they face dismal futures as captive spouses.

No one knows exactly how many thousands of Burmese women are trafficked into China each year. What is clear is that the numbers are rising. 'I can only go by how many women come to our safe-house in Ruili and the number has doubled in the last year,' said Julia, a Kachin woman working for a Thailand-based organisation which assists the tiny percentage of women who are rescued, like Aba, or escape.

Julia was twenty-seven, small and serious and passionately proud of being Kachin. She was also paranoid and had good reason to be so. She flitted between Ruili and Kachin State via the holes in the border fence, just like the smugglers do, and her work took place in the shadow of the state in the same way as the trade in women does. With the Myanmar authorities uninterested, as most of the women being sold are from ethnic groups fighting the government, and the Chinese more concerned with the kidnapping and sale of children inside China, a major problem in itself, Julia was on her own.

For those snared by the trafficking gangs, it is an exceptionally nasty and humiliating experience which leaves the victims with emotional scars that last a lifetime. 'The Burmese traffickers bring the women to the border, where they are handed over to the Chinese traffickers. Sometimes the sale has been arranged in advance, but often the women are sold in markets held in parks in Ruili,' explained Julia. 'The traffickers will put them in nice dresses and make-up and then they are sold. It's very cruel because the women are happy to be in nice clothes, which they've never had before, and then they are sold like vegetables.'

Thankfully, Aba avoided being paraded in front of a crowd of potential buyers as if she was an animal at auction. She was very young to be taken too, which is why she was sold as a future bride, but around a quarter of all the women trafficked are under the age of eighteen. 'The men buying them always want women who can produce babies. They always ask about that first. They want healthy young girls,' said Julia.

Prices for a bride range from 6,000 to 40,000 yuan (£600–£4,000), depending on the woman's age and appearance. Some will be bought again, once they have provided the man with an heir, according to Julia. 'The women are really just regarded as baby-making machines. After they give birth, they'll be sold on to another family, or sometimes into the sex industry to work as prostitutes.'

While Yunnan is the principal destination for trafficked women from Myanmar, some like Aba are sent to the other side of the country. Aba had no idea which province she ended up in. 'I was taken a long way away, first by bus for a day and then two days on a train,' she said in her small voice. 'It snowed a lot and was very cold in the winter and they spoke a different kind of Chinese to what they speak here.' From her description of the weather and the length of the journey, I thought Aba was transported to somewhere in the north or north-east of China. They are both regions where the lack of women in the countryside is most acute.

Thousands of kilometres away from home and living with strange people speaking a different language who treated her as an unpaid servant, Aba was terrified. 'I was afraid a lot of the time and very lonely because I had no friends I could talk to. I cried a lot. In the beginning, they told me gently to stop crying. Later on, they would shout at me when I cried.' She was also physically abused. 'I couldn't speak Chinese at first, so I couldn't understand what chores I had to do around the house and farm so I would make mistakes. Then the mother would beat me,' said Aba.

That she was still traumatised by her ordeal was obvious. 'I feel scared going out on my own, especially in the evening,' she told me. Her life up to the time she was kidnapped had been far from easy anyway. One of three children of a casual labourer in Muse, Aba had already left school and was looking for work to help support her family when she made her fateful journey to Ruili.

Escaping from the farm was impossible. Aba had no money and no idea where she was and the family made sure she couldn't slip away. 'They watched me all the time. I wasn't allowed to go out on my own.' Nor could she call her parents; they are too poor to own a phone. So Aba resorted to pleading with the family to let her leave. 'All the time I wanted to go home, to go back to my parents. I would ask them to let me go, but they would say no and that I had to stay.'

Eventually, she discovered why she had been abducted and was being guarded so closely. One day, the family revealed she was to be the wife of their twenty-year-old son. 'I had been there almost three years when they told me I was to be married to him,' said Aba, her voice becoming even more inaudible. 'I had no idea that was why they had taken me until then. Of course, I refused but they told me I had to marry him.'

Virtually all the women sold as forced brides have no choice but to marry the men who have bought them because they have no chance to run away. Just as Aba was, they are trapped in what is to all intents and purposes a domestic prison. 'Most trafficked women don't escape. We can't help them,' Julia said. Faced with the hopelessness of their situation, some choose to end their lives by swallowing the highly poisonous chemical pesticide used on farms – the most common way to commit suicide in the Chinese countryside.

A few resourceful women do manage to flee, although they tend to be the ones living much closer to home in Yunnan. 'Sometimes, kind people will tell us there is a trafficked woman in their village, or a woman will call us on her own initiative,' said Julia. 'Then we'll call the local police. Often they can't be bothered to help, but if we know the exact village they will go. Otherwise, we tell the woman to try and get to the nearest police station. Because they have no Chinese identity card, they'll be arrested and eventually returned to Myanmar.'

Not having an identity card saved Aba too. Two months after learning she was to be married, she was working on another farm with the grandmother and daughter of the family. They were being paid 1,000 yuan (£100) a month each, although Aba's salary was being kept by the grandmother. 'One day the police came and asked to see everybody's identity cards, because there were many migrant workers on the farm. I didn't have one, so they took me away.'

Once in the hands of police, Aba explained what had happened to her. 'The police went to see the family and told them, "You can't buy people, they're not animals." They asked me if I wanted to prosecute

the family, but I said, "No." I just wanted to forget it and go home.'
Aba was treated well by the police, a new development in itself. Until
recently, the Chinese authorities regarded all trafficked women as
illegal immigrants and imprisoned them until they could be returned
to their home countries.

Three years after disappearing from her parents' lives, Aba walked
alone across the official border crossing to Muse and returned to her
house. 'My mother and father were very shocked to see me,' said
Aba. 'They started crying and so did I. I was so happy to see them.
They didn't ask me questions about what had happened. My parents
knew I was taken and just said it was all in the past.'

They had tried to find their daughter. After Aba disappeared, her
parents went to the Muse police and told them she had been
kidnapped and taken to China. 'They asked for money to investigate.
They wanted 6,000 yuan [£600], but my parents couldn't afford to
pay,' said Aba. Julia told me that is the standard response of Myanmar
officials to cases of trafficked women. 'Unless you pay, the police
won't refer the case to the Chinese authorities.'

Ruili's status as the women-trafficking capital of China is just its
latest dubious claim to fame. The city has been known for smuggling
ever since the late 1980s, when China started to relax its controls on
its frontiers, which were technically sealed at the start of the Cultural
Revolution. Closing the borders in Yunnan was never possible and
people carried on crossing them to visit friends and family, or to
escape the Red Guards. But it was the official reopening of the crossing with Myanmar in 1986 that led to Ruili becoming a byword for
crime.

An extreme incarnation of a debauched frontier town, Ruili was
China's original sin city, a place people flocked to for wild weekends
where anything went. In a country where everyone had been under
the rigid control of the CCP for decades and subject to its twisted
and puritanical version of morality, Ruili was not unique in the way
it embraced the seamy side of life. But its location next door to the

lawless borderlands of Myanmar ensured that nowhere else in China could match Ruili's capacity to provide depraved entertainment for those in search of it.

Gambling dens and jungle casinos flourished just across the border, so many that the village of Maijayang became known as the Macau of Myanmar. When I first visited Ruili, prostitution took place on an immense scale with hundreds of shop-front brothels where Han and Burmese women, as well as women from the local ethnic minorities, sat on display. Heroin from the Golden Triangle was readily available and, as addicts shared both needles and female company, Ruili soon had the highest incidence of HIV/AIDS in China.

Over the last few years, the local government has attempted to rid the city of its sleazy image by touting it as the jade centre of south-west China. Jade has a mystical resonance for the Han, both as jewellery that indicates wealth and status and as a metaphor for honesty and virtue. Countless Chinese women have been told to stay as pure as jade, while Confucius employed it to symbolise the character of the most upstanding of men.

Hotan in Xinjiang is the source of white jade, the most coveted of all. But Myanmar's jade, known locally as 'green gold', is almost as popular. The jade market in Ruili had doubled in size since my last visit. Despite the surfeit of shops, the traders claimed business has never been better. 'Prices are going up, mainly because the Burmese are hoarding the jade,' explained one Han dealer. 'There's still plenty being produced in Myanmar, but there's a quota on how much can be exported.'

Rising incomes have made jade far more affordable for ordinary Chinese than it was in the time when it only adorned emperors, high officials and their wives and concubines. Such is the insatiable appetite for 'green gold' that the Burmese export quota has simply fuelled the black market for jade and it continues to be illegally imported into Ruili in large quantities, along with rubies and teak.

Many Burmese have moved to Ruili to take part in the jade trade, enough to make some streets in the city resemble those of Yangon. *Longyi*-clad Burmese men sit late into the night in restaurants sipping glasses of milky tea, while ladies with cheeks smeared with *thanaka*, a natural sunscreen worn by all Burmese women, sell betel nut wrapped in banana leaves from mobile stalls. Some Han mutter darkly about the influx of Burmese, claiming they are responsible for much of the crime in the city. Given Ruili's perennially seedy reputation, I regarded that as wishful thinking.

Jade apart, Ruili is also being trumpeted as a future holiday destination, the authorities pointing to yet another of the projected high-speed rail lines that will run from Kunming to Yangon via Ruili. But I doubted that Ruili was on the cusp of a tourist boom, or would ever be. Until as late as the 1960s, the area that is now Dehong Prefecture was regarded with dread by the Han, a malarial morass of a land populated by largely unknown and unfriendly minorities.

Western travellers, too, steered clear of the region. Marco Polo wrote, 'the air in the summer is so impure and bad', and warned that any foreigner 'would die for certain'. When Reginald Fleming Johnston, a Scottish diplomat based in eastern China, passed through in 1906 on his way to Mandalay, he struggled to persuade his porters to accompany him. Fleming Johnston survived to become the tutor to Puyi, the child who was China's final emperor, a role which resulted in him being immortalised by Peter O'Toole in the Bernardo Bertolucci movie *The Last Emperor*.

Nor have the Dai and Jingpo in Ruili prospered as the Dai in Banna have, despite the banana plantations surrounding the city. 'The Dai here aren't locals like the Dai in Banna are. They're more like Burmese people and so are the Jingpo,' one Han man told me over *shaokao*: barbecued meat and fish served on skewers at outdoor stalls and the most popular eating option in Ruili.

Throughout Dehong Prefecture, the Dai and Jingpo are almost indistinguishable from their relatives across the frontier, a telling fact considering the huge wealth gap between Yunnan and Myanmar. All the minorities resent the way Ruili has been smartened up, superficially anyway, while they have not benefited. That discontent surfaces in their ambivalence towards visitors, Han or foreign, and they are far from welcoming. Ruili is the only place in China I have been to where I felt the need to look over my shoulder at night.

There are no beautiful Dai girls in dancing shows for Han tourists to goggle at in Ruili, just lots of hookers trying to make enough money to support their families or a drug habit. Prostitutes are the most obvious sign of Ruili's underbelly. The shop-front brothels that once dominated the centre of town have been closed down, but working girls still congregate on streets not far away. Others do as prostitutes do all over China, and paper every hotel room in town with business cards and wait for a phone call.

Heroin use remains widespread too, with any number of innocuous-looking shops selling it, and *yaba* too, under the counter. Walking down Ruili's main street early one evening, I almost fell over three men slumped against a wall. They were dirty, oblivious to everything, and a syringe was sticking out of a vein in the arm of one of them. Across Ruili, and especially in the Jiegao district by the border, discarded syringes half full of blood are a common sight.

But compared to the trade in women, the drugs, prostitution and jade smuggling fades into insignificance. Selling innocent young girls into lives of misery is so sordid that it makes everything else going on in Ruili appear almost wholesome. Even more depressing is the fact that many of the traffickers are Jingpo themselves, like the women they fool into travelling to China. 'Sometimes, Jingpo people come to Kachin State to find a bride and because we see the Jingpo as our brothers and sisters, we say yes when they ask for one. But often it's a fake marriage and the women are sold when they come to China,' said Julia.

Their collaboration in the trafficking trade is probably a result of them being almost as poor as their cousins in Myanmar and willing to do anything to rectify that. Possibly, it is just sheer ruthlessness. But there is no question that poverty drives the sale of women. China's gender imbalance ensures a market for forced brides, but it is the dire economic and political situation in Shan and Kachin State that prompts young women to leave. It wouldn't matter if the barrier between Muse and Ruili was ten metres high and electrified; people would still find a way to come to China in search of better lives.

Aba's return to Ruili was proof of that. Just three months after she had been rescued, Aba climbed back through one of the holes in the border fence. This time, she was alone and looking for a job to help keep her parents. Now she earns £60 a month working seven days a week as a waitress in a restaurant. Her time as a trafficked teenager has left her speaking fluent Mandarin, enabling her to blend in with the locals. Learning Chinese, though, is scant consolation for the three years of her life that were stolen from her. 'I still hate the family for what they did to me,' Aba told me when we last met. 'I think I always will.'

Part IV

DONGBEI – PUSHING THE BOUNDARIES

There is nothing like being an imperial people to make a population conscious of its collective existence . . .

Eric Hobsbawm, *Nations and Nationalism since 1780: Programme, Myth, Reality* (1990)

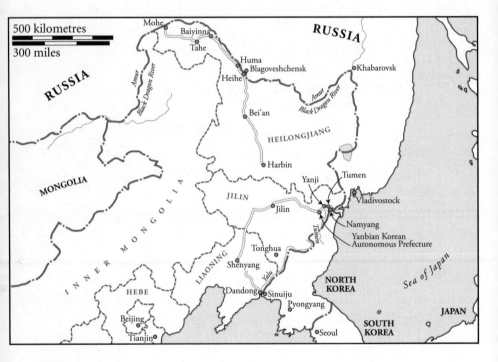

21

The Pyongyang Express

I thought the two men were Han at first. They wore the black trousers and shoes and casual but smart sweaters which are almost a uniform for provincial Chinese businessmen. Swaying in the area between carriages, cigarettes burning between their fingers, they could have been any aspiring entrepreneurs returning home after a trip to Beijing. But over the roar of the train, I heard them speaking a different language to Mandarin. Then I glimpsed the tell-tale badges of Kim Il-sung fastened to their sweaters.

'Where are you from?' I asked. 'North Korea,' one replied in surprise. I tried not to smile. For the last couple of hours, I had been prowling through the carriages in search of North Koreans. It was the reason I had caught this particular train: the K27. Twice a week, it departs Beijing for Pyongyang, capital of the Democratic People's Republic of Korea (DPRK), better known as North Korea. Apart from a handful of flights and a train from Moscow, the K27 is the only public transport link between the DPRK and the outside world.

Neither of the men conformed to the popular image of starving North Koreans. Years of famine over the last two decades have left many in the countryside stunted, or with the large heads and spindly legs that are evidence of malnutrition. But these two didn't look like they had skipped any meals. One was stout, the other over six foot tall. I asked them about the man whose face stared out from the small badges they were wearing. 'It is our great leader Kim Il-sung,' said the taller one.

Kim Il-sung was the first president of North Korea, installed with Soviet backing after the Second World War, and its absolute ruler until his death in 1994. Still known as the 'Eternal President', he was succeeded by his late son, Kim Jong-il. Now his grandson Kim Jong-un, the 'Great Successor', is the leader of the DPRK, the only country in the world where a hereditary communist dictatorship maintains power. As with Lenin and Mao, Kim Il-sung's godlike status in his home country is such that his body was embalmed and is on public view in Pyongyang, while hundreds of statues of him are dotted around the country.

Asking about their badges was just my opening gambit. I offered each a smoke to keep them from fleeing. 'North Korean cigarettes are cheap and very strong,' said the taller man, fingering the one I handed over. He revealed that they were returning from a two-day holiday in Beijing. I wondered if Pyongyang was similar to the Chinese capital. 'No, it's not very much like Beijing.' He asked me where I was from. 'England? I've never met anyone English before.'

He and his friend were living temporarily in Dandong, the city on the border with the DPRK I was bound for. 'I like Dandong. There are lots of new buildings and restaurants and many Koreans living there,' he said. I asked what they did there. 'We are working in the electronics business.' Just when I thought he was warming up and would talk on, his silent stocky partner muttered something to him in Korean. 'We have to go,' he said, shaking my hand and turning away quickly.

They were the first North Koreans I had ever met, citizens of what is perhaps the world's most reclusive country. The DPRK's twenty-four million or so people live in a rigidly controlled society largely closed to visitors, pounded by propaganda into believing they are blessed to be under the benevolent rule of the Kim dynasty. A vast army and the Workers Party of Korea, the North Korean version of the CCP, are the sharp teeth behind the dictator's smile, and the state intrudes into every aspect of life, a means of making sure no one questions, in public at least, why this Cold War relic of a country still exists in the twenty-first century.

In many ways, North Korea is reminiscent of China before the death of Mao in 1976. There is the same cult-like worship of the leader and an all-powerful ruling party that has to be obeyed no matter what. A belief in the country's supremacy results in an extraordinary insularity, while an archaic, barely functioning economy ensures the vast majority of the population don't live but merely subsist. Food is rationed, like it was in China until the late 1980s, while fridges and TVs are luxury items, just as they were in China before Beijing embraced capitalism.

My brief companions on the train were part of the select few: well-fed party members who live in Pyongyang and are trusted enough to travel overseas. Ordinary North Koreans are not allowed to leave the DPRK, in case they abscond after being seduced by the home comforts which are now taken for granted in China and elsewhere. Worse still is the possibility that they might return to challenge the state's insistence that life in countries like neighbouring South Korea is a hell of American-sponsored repression and depravity.

Just as most North Koreans can't get out, so westerners can't get in to the DPRK except on brief, restricted tours that make Beijing's rules on travel for foreigners in Tibet look lax. Dandong was as far as I could go on the Pyongyang express. After an overnight ride, I emerged from Dandong's train station on a blustery and cold late-October morning, while the K27 prepared to rumble on across the bridge that links China to North Korea here.

Almost every visitor to Dandong heads first to the Yalu River, which separates the city from North Korea. I joined the Chinese tourists, and a few South Koreans, snapping away with their cameras at Sinuiju, the North Korean border town a few hundred metres away on the opposite bank. There is little to see. A solitary factory with no smoke emerging from its chimneys, some functional one-storey buildings and a stationary Ferris wheel, a remnant of an amusement park built in the 1970s, are the only signs of life.

'It looks like a village,' said one of the Chinese. Another was more scathing. 'It looks like China thirty years ago.' Such disparaging comments are the typical reaction of Chinese tour groups when they assemble in Dandong and first see the DPRK. But the lack of progress in North Korea is also part of its attraction for many Chinese. The fact that it is frozen in time, a throwback to the China of the Mao era, makes a trip to the DPRK a nostalgic experience, as well as enabling the Chinese to crow over how their country has changed for the better.

Evidence of that was all around. Dandong spreads west, south and north of the Yalu, and for the North Koreans who can occasionally be glimpsed pottering around on the other side of the river, it stands as a sobering reminder both of their country's stalled development and of the sheer lack of vitality in the DPRK. The regime in Pyongyang can bombard its people with as much misinformation as it likes, but North Koreans living along the border with China only have to lift their eyes to see how very different life is outside their country.

Music was bellowing out of loudspeakers on the river promenade as old ladies danced in keep-fit classes. Lines of people waited to board the boats that run their passengers within twenty metres of North Korea for a close-up view of stagnant Sinuiju. Cars and trucks crowded the road that runs parallel to the river, which is lined with newly built apartment blocks. In the distance, giant cranes were hoisting seemingly unlimited quantities of raw materials to construct yet more of them.

When I returned to the promenade at night, the contrast between Dandong and Sinuiju was far crueller. A yellow moonbeam shone down on the river like a searchlight, but the buildings along Dandong's waterfront were already lit up by thousands of watts, a riot of multi-coloured neon. Over in electricity-starved Sinuiju, there were only a few isolated lights. They looked like torches vainly trying to stab through the impenetrable darkness that has enveloped North Korea for decades.

China's border with the DPRK runs for 1,416 kilometres along two rivers. The Yalu marks the boundary in Liaoning Province, where Dandong is located, and in the south of neighbouring Jilin Province until it gives way to the Tumen River. That waterway winds slowly north-east across Jilin and then turns abruptly right and flows south along the DPRK's far northern border. Eventually, it reaches a tiny sliver of land where the frontiers of China, North Korea and Russia meet, before running into the Sea of Japan.

Along with Heilongjiang further north, Liaoning and Jilin make up the three provinces known collectively in China as Dongbei: the north-east. Surrounded on three sides by Mongolia, Russia and North Korea, it is a region of climactic and geographical extremes. In the winter temperatures can drop to -40 degrees Centigrade. Summers, though, are baking hot and humid. Forests that are home to a dwindling number of Siberian tigers cover much of Dongbei, but it was also China's heavy manufacturing base until Beijing turned off the money tap in the 1990s and began denationalising many industries.

To the rest of China, the north-east is still a place of grim and grey cities, its factories the Chinese equivalent of the dark satanic mills of the English industrial revolution. Its people are typecast too. The men are regarded as rough and ready with an appetite for alcohol and fighting. They are bigger than most Han, and a disproportionate number of China's soldiers and nightclub bouncers are what the Chinese call Dongbeiren, or north-eastern people. The women, too, are taller than average and many have the milky white skin and big eyes that are the ideal of beauty in China.

Dongbei, though, is also the place where China is most likely to push its boundaries again, as it seeks to take advantage of its neighbours' frailty and geographical isolation and turn them into de facto colonies. Sitting opposite the north of Dongbei is the Russian Far East, a vast, little-populated, underfunded region rich in natural resources that many Russians believe Beijing can't wait to snap up.

North Korea is in an even worse position as it stubbornly sticks to its own unique version of an authoritarian state-controlled economy, a model that has been abandoned everywhere else in the world. A political pariah unable even to feed its own people or power their homes, the DPRK can only look to Beijing for support and is already little more than an economic vassal of China.

That Dongbei is the new front line of the Chinese empire is a historical irony, because until the seventeenth century it was not even part of it. Before then, the north-east was known to the Han as the 'Land of the Northern Barbarians'. Just as the fort at Jiayuguan in Gansu Province marked the end of the Chinese realm in the west, so the Great Wall in Liaoning separated Han China from the untamed lands to the north. Outside Dandong, the remains of the Wall stand as a reminder that this was once the far northern frontier of China. Everything beyond it was Manchu territory, known in the west as Manchuria.

Originally, the Manchu were semi-nomadic tribes who roamed across what are now Dongbei, the Russian Far East and eastern Mongolia. Subdued, like everyone else, by Genghis Khan, the various Manchu clans were later allied to the Ming dynasty. But in the early seventeenth century they unified themselves under one leader and began marching south. In 1644, they seized Beijing and established the Qing dynasty. The Manchu were to be the last of China's emperors, ruling until 1912.

Uniquely, the Manchu are the only one of China's fifty-five minorities to have run the country, although various Mongolian dynasties displaced the Han throughout the country's early history. That they did so for almost 300 years is all the more remarkable. But their reign came at a huge cost to the Manchu. It is a supreme paradox that the Qing extended the Chinese empire further than any Han dynasty, establishing the borders of what is essentially the China we know today, while losing much of their own homeland. Not only that, but their very identity was steadily diminished throughout their rule.

By the mid-nineteenth century, the Qing emperors had begun to lose control of provincial China to warlords and rebellions. As they retreated further into the fantasy land of the Forbidden City, Russia appropriated much of northern Manchuria and absorbed it into the Russian Far East. At the same time, millions of Han were moving north to the then under-populated lands of Dongbei, a result of the Qing lifting their two-centuries-old ban on Han emigration to the region.

As the Qing grew ever weaker, Han resentment of their Manchu conquerors became far more pronounced and the familiar disdain and hatred of minorities began to emerge. In 1903, the proto-revolutionary Zou Rong made that explicit. He called for 'the annihilation of five million or more of the furry and horned Manchu race, cleansing ourselves of 260 years of harsh and unremitting pain, so that the soil of the Chinese sub-continent is made immaculate'. Zou's extreme theories on racial purity were espoused by Han intellectuals of the time including Sun Yat-sen, who became China's first president in 1912.

But the Manchu weren't wiped out in some Chinese precursor of the Nazi's Final Solution. Instead the Han migrants to Manchuria began to marry the Manchu and make them Han. The Manchu tongue, which was always subordinate to Mandarin, became redundant, while their tribal culture and customs faded away until they were no more than a distant memory. So successfully were they assimilated that the number of pure Manchu left in China like Fei Fei, the woman I met in Urumqi, is tiny. Now, it is estimated that barely 100 people can speak their language.

Yet, in a contrary example of some Chinese opting to be classified as a minority, more and more people are claiming to be Manchu. Since the early 1980s, their numbers have doubled to over ten million, making them the third largest of China's minorities. The increase is due to Han with Manchurian roots choosing to be registered as Manchu. They do so to avoid being subject to the one-child policy, or so their kids can score fewer points on the *gaokao*, the university entrance exam, and still win a place at college.

One of my former Chinese teachers defined herself as Manchu and liked to boast that her family had been friends with Puyi, the last of the Qing emperors, who ended his days as a humble gardener in Beijing. She believed that the Han still look down on the Manchu, making life difficult for them. But if that was the case, their numbers would surely be dropping. Becoming Manchu is regarded as a positive choice: a way of benefiting from the state's preferential policies for minorities while knowing that nothing else, like language, religion or culture, marks them out from the Han.

A similar phenomenon has occurred in Guangxi Province in the south-west, where the Zhuang minority has increased to well over sixteen million people in recent years, making them the most numerous of all China's minorities. Intermarriage between the Zhuang and Han is common, allowing people of mixed ancestry to claim to be Zhuang. But deciding to become a minority viewed as no threat by Beijing is very different from identifying yourself as Uighur or Tibetan. I have never heard of any Han choosing to do that, despite the opportunity to have more kids or go to university.

Around half of the new Manchu live in Liaoning in the five autonomous counties named for them, one of which is outside Dandong. But they are an irrelevance in the area, just like Manchuria is as dated a name for Dongbei as Formosa is for Taiwan. In Dandong, the Koreans are the only people of any significance who are not Han. The city has a large population of both North Koreans and ethnic Chinese Koreans, a result of it being China's official gateway to the DPRK – a position which gives Dandong an importance out of all relation to its size.

Dandong is a springboard that allows China to plunge into the DPRK and expand its influence beyond its borders. Pyongyang has no choice but to acquiesce, because without Beijing's support the Kim dynasty could not survive. China is its closest ally and regards the DPRK as a bulwark in a region where Japan and South Korea are firmly aligned with the United States. So Beijing props up North

Korea, supplying it with up to one million tonnes of food aid annually, as well as a similar amount of crude oil and other essentials to keep the country from total collapse.

Virtually everything of any value in North Korea originates in China, and it mostly reaches the DPRK via Dandong. North Korean officials and businessmen, like the men I met on the train from Beijing, coming cap in hand on state-sponsored shopping trips are everywhere. Easily spotted by their badges proclaiming their loyalty to the various Kims, at night they haunt the Korean restaurants and karaoke bars within view of the DPRK itself. During the day, they congregate on the street by the border post beneath the bridge that leads to North Korea.

From the early morning to the late afternoon, the line of trucks waiting to cross into the DPRK tails back down the road. There are warehouses and wholesale shops all along it and a constant procession of North Koreans going in and out of them. They buy spark plugs and coils of wire, generators and tyres, household appliances and kitchenware. The goods are destined for North Korea's armed forces, more than a million strong, for the few industrial concerns still working, or for the Pyongyang elite.

Other less legitimate trade opportunities abound in Dandong too. Photocopied sheets of paper taped to lampposts offer the chance to invest in dubious business schemes inside North Korea, while the smuggling of everything from mobile phones to rice is rampant. These illicit enterprises are largely controlled by the 5,000 or so North Koreans who live permanently in China and their equivalents across the border: the few thousand ethnic Chinese who are residents of the DPRK.

Some of China's two million ethnic Korean citizens are also involved in trading with North Korea. Almost all of the Chinese Koreans, who mostly live in Jilin and Liaoning, have their roots in the DPRK and many still have relatives there. As such, they have the right to cross the nearby frontier, just as the minorities in Yunnan can travel to Myanmar and Laos. It is an easy matter for them to bribe the DPRK guards with a carton of cigarettes, so a blind eye is turned to what they bring in with them.

With China playing such a dominant role in the DPRK economy – the yuan has already superseded the North Korean won in some border areas – North Korea is on its way to becoming just another province of Dongbei. In return for Beijing's aid shipments, Chinese companies have been allowed to set up joint ventures in the DPRK that are busy plundering some of the world's largest untapped reserves of coal, iron ore and an assortment of minerals. New roads, almost certainly funded by China, are being built in North Korea too, despite the fact that hardly anyone in the DPRK owns a car, simply to facilitate closer economic ties with Dongbei.

Beijing does not even bother to treat North Korea as a country in its own right any more, much to the fury of South Korea, except when the DPRK is being targeted with sanctions by the United States or the UN and China is forced to offer public support to Pyongyang. Relations with North Korea are handled not by the Foreign Ministry, which deals with all China's other neighbours, but by a combination of the CCP, the PLA and the Ministry of Commerce, as if the DPRK had already been absorbed into the Chinese empire.

Pyongyang is in no position to complain about Beijing's blatant disregard for its sovereignty. So hungry is it for Chinese cash that a number of official North Korean restaurants are located in Dandong, as well as one in Beijing, their profits being remitted back home to the government. Despite my misgivings about helping to subsidise the Kim regime, I decided that a North Korean meal could be justified in the name of research. One night, I walked into one of the restaurants close to the Yalu River to be greeted by an attractive waitress in a red, flight-attendant-style uniform.

She spoke decent Chinese and was clearly used to westerners turning up and trying to pump her for tales of life inside North Korea. Like the businessmen in Dandong, the waitresses in the official

DPRK restaurants are loyalists, otherwise they wouldn't be in China at all. She soon became impatient with my attempts to make conversation, shoving a menu in front of me and brusquely telling me to hurry up and order.

I chose *bibim naeng myun*: cold buckwheat noodles served in a spicy soup – North Korea's one notable contribution to world cuisine. The waitress marched off, leaving me alone in the restaurant apart from two middle-aged ladies who were downing glasses of *songak*, a white spirit that is the North Korean equivalent of China's *baijiu*. I asked where they were from, already knowing the answer. They said almost nothing but did press a couple of glasses of *songak* on me, a drink as vile as *baijiu*. Then, like every other North Korean I had met, they disappeared, leaving me to my noodles.

Dandong's North Koreans were not proving to be a profitable source of information. I hadn't expected them to be. They are too tied to the regime to be anything but circumspect when a foreigner accosts them wanting to talk. Nor does Pyongyang trust even those people it allows out of the country. Agents from the State Safety and Security Agency, the DPRK's intelligence service, criss-cross Dandong keeping a watchful eye on their citizens. Any North Korean spotted talking to a westerner would instantly arouse suspicion and face uncomfortable questions, or worse, on their return home.

Only those who have escaped the regime are willing to talk about what really goes on inside the DPRK. It is the refugees to China, the thousands of people who each year flee the food shortages and the crushing control over their lives for Dongbei, who know better than any official or businessman what is happening outside Pyongyang. But Dandong is not the place to find them. Security on both sides of the border here is tight; the area around the city is the one part of the frontier that is fenced. The Yalu, too, is far too wide to make crossing it without a boat feasible.

Instead, most refugees and defectors from North Korea arrive further north in Jilin Province. Not only is the Tumen a far narrower river than the Yalu but the borderlands of Jilin are part of the Korean Autonomous Prefecture, the heartland of China's ethnic Koreans. Every North Korean knows he or she will find people there who can speak their language, and maybe even a relative. The peak times to cross the border are in June and July before the summer rains arrive, when the Tumen is easy to wade across, or in the deep winter when it freezes and escapees can walk to China.

There is one spot near Dandong where crossing from North Korea looks easy. It lies in the shadow of the Great Wall, once the dividing line between Han China and the Manchu empire. Twenty kilometres north-east of Dandong, a steep stretch of Ming dynasty-era Wall known as the Tiger Mountain Great Wall runs parallel with the border with the DPRK. From the top of its heavily restored watch-towers, you can gaze down on North Korea.

Like the view across the Yalu River in Dandong, the prospect offers little insight into the country. A treeless expanse of muddy land runs towards far-off hills and is empty save for a few houses and a larger building that is a barracks for frontier guards. But if you descend from the Wall, scrambling down its sides, you reach a point where the Yalu River narrows dramatically. Now North Korea is just ten metres away and the partially collapsed border fence appears in close-up. Continue walking to the left and the river tapers still further until the DPRK is right in front of you.

Known to the Chinese as *yibukua*, or 'one step across', it is a mere long jump to North Korea from here. I wanted to leap over the water just so I could set foot on its soil. Adding to the temptation was the lack of any visible guards in the vicinity. But I knew soldiers were near by, ready to emerge from their hiding places should I do so. *Yibukua* is far too obvious a route out of the DPRK and no North Koreans escape their bleak lives this way. I turned back. Some borders are not meant to be crossed.

22

The Third Korea

The bus to Yanji was half full, its other occupants Chinese Koreans returning to the capital of their homeland. We ran roughly parallel with the Yalu River and then the Tumen past farms and through small towns for fourteen hours, until I was deposited outside Yanji's train station just after dawn. It was November and much colder than in Dandong. From here on, I would be moving only north, and every day the temperature dipped lower as the frigid Dongbei winter clamped the region in snow and ice, while a bitter, freezing wind blew down from the Siberian plains.

Yanji was still the same tightly packed mass of greying apartment and office blocks, divided by the Buerhatong River, I had encountered on previous visits. But if Yanji looks like a typically undistinguished third-tier Chinese city, it feels very different from one. The first hint of its dual nature is the fact that the street signs are in same-sized Chinese and Korean characters. They are symbolic of the way Yanji's 400,000 people are divided almost equally between Han and ethnic Korean, and how they coexist in a far more amenable atmosphere than is normal for Chinese and minorities in the borderlands.

There is no sense that the city is segregated, as Lhasa and Urumqi are rigidly divided between Han and Tibetan or Uighur neighbourhoods. Stand at a bus stop in Yanji and you will hear Korean in one ear and Mandarin in the other until they seem to blend into one bizarre new tongue. And the longer you stay in Yanji, the more South Korean it feels. Restaurants offering Korean delicacies like dog meat outnumber Chinese eateries. The city has its own TV channels in Korean, along with newspapers and magazines offering the latest updates on celebrity scandals in Seoul.

Security is unobtrusive here too. There are plenty of soldiers in the surrounding Yanbian Korean Autonomous Prefecture, the official Chinese name for the region, mounting guard along the nearby border with the DPRK. But in Yanji itself the main hint that the military is around are the jets from a nearby air-force base that scream over the city at regular intervals, coming in so low that the red stars on their fuselages are clearly visible.

Yanbian, Yanji apart, is one of the least densely populated regions of China outside the high plateau of Tibet and the deserts of Xinjiang. Around 2.2 million people live in an area of Jilin Province about half the size of South Korea, which has a population of fifty million. After the packed cities and countryside of eastern and southern China, where every inch of land is utilised, the empty landscape is both a shock and a relief. Forty per cent of the residents of the prefecture are ethnic Korean, the rest Han, with the remaining million-plus Chinese Koreans mostly spread throughout the rest of Jilin, or in neighbouring Liaoning Province.

My contact in Yanji was from Shenyang, the capital of Liaoning. Christina was tall with the narrow eyes that mark out Koreans from the Han. She was deathly pale, which I put down to the sun disappearing in the mid-afternoon during the long Dongbei winter, and a student at Yanji's Yanbian University. Set up specifically to educate Chinese Koreans, Yanbian is unique among China's universities in that some of its courses are not taught in Mandarin. Ethnic Koreans are allowed to study in their language as well, a privilege not granted to any other minority.

When we met in a restaurant, Christina greeted me with a penetrating, disappointed gaze. 'From your voice and emails, I thought you'd be younger,' she said. No one in China, whether Han or a minority, is ever shy about commenting on the age or looks of a foreigner. Christina had been recommended to me because she spoke good English, as well as Mandarin and her native Korean. Her English was fine, but over barbecued beef, cold noodles and *kimchi*, the spicy cabbage that accompanies every Korean meal, she confessed that her Chinese was not perfect.

'At home we speak Korean, so it's much better than my Mandarin,' she revealed. 'Some Chinese Koreans want their children to speak Chinese first, but it really depends on your family. My grandmother can't speak any Chinese and my mum's is pretty bad, so we've always spoken Korean. I think I'll do the same and teach my children Korean before Mandarin. It's very much my first language. Even if I have to speak Chinese when I get a job, I'll always talk to my friends in Korean.'

Ethnic Koreans are known in China as Chaoxianzu, which translates as 'North Korean race', Chaoxian being the Chinese name for the DPRK. It is a way of distinguishing them from South Koreans, but also an accurate description of their origins because nearly all Chinese Koreans come from areas that are now part of North Korea. Christina's roots were in North Pyong'an Province, the region across the Yalu River from Dandong. 'My family came to China in 1930. It was a bad time in Korea then and they thought life would be better here. I still have relatives there, although I've never met or even spoken to them.'

Christina's great-grandparents were relatively late arrivals in China. Koreans started moving across the Yalu and Tumen Rivers from the 1860s as, in a brutal harbinger of what would happen in the DPRK in the 1990s, a series of famines struck what was then the north of the undivided country of Korea. Others left after 1910 when the Japanese invaded. Among the emigrants was the family of Kim Il-sung, the future founding father of North Korea. His parents moved to Jilin City in 1920 when he was eight, and Kim didn't return home for twenty-five years.

By the time he did, there were 1.7 million Koreans living in Dongbei. With Japan occupying Korea, almost all supported or

fought for the CCP in its battles against the Japanese and the nationalist armies, including Kim Il-sung who would later wildly exaggerate
his success as a guerrilla leader, despite having spent much of the
Second World War living safely in the Russian Far East. Even after
the defeat of Japan in 1945, most Koreans in China chose to stay on,
with only half a million returning to their homeland.

As Korea was plunged into the war that formalised the division of the
peninsula into two separate countries, another Korea was being created.
Beijing didn't forget the sacrifices of the Koreans in Dongbei during the
Sino-Japanese War and the Chinese Civil War. They were given land
and, in 1952, became one of the first ethnic groups to be granted their
own official region. Now Yanbian is a third Korea, only one inside
China. With its people hailing from North Korea but bound culturally
to South Korea, it presages what a reunified Korea might be like.

China's Koreans enjoy advantages denied to other minorities,
which only reinforces the sense that Yanbian is more like a mini-state
than just another autonomous area. The most notable of these is the
right to education in their own language at school as well as college.
Unlike in Xinjiang, where the government has closed down Uighur-
only schools, or Xishuangbanna and Tibet, where the only way to
study Dai or Tibetan is to become a monk, the Yanbian government
actually funds schools that teach in Korean.

Nor are the Koreans as obviously subordinate to the Han as most
other ethnic groups, being well represented among local officials.
Apart from during the Cultural Revolution, when the Chaoxianzu
suffered along with all the minorities, the Han have always maintained
a mutually respectful relationship with the Koreans. On the surface at
least, the Han approach in Yanbian seemed to me to be a model which
if followed elsewhere would certainly reduce, while not eliminating,
tensions between the Chinese and the most restive minorities.

In Yanbian, there is no conflict between being Chinese by nationality and Korean culturally and that gives the Chaoxianzu little
reason to resent the Han. Christina's family epitomised the way they

exist in a cosy space alongside the Chinese, speaking Korean, eating Korean food, following Korean traditions and watching South Korean soap operas. Yet her father, a teacher, is also a CCP member.

Few Han care that the Koreans maintain their language and separate culture. 'Some things are different with the Chaoxianzu,' one Chinese businesswoman in Yanji told me. 'The food obviously but also how they don't think New Year is as important as we do. Weddings and birthdays are more important to them. I think maybe in the old days there were more differences because Han and Koreans never married then, but now they do. Actually, I think Korean men are quite handsome.'

Like the Manchu before them, it is intermarriage which poses the greatest risk to China's Koreans and to Yanbian's status as the third Korea. With many moving away to the big cities of Dongbei where the Han are the majority, more and more are marrying Chinese. The number of ethnic Koreans is dropping anyway because they have a lower birth rate than the Han, even though as a minority they are not constrained by the one-child policy.

Christina was under strict instructions to marry a fellow Korean. 'My dad said our relationship would be over if I marry a Han guy,' she said, giggling. 'It's because my sister married a Chinese.' Christina, though, wasn't happy with her father's stricture. 'I want to marry a Han man. They're kind and do housework and drink less than Chaoxianzu men. I think Korean men feel they have to be the king. They want to provide for the family, but they don't want to do the small things.'

But it was her father who raised Christina, after her mother left for South Korea to work in a restaurant when she was eleven. 'She stayed there for eight years and didn't come back to China once,' said Christina. 'When she did come back, I cried because I didn't think she was my mum any more. Eight years away was such a long time. I didn't feel angry with her because I knew she did it to earn money for my university education. I just felt sad she'd been away so long.'

Many ethnic Koreans leave China in search of better-paid jobs. At any time, one in ten Chinese Koreans are working overseas, mostly in South Korea but also in Japan. Obtaining a passport is easy for them – another sign of how trusted they are. Yet that freedom of movement is also contributing to their declining population because, inevitably, some of those migrant workers never return to Dongbei.

Assimilation with the Han is why Koreans now make up only 40 per cent of Yanbian's population, down from two-thirds when the prefecture was established. Many Korean schools are shutting down, both because there are fewer children to attend them and due to the fact that the offspring of Han–Korean couples tend to be raised speaking Mandarin and so are sent to Chinese schools. And with the Koreans increasingly spreading to other parts of Dongbei, or even further afield, a Korean education is now regarded as less useful than a conventional Chinese one.

A highly emotive example of how the closing of Korean schools and mixed marriages are diluting Chinese Korean identity can be glimpsed on the football fields of Yanbian. Just as the Koreans are the only minority who still have their own education system, so they are the one ethnic group with a soccer team. Yanbian Baekdu Tigers FC started life in 1955 as Jilin Three Stars, and for much of its history was famous throughout China as one of the country's top clubs. More than forty of its players have graduated to the Chinese national side, an astonishing number given how few of China's people are ethnic Korean.

'Football is like the calling card of Yanbian. Koreans are known in China for football in the same way that some minorities in Yunnan are known for singing or dancing,' said former player Jin Guangzhu. 'When I was playing, we'd pack out the stadium in Yanji. There'd be 50,000 people watching us. We all felt very proud when we were the number-one team in China. All the players were Chaoxianzu and we were the only minority to have our own football team, so we were really representing Yanbian and our people.'

Those glory days are long gone. Yanbian haven't won the Chinese championship since 1990 and are now marooned in the second division, attracting a crowd one-tenth of the size they used to draw. I met Jin Guangzhu in the concrete block of a building that is the administrative home of the Baekdu Tigers. Paint was peeling off the ceilings and walls of the unheated corridors, while a few men in tracksuits sat in offices smoking. Old Trafford it wasn't.

Slim and still fit at forty-three, Jin was a defender for Yanbian in the late 1980s and early 1990s, as well as representing China between 1993 and 1995. Born in Helong, a town south of Yanji close to the border with the DPRK, he believes the popularity of soccer in Yanbian is an expression of a wider, pan-Korean identity. 'Football is the traditional game for Koreans, whether you're from North or South Korea or Yanbian.'

He traced Yanbian FC's decline to the way more ethnic Koreans are going to Han schools. 'They don't care about football in the way Korean schools do,' he said. 'It's our biggest worry. If the young people go to Han schools then we won't get the players, and then we won't be a Chaoxianzu team any more. You know, there's a lot of financial pressure in China now. Parents think their kids will get better jobs if they go to Han schools, so even if they are good at football their parents will stop them playing because they want them to study hard instead.'

To make up the shortfall in numbers the club takes North Korean footballers on loan. 'The DPRK sometimes offers us players and we'll always sign them if they have good skills. They speak the same language as us, so they fit into the team very well,' said Jin. 'But what we really need is a proper sponsor, so we can make playing for Yanbian an attractive option for Chaoxianzu. At the moment, we can only pay the players 7,000 yuan [£700] a month.'

Professional football players everywhere are usually from urban areas and Yanbian FC's struggle to attract fresh talent reflects the divide between the cities and the countryside in the region. In Yanji, ethnic Korean children are going to Chinese schools and are much more likely to end up marrying a Han partner. But out in the rural areas, along the border with the DPRK, Korean schools still flourish and there are far fewer Han. The grandmother of one of Christina's classmates lived in a village near Tumen close to the frontier with the DPRK. When she told me she was due to make a visit, I asked if I could come along.

We caught a local bus to Tumen, travelling past fields where corn, the main crop in the area, had been harvested for the winter and then through hilly, thickly wooded country; the lack of people in Yanbian means much of the land has yet to be cleared for farming. From Tumen, it was a taxi ride down back-roads to the village, a collection of single-storey brick buildings populated entirely by Chaoxianzu and overlooked by an unsightly natural-gas plant.

Granny was waiting for us at the end of the path that led to her house, a tiny, smiley, bright-eyed widow standing by a neatly stacked pile of firewood. She was excited at seeing a fresh face, showing me the herbs and vegetables she cultivated in a small plot outside her front door. 'I've only met Russians before, never a westerner,' she told me. She was seventy-two and first-generation Chinese, born in Heilongjiang to Korean immigrants, but her Mandarin was worse than mine and she spoke in Korean.

Inside, the two-room house was spotless and compact, the walls covered with photos of her children and grandchildren, some of whom were living in South Korea. The house was heated in the traditional Korean way: a wood-fired oven under a raised platform, known as a *gudeul*, which covered much of the main room. We sat on it to eat a delicious lunch of soybean soup, cold fish, beef and rice, along with Granny's homemade *kimchi*.

She had moved to Yanbian after her marriage. It was the time when China was in the throes of the Great Leap Forward, Mao's catastrophic attempt to transform a then overwhelmingly agricultural country into a modern industrialised economy in a few short years.

As harvests shrank because people were taken off farms to work in backyard factories, two years of severe drought further reduced the amount of food being produced.

Officials doctored the grim statistics, too scared to report the truth. Mao's egotistical policy of continuing to export grain to Russia and Africa, in an effort to convince the world of the superiority of the Chinese communist system, only accentuated the food shortage. Instead of turning China into a manufacturing nation, the Great Leap Forward resulted in up to forty-five million people dying in one of the world's worst famines.

'It was 1959. I worked on the farm, growing corn and some vegetables. But we had no rice or meat to eat,' recalled the grandmother. 'Life was so hard then and in the early 1960s that there was no time to do anything but survive. From sunrise to sunset we worked on the land and often we would work into the night. We were always hungry. Some people died of starvation, or they were so hungry they ate weeds that caused them to die.'

Death denuded the village of many of its residents during those years, but some just disappeared. 'At that time, many people left. They ran away to North Korea. It wasn't just that they had more food there, but because it was their country. They are regretting it now,' said Granny with a grim chuckle. 'I never thought about it. I was born here and feel totally Chinese, even if I don't really speak Chinese and all my family and friends are Korean.'

Since the early 1990s, the movement of people across the Chinese–DPRK border has been exclusively one way as North Koreans escape for Dongbei. But before then it was almost entirely in the opposite direction. Unknown thousands of China's Koreans returned to North Korea during the Great Leap Forward, and more followed once the Cultural Revolution started. Some may have been motivated by a desire to return to their ancestral homeland. Most, though, left because until the mid-1980s North Korea was a more prosperous place than China.

Propped up by China, the old Soviet Union and its allies in Eastern Europe, North Korea had access to both cheap imports and markets for its goods. The fall of the Berlin Wall in late 1989 and the demise of the USSR in 1991 brought that support to an abrupt end, just as China was opening up to the world. Around the same time, the DPRK started investing huge amounts of money in developing nuclear weapons, a further drain on its dwindling resources. Unable to pay for oil imports, North Korea's economy collapsed and people started to go hungry.

From 1992 on, a famine began to take hold in the DPRK that was as devastating as the one Mao had inflicted on the Chinese country-side during the Great Leap Forward. It lasted for almost a decade and was especially severe in the north of the country, the regions bordering Dongbei, resulting in an estimated 100,000 North Koreans fleeing to China. Granny remembered it well. 'About ten to fifteen years ago, there were people coming to the village from North Korea. None come now – they know it's too dangerous because the police will find them and send them back.'

Her reaction to the North Korean refugees was a mix of sympathy and fear. 'I felt very sorry for them and I wanted to help them, but I was too scared. I was afraid they would be a burden,' she confessed. 'We never told the police there were North Korean people living here, but they always found out. There was one woman married to a man from the village and they came and sent her back. We got into trouble if we helped them.'

Nearby Tumen houses a detention centre where captured North Koreans are held before being repatriated to the DPRK. It lies north of the bridge across the Tumen River that divides Tumen from the North Korean town of Namyang. The DPRK is far closer to China here than it is in Dandong, but the view from the river bank is no more inspiring. Namyang is a series of decaying apartment blocks separated from each other by wasteland, criss-crossed by a few roads mostly empty of traffic. Behind the town, barren brown hills rear up and just like Sinuiju, the town opposite Dandong, there is little obvious sign of life.

Chinese tourists can pay to be escorted halfway across the bridge that leads to the DPRK to take photos. I was waved away when I tried to buy a ticket. There are a few souvenir shops on the river bank, selling badges of the various Kims, as well as North Korean stamps and cigarettes. Wavering over buying a pack of DPRK smokes, wondering if they were real or Chinese-produced fakes, I noticed a middle-aged woman eyeing me curiously. I asked her if they were genuine and she looked at them and nodded.

Mrs Lee was a primary school teacher in Pyongyang with alarming bridgework on her upper teeth. Dressed in what was the height of fashion in rural China two decades ago – a pink windbreaker, black polyester trousers and pointy black shoes – she was about to cross back into North Korea after visiting her aunt, who was married to a Chinese Korean. Mrs Lee told me I should come to Pyongyang. 'It's a better place than Tumen.' I wasn't so sure. Tumen is tiny but at least I was allowed to walk around it unescorted.

Both her children were in the army and she proudly showed me her royal-blue DPRK passport. Mrs Lee was a true believer – faithful to her country and leader and no fan of China. 'The country is too free and the people are too free. It's because there are so many countries with such free ways that we are poor,' Mrs Lee said sternly. Christina, who was translating, began to look bewildered. 'In North Korea, healthcare and education is free. You can go to the hospital with no money and they will still treat you. Even if there are just three children in a village, there will be a teacher for them. It's not like that in China.'

Telling her that the reason there might only be three kids in a village could be because all the others had died of hunger or disease seemed a little harsh. I compromised by saying that surely there is more to eat in China than there is in the DPRK. Mrs Lee paused before replying, as if she was trying to remember her lines.

'Nowadays, we have enough food. We'll have even more soon.' She made it sound like a warning.

Before Mrs Lee left, she tempted me again to visit North Korea. 'The young people are all good at singing and dancing.' I had a momentary flashback to my time in Yunnan, and the beautiful Dai girls performing their fake dance rituals for Han tourists in Jinghong. Conjuring up images of sultry and sexy North Korean women seducing me with a glance proved impossible, though. It was too much of an imaginative leap, with desolate Namyang over my shoulder and the desperate inmates of Tumen's detention centre down the road.

23

Spreading the Word

Christina had a secret life. I had noted the wooden cross around her neck when we first met, but in China some people wear them as a fashion accessory rather than as a sign of religious devotion. Then one day Christina asked me what I believed in and I realised that being a Christian was the most important thing in her life. Answering such a deceptively simple question was not easy. I settled for saying that I didn't know if there was a God and maybe I'd find out later.

She is one of many Christians in Yanji. Although they probably now outnumber the eighty million-plus members of the CCP, followers of Christianity are not spread evenly across China. Instead, they tend to be concentrated in regions which were exposed to foreign influence before 1949. Many of Yunnan's hill tribes were converted by missionaries who slipped across the borders from then British Burma and French Laos. Missionaries were active in Dongbei and neighbouring Korea too, and Yanbian and Jilin Province have always been strongholds of the faith.

Yanji is full of churches, mostly Protestant but some Catholic, and nor are they small or tucked away out of sight like many houses of God are in China. The largest is an imposing redbrick building in the centre of town by the banks of the Buerhatong River. Two giant white crosses are etched into the brick, visible from hundreds of metres away. The main Catholic church is less impressive, a grey pebbledash affair in the east of Yanji, but its tall steeple still overlooks the surrounding apartment blocks.

Those churches are official ones, part of a network across the country controlled by Beijing. The CCP is an atheist organisation and dislikes religion to the point where none of its members are allowed to follow one. But it is more suspicious of Christianity than any other creed, principally because it perceives it as an alien, western faith. Even Islam raises official hackles only in Xinjiang, and that has more to do with it being a rallying point for the Uighurs than its origins overseas.

Catholicism is particularly problematic, because the party believes the allegiance Catholics owe the pope is a direct challenge to its authority. Beijing severed diplomatic ties with the Vatican in 1951 in an effort to assert its control over China's Catholics, ordering them instead to join the Chinese Catholic Patriotic Association. That organisation does not recognise the primacy of the pope, and instead it is the CCP which anoints China's Catholic bishops. Since 1954, Protestants have been monitored in similar fashion.

The majority of Christians, though, perhaps as many as three-quarters of them, do not attend the churches overseen by Beijing. Instead, they worship in house churches: underground gatherings of the faithful who meet in apartments, empty offices or the back rooms of restaurants. Christina did the same. Her house church, which Christina referred to as a 'family church', was made up of university students and recent graduates, all of whom were ethnic Koreans.

Neither of her parents knew that Christina was a Christian. 'My dad would probably be angry,' she said. 'He'd say I should be concentrating on studying. I'll tell them after I graduate.' She was taking a risk too by attending a house church. Tolerated to some extent by the authorities, they are also regularly raided and their pastors arrested and members of the congregations detained.

I had been to a house church in Beijing and was keen to see Christina's. She wasn't sure I would be welcome but after consulting with her preacher, it was agreed I could meet him and some of Christina's fellow worshippers in a neutral setting. Early one evening, I joined them in a café near Yanbian University. The pastor was in his late twenties, short with thick round glasses. He told me to call him Mr Kim. Two young women, both fellow students of Christina's, were with him.

None had been brought up as Christians. In the past, Christianity tended to run in families in China and was more prevalent in the countryside than the cities. Now, urban young people are discovering religion for themselves and large numbers of them are university educated. At the house church I visited in Beijing nearly all the congregation were under forty and many were students or new graduates.

Mr Kim traced his conversion back to his first year at college. 'I started to think about the life I was going to live. I thought if I buy an apartment for my parents, I'll have to save for twenty years. Then if I want to buy one for myself, I'll have to save for another twenty years. I'd be sixty and would have spent my life just working to buy two homes. I thought it was a depressing, meaningless way to live. I talked to one of my friends about it and he suggested I go to church with him, one of the official ones in Yanji. I felt more peaceful after the service. That's when I started to realise there was more to life than work and money.'

Like her pastor, Christina was dissatisfied with the prospect of an existence centred only on her material needs. 'It was when I went to university that I realised I really wanted to believe in something. A lot of people don't want to believe in anything, or they just believe in the CCP, but that wasn't enough for me. I knew when I was eighteen that just studying, playing and going to karaoke didn't make me happy or bring me any peace,' she said.

For the CCP, the rise in faith among educated people like Christina, the daughter of a party member, is an unwelcome development. Not only are they the demographic it traditionally recruits its future leaders from, but their turning to religion is proof of a widening disillusionment with the party's credo of the last two decades, which has been to allow people to make money as long as no one questions its right to rule. More disturbing still, the increasing number of Christians is a challenge to Beijing's unspoken assertion that there is no need for God when the CCP already acts as if it is one.

Although Christina and her friends were breaking the law by attending a house church, it didn't concern them. 'Every church has its own vision and I was called to this one,' stressed Mr Kim. 'In this region there are lots of churches so Christians have a choice, but in many parts of China a house church is the only option. We don't worry about the police because we're not such a big church. If there are less than thirty of you meeting regularly, you're normally OK.'

Far more dangerous is how Mr Kim and his congregation believe it is their duty to evangelise. It is one thing to be a Christian in China, but proselytising verges on what the CCP regards as organised dissent. Beijing has a longstanding antipathy to western missionaries – who are viewed as yet another example of outsiders meddling in China's internal affairs – and is equally unhappy with its own citizens doing similar work. 'It's OK for me to talk to a fellow student about Christianity, but we'd get into trouble if we did it on a big scale and started handing out Bibles,' said one of Christina's friends.

Despite the risks, they still roam across Jilin Province trying to convert people. 'We went to Tonghua for ten days earlier this year to spread the gospel. We just walked the streets, stopping people and trying to talk to them about God,' said Christina. 'We'd say "have you heard of Jesus Christ?" Lots of people said "no" or "I'm not interested" or "I don't believe". But a few people were prepared to stop and listen. It's about spreading the word, sowing the seeds of faith.'

One of Christina's classmates had gone as far as Ningxia, the Hui autonomous region in the north-west, to seek converts among the local Muslims. Mr Kim had come close to arrest when he travelled to Guizhou in south-west China to preach to people from the Miao minority. 'I supported myself by teaching, and I'd meet some of my students after school and tell them about God. I got into trouble when the parents of one of the students found his notebook with his thoughts about the Bible. He was a policeman. Luckily, I'd already left Guizhou but now I can't go back. I've been much more careful since then,' he said.

Rather than traditional Catholicism or Protestantism, it is evangelical Christianity which is surging in popularity in China. Many house churches are similar to the Pentecostal churches found across the Bible Belt of the USA, where worshippers raise their hands to heaven, cry 'Hallelujah' during sermons and pray aloud for the Holy Spirit to enter them. It is a tradition that has also taken hold in South Korea which, along with the Catholic Philippines, is the most Christian of all nations in Asia.

But long before Seoul became known as a spiritual centre – the home of the extraordinary Yoido Full Gospel Church with its million-strong congregation – Pyongyang was the heartland of Korean Protestantism. The many missionaries who came to the north of the still undivided Korea in the late nineteenth century met with such success that in 1907 Pyongyang was dubbed the 'Jerusalem of the East'. It was a city of churches, and almost a third of its population were Christians.

They included Kim Il-sung's parents. His mother and father were both devout Protestants, and his maternal uncle was a pastor. But when Kim became president of the new North Korea he launched an all-out assault on Christianity. It was reviled as an American import, its ministers and priests no more than CIA-backed Fifth Columnists out to subvert his glorious regime. Soon after the end of the Korean War in 1953, North Korea's churches were burned down and an estimated 100,000 Christians were imprisoned in the DPRK's notorious gulags.

By then, many of the north's Protestants had fled south to play a major role in turning South Korea into the stronghold of evangelicalism it is today. Now South Korea sends out more missionaries than any other nation apart from the United States. Yanbian is one of the principal regions they operate in. Not only is it home to almost a million ethnic Koreans but it is adjacent to the DPRK, the country whose people were once such fervent believers until their devotion was forcibly transferred to its new leader – a twisted exorcism performed by the state, one that mimicked the way Mao was presented as a godlike figure to the Chinese.

With so many Chaoxianzu working in South Korea, or having relatives who do, awareness of Christianity is far higher among Yanbian's Koreans than elsewhere in China. But more often than not, it is missionaries who reel them in. Many work as teachers, just as Mr Kim did during his time in Guizhou. A high proportion of the members of his house church were converted once they started college. 'Some of my lecturers at university are South Korean and they are all Christians,' said Christina. 'God and Christianity is a big part of South Korean culture now, and so we always talk about it.'

Around 10,000 South Koreans live in Yanji. 'I'd say about half are missionaries,' said Paul. He was one of them, a youthful forty-nine-year-old from Seoul in jeans and a check shirt with a broad face and bushy hair cropped close at the sides. Paul had followed his sister, a teacher and fellow missionary, to Yanji a couple of years before. Now he owned a restaurant popular with students, a way of disguising his real purpose in China.

'Most of us in Yanji run businesses or teach because we don't want to draw attention to ourselves,' said Paul. 'We do worry about the government's attitude to us, but we're not doing anything political. We think the Chinese understand that, but we also know they are watching us. You have to be careful. People who've been here a long time know what you can do and what you can't. Officially, we don't spread the gospel. But we try and show people what a Christian life is and introduce them to the Bible.'

Paul gave up his job as the manager of a foreign trade company to come to Yanji. 'A lot of South Koreans feel the Chinese need faith as

China develops. If they have no faith and a western economic system, then people will just become corrupt,' he said. 'It's easier for us to spread the gospel here because the people are Koreans and we speak the same language. Then the Chinese Koreans can go on and spread the word to the Han Chinese.'

Sentiments like that ring alarm bells in Beijing. The very idea of South Koreans disseminating Christianity, a creed the CCP associates with its traditional enemies in the west, to Yanbian's Koreans feeds Beijing's belief that religion serves only to foster separatist tendencies among its minorities. Tibet and Xinjiang are glaring examples of how the power of faith unites the peoples of those regions against the Han. For the CCP, it is one small step from China's Koreans being converted by South Koreans to them starting to regard their shared religion as proof they are part of a greater Korea.

South Korean nationalists believe that already and advocate the incorporation of Yanbian into one super-Korea along with the DPRK. They point to the way the Koguryo Kingdom, the most powerful of the three dynasties that ran ancient Korea until the seventh century AD, stretched into what is now Jilin Province. South of Yanji in Jian, the ruined pyramids and tombs of a former Koguryo city are a permanent reminder of how this part of Jilin was once Korean territory.

Reinforcing Yanbian's claims to be part of a larger Korea is the way it is so culturally intertwined with South Korea. 'I think there's very little difference between Chinese Koreans and South Koreans,' said Paul. 'Actually I think Chinese Koreans get a more traditional Korean education in Yanbian than they do in South Korea. The family relationships are closer and more traditional too. The different generations of Korean families all used to live together, but nowadays in South Korea parents and children live separately. It's not like that here.'

Almost sixty years of a divided Korea has drawn Yanbian and South Korea closer together, so they now have far more in common

than the South does with the DPRK. 'There's a much bigger difference between us and the North Koreans. We still regard them as
brothers – we are one nation – but there's a wall between us and them
now. They've been brainwashed and think their leader is a god, and
breaking down those barriers takes a long time,' said Paul.

Yet, despite their ties to South Korea, the overwhelming majority
of Chinese Koreans are not Korean nationalists – at least not in the
sense of wanting to be part of one Korea. But, for Beijing, the activities of missionaries like Paul are seen as bringing the day closer when
the Chaoxianzu will no longer be content with just being culturally
Korean. House churches can be found across all China now, but only
in Yanbian does Christianity pose a real threat as a potential vehicle
for separatism.

During my time in Yanbian, I encountered only one Chaoxianzu
who regarded himself as Korean rather than Chinese. 'Call me Piao,
like *mai piao*,' he told me when we met. *Mai piao* means 'to buy a
ticket' and, as I got to know Piao, I came to think of his nickname as
an astute, self-mocking comment on his sad life. He was in his early
thirties: chubby-faced with longish hair, the beginnings of a pot belly
and always dressed in a leather jacket and jeans. We were introduced
by an acquaintance of mine from Beijing, a Han woman who had run
a bar in the capital before returning to her hometown of Yanji to
open a place there.

Her customers were mostly ethnic Koreans, proof perhaps of
their reputation in China as party people. 'We think differently from
the Han,' Christina said often. 'Korean people like to play, to enjoy
life. I think the Han just like to work and save money. They don't
have as much fun as we do.' It is a common belief among China's
minorities. I never met one who wasn't convinced they are more
gregarious than the Han, and mostly they are.

Fun for Chaoxianzu men involves downing beers and *baijiu*. Even
among the hard-drinking males of Dongbei, Chinese Koreans stand
out for their love of alcohol. Their tippling was the reason Christina

wanted to marry a Han man, and Piao spent his evenings traversing unsteadily across Yanji's many watering holes. One night, I bumped into him as I was leaving a bar in the centre of town. Piao was already half cut. He put his arm around my shoulders and insisted I stay for another drink.

Other friends of his joined us and Piao got progressively drunker. It was then that he revealed his patriotic streak. 'I am a Korean man,' he kept telling me, 'a Korean man.' I asked if he meant he was Chinese Korean. He shook his head and started to draw a rough map in the beer spilled across our table. 'This is the DPRK, this is Yanbian and this is South Korea,' he said, slurring as he sketched the outlines of the borders. 'We are the same people, whether you live in North Korea, the South or here. You know, a long time ago this was all one big powerful country, not two countries and a bit of China.'

Not even Piao's friends agreed with him. They all defined themselves as Chinese Koreans, rather than as Koreans living in China. Piao ignored them and became increasingly aggressive and maudlin, repeating 'I have no country' over and over again. He perceived himself both as an exile in a foreign nation and as someone living in territory which rightfully belonged to Korea.

Later, I learned why he was so angry. He told me how six years before he had met and married a North Korean refugee. Most of those who escape the DPRK are women, with some sources claiming they make up around 80 per cent of all people who defect. The gender discrepancy in rural Jilin Province, where females are in short supply and farmers have always looked to North Korea as a source of brides, means some of the women are trafficked or tricked across the frontier. But many come of their own accord.

That is a direct result of the famine that gripped the DPRK for much of the 1990s. While men remain tied to their work units – the system by which Pyongyang regulates North Korean society – it was women who scrounged what food they could and set up tiny business operations in the makeshift markets that sprang up in place of the inert state economy. Out of necessity, North Korea's females grew more resourceful than their husbands, sons and brothers, and that newfound spirit propelled many across the border in search of something better.

Piao and his wife had a son, now five. But soon she began pressing him for help to leave for South Korea. 'It was too dangerous for her here. She was afraid of being caught and sent back,' said Piao. Initially, China turned a blind eye to the refugees who started coming to Yanbian from the early 1990s on. Then, as food became scarcer, more and more arrived. Senior DPRK defectors have revealed that Pyongyang itself put the number who died during the famine at between one and two and a half million, or around 10 per cent of North Korea's people. In the regions close to Dongbei, it may have been as high as 20 per cent of the population.

Faced with an ever-increasing influx of North Koreans, Beijing grew uneasy and began hunting down the refugees and returning them to the DPRK. They were seen as a threat to the stability of Yanbian, their presence redressing the decline in the number of Chinese Koreans caused by their low birth rate and emigration to other parts of Dongbei. The CCP feared also the impact of the migrants on Yanbian's already precarious economy, as they were prepared to work for lower wages than the locals.

Beijing's nightmare scenario in Yanbian is the sudden and total collapse of the DPRK. Inevitably, that would lead to people coming across the border in far greater numbers than ever before. One of the unspoken reasons why the CCP prefers to keep the Kim regime in power is the risk of the Han becoming a minority in Yanbian, which would only support the claims of the South Korean nationalists who believe it is part of a greater Korea. Returning the refugees was a tacit admission of Beijing's determination to keep the Korean peninsula divided.

Border patrols were stepped up on both sides of the frontier. As the grandmother I met near Tumen recalled, the authorities started descending on villages checking identity cards and searching for North Korean women married to local men. The Chinese allowed plainclothes DPRK police into Yanbian to assist in the round-up as well, while rewards were offered to those who turned people in.

As they were fleeing both a desperate famine and a despotic regime, the North Koreans qualified for protection under the UN Convention Relating to the Status of Refugees. But Beijing insisted they were just illegal economic migrants and so had no right to stay in China, a position it continues to maintain. North Koreans who are caught in China end up in detention centres like the one in Tumen, and face a prison sentence on their return to the DPRK.

North Koreans reacted to China turning on them by following the dispersal of the Chinese Koreans across Dongbei and beyond. Many of those who cross the border now leave Yanbian quickly and make for the big cities, where the police are not looking for DPRK refugees and they can blend in by claiming to be Chaoxianzu. Others, like Piao's wife, try and escape to South Korea. There are two routes used to reach Seoul: either via Mongolia, which deports all North Korean illegal immigrants to South Korea automatically, or across China to Yunnan and then on to Thailand.

Both the escape lines are run by the South Korean missionaries in Yanji. They fund them by raising money at home and from the American Korean community. One day, Piao's wife was spirited south-west to Kunming, then to Laos and Bangkok and finally to Seoul. Piao had seen neither her nor his son for four years. After hearing that, I understood why he was out every night getting so drunk, as well as his unhappiness with Korea being divided while he was stranded in China.

Nevertheless, I wasn't sure if Piao was telling me the whole story. Some North Korean women marry Chinese Korean men, but stay in Yanbian only until their Mandarin is fluent enough for them to pass as Chaoxianzu elsewhere in China. There is an orphanage in Yanji full of children who have been abandoned by their fathers, after their North

Korean wives decided it was time to move on. Perhaps Piao's wife used him just to hide from the police before she could leave for South Korea, or maybe she was more scared of being sent back to the DPRK than she was in love with him. Either way, Piao is on his own now.

No one knows exactly how many North Koreans are living illegally in China. Most rational estimates settle on a consensus of somewhere in the region of 30,000 long-term refugees. What is certain is that DPRK citizens continue to come to China, even if their numbers are down from the time of the 1990s famine, despite the increased security presence along the border. Food remains desperately scarce, with ordinary people surviving on around 1,500 calories a day, according to the few NGO workers allowed into the DPRK. More than half of all defectors say it is the shortage of sustenance, rather than the lack of freedom, that drove them to leave.

What has changed is that some of those crossing the border are no longer staying permanently. Instead, they come to Yanbian in search of assistance, or to work illegally on a construction site or farm for a month or two, before returning home. In Yanji, most make for the churches or the undercover missionaries like Paul. 'People in North Korea know they will get help if they go to a church,' one ethnic Korean Catholic priest told me. 'They ask for rice, clothes and money, the things that are essential for life. I don't give them anything personally, but I'll make sure a member of my congregation does.'

When I first met Paul, he told me he wasn't involved in assisting refugees either to escape or to find supplies. Yet I knew North Koreans came to his restaurant, which suggested that people on the other side of the frontier were aware he could help them. 'DPRK people do come here,' he conceded one day. 'But I never give them money, only food and clothes. If they get caught by the Chinese or the North Korean police, they'll ask where they got the money and then I'll get into trouble.'

It was a matter of national pride for Paul to be there for the North Koreans. 'If I see a fellow Korean, a brother, who is hungry then of course I will help him.' But it was also another way of fulfilling his messianic mission. Now Bibles have joined the long list of goods being smuggled into North Korea. Its people are too preoccupied with finding their next meal to be ideal converts just yet, but given what is happening in South Korea and Yanbian it is perfectly possible that Pyongyang will be a city of churches again one day.

A Protestant revival apart, Paul had no doubt that the Kim dynasty will not last. 'I think there'll be huge changes in the next five to ten years. People live such a poor life and are so hungry that I don't see them agreeing to go on the way they are. I don't see Kim Jong-un being able to maintain power for as long as his father did. Years ago, North Koreans thought their leader was a god. Now they don't. They know it's wrong they have no food. Only a few people are against the system now, but their numbers will increase,' he stated.

If and when the regime goes, it won't be with the help of Beijing. Not only will the fall of the Kims threaten China's strategic interests and the DPRK's current status as little more than an ancillary province of Dongbei, but it will result in increased uncertainty in Yanbian. The people of the third Korea come from North Korea, but have been cut off from their roots for the last sixty-odd years. Given the opportunity to rediscover their ancestral homeland, allied with their solid cultural ties to South Korea, more Yanbian residents could well join Piao in claiming to be citizens of one Korea. But, unlike Piao, those people are likely to be Christians as well.

24

The Arctic Borderlands

The full force of the Dongbei winter had been unleashed by the time I left Yanji. It was cold even inside the bus to Harbin, travelling through the west of Yanbian before veering right outside Jilin City and entering Heilongjiang, China's northernmost province. We ploughed along a two-lane highway bordered by snow-covered fields and rivers freezing over, spraying slush over the farmers passing in the opposite direction on their tractors.

Snow was thick on the ground in Harbin, the capital of Heilongjiang, and fell every day and night, turning it into a monochrome city. The giant green onion dome atop St Sophia, a former Russian Orthodox cathedral and the city's most famous landmark, was dusted white, while cars churned along roads of black sludge. People slithered along the treacherous pavements, despite the efforts of the teams of workers who chipped away at the ice with hoe-like implements or shovelled the snow into neat piles which bulldozers removed at night.

Shrugging off the weather, the tall Harbin women strode out in short skirts, leggings and knee-length boots, although a fair few still tapped along in high heels. I was wearing multiple layers, thick gloves and a woolly hat pulled low over my ears. The contrast between the toast-warm interiors of apartments, hotels and restaurants and the freezing conditions outside ensured I spent much of my time either stripping off clothes or putting them on.

Heilongjiang was the Manchu heartland, the place where their forebears the Jurchen tribe hailed from. It is still home to a dwindling number of minorities such as the Oroqen and Hezhen who straddle the border between Heilongjiang and the Russian Far East, just as they did when those lands were part of what was then known as Outer Manchuria. Harbin, though, is essentially a Russian creation. Disused churches like St Sophia and pockets of European-style buildings stand as testimony to how the tsar's empire absorbed much of Manchuria, even while a Manchu emperor sat on the Dragon Throne in the Forbidden City.

In 1858, the Treaty of Aigun formalised the division of Manchuria. Everything north of what the Russians call the Amur River and the Chinese the Heilongjiang, or Black Dragon River, was assigned to Russia. Two years later, more Manchu lands went north under the Treaty of Peking. In all, Russia acquired a million square kilometres of Outer Manchuria. It is a massive area. Stretching from the present Sino-Russian border to the shores of the Sea of Okhotsk, it includes what are now the major cities of the Russian Far East – Vladivostok, Khabarovsk and Blagoveshchensk – yet the tsar's army barely had to fire a shot to attain it.

Faced with internal rebellions and in the midst of the Second Opium War with the British and French, the Qing dynasty was so enfeebled by the late 1850s that Russia was able to take Outer Manchuria simply by threatening Beijing. The once mighty Manchu, who had expanded China's frontiers in the west and south-west, conceded the territory in the bitter knowledge that they were now unable to defend even their own homeland.

With the western colonial powers establishing themselves in China's major ports in the aftermath of the Opium Wars, Russia's takeover of northern Manchuria was supposed to be the prelude to it conquering all of Dongbei. The extension of the Trans-Siberian Railway, first to Harbin and then south to Port Arthur, now known as Lushun, was another step towards that goal. From 1897, Russian workers started arriving in Harbin, then not much more than a fishing village on the Songhua River, to build the new rail line. So many

Russians came over the border that they dominated Harbin for the next couple of decades.

Russia's dreams of turning Dongbei into a colony were dashed by its defeat in the Russo-Japanese War of 1904–5. Instead, it would be Japan which occupied Manchuria from 1931 until the end of the Second World War. But Harbin remained primarily a Russian city. Like the Koreans who escaped the Japanese occupation of their country by moving to Yanbian during the same period, Russians sought refuge in Harbin from the chaos at home.

Well over 100,000 White Russians arrived after the Russian Revolution of 1917, joining 20,000 or so Russian Jews who had fled tsarist pogroms a decade earlier, making Harbin the largest community of Russians anywhere outside the old country. Far outnumbering the Chinese population, and with the new rail link boosting the local economy, the Russian residents, known as Harbinets, created a city which imitated distant St Petersburg and Moscow.

Harbin's main shopping street, Zhongyang Dajie, offers an architectural history lesson. Art Nouveau hotels and department stores sit alongside baroque-style buildings, and once grand houses with large arched windows and iron balconies line the streets running off it. Former Russian Orthodox churches, as well as synagogues with window frames in the shape of the Star of David, are scattered throughout the city.

Along with other Chinese cities which have an extensive foreign heritage, such as Shanghai and Tianjin, Harbin is ambivalent about its cosmopolitan past. The buildings, even the crumbling houses which have been chopped into apartments, are much more distinctive and impressive than anything built in the communist era. Yet they are also evidence of how Harbin was more Russian than Chinese until 1949. To admire them is unpatriotic, and locals claim to be indifferent to structures like the former St Sophia Cathedral, regarding them only as unique backdrops for wedding photos.

Most Harbinets returned home after the Second World War or emigrated to the west. By the 1960s only a handful remained, although Harbin's last Russian resident didn't die until the early 1980s. But the city attracts many tourists from across the frontier – enough for the Chinese to assume that any foreigner in town is Russian. They come on shopping trips from Khabarovsk and Vladivostok, in search of a far wider and cheaper range of products than are available in the Russian Far East. There are also many Russians studying Mandarin, the language which may one day be the lingua franca of the former Outer Manchuria.

Others arrive in search of work, prompted by the slump in the Far East's economy that was precipitated by the break-up of the old USSR in 1991 and continues today. In an echo of 1920s Shanghai, when the refugee daughters of the Russian aristocracy were reduced to dancing in nightclubs to survive, all Harbin's premier nightspots feature a show with Russian dancers. Those who can't perform professionally come on month-long tourist visas as working girls, crowding out the same clubs in search of clients. It is not uncommon in Harbin to see a tall, blonde Russian woman on the arm of a Chinese man.

There is a significant Russian population in Beijing too, but it is Dongbei which is receiving the most migrants as people abandon the Far East for the chance of earning a better salary in China. Whether they are tarts, traders or translators, the latest generation of Russian immigrants are the most obvious sign of how China is now far more powerful and influential than Russia. It is a reversal of roles no one could have foreseen in 1949 when Moscow was the big brother to Beijing's eager little sibling, the cradle of communism and the place where many of the original CCP leadership were trained.

China and the Soviet Union began drifting apart after 1960, as Mao came to regard his political philosophy as superior and the USSR regrouped after the trauma of the Stalin years. That split became gradually more toxic until it culminated in a brief border skirmish in March 1969, when the Soviet Red Army and the PLA exchanged shots over one of many disputed islands in the Ussuri River, a tributary of the Amur.

Still smarting over the loss of Outer Manchuria, China long refused to recognise the demarcation of sections of the frontier between Heilongjiang and the Russian Far East. Only in 2008 did the two countries agree on the border, which tracks the Amur River as it wiggles east for almost 3,000 kilometres from just west of Mohe, China's most northerly town, towards the Sea of Japan. By then, China was the dominant partner in what is an increasingly unequal relationship, and Beijing was able to claw back a tiny portion of the land it lost in the nineteenth century.

Those formerly contested borderlands were my ultimate destination in Dongbei. I intended to follow the Amur River and the Chinese–Russian frontier south from Mohe, travelling through the counties where the remaining minorities of the north-east live to Heihe. A flourishing trading town, and compelling symbol of how China has prospered as its neighbour and one-time enemy has declined, Heihe lies opposite Blagoveshchensk, where my journey around China's far edges would end.

Dongbei's minorities are the most obscure of all China's ethnic groups. Persecution in the pre-1949 era and now intermarriage with the Han means only around 15,000 Oroqen, Hezhen and Daur people are left in Heilongjiang, although more live across the frontier in Russia. Like the Manchu before them, their languages will likely die out completely within a generation or two. They are the last reminders of what Outer Manchuria once was: a barely populated land whose tribes congregated on both sides of the Amur, roaming through endless taiga where frontiers were unknown.

Even now, the extreme north of Heilongjiang remains relatively inaccessible. Harbin is the starting point for any journey to the borderlands, but it is still a considerable distance from where Outer Manchuria once began. Rather than risk the roads which are often closed because of heavy snow and ice, I was faced with a twenty-one-hour train ride to Mohe. My berth was in a carriage full of people chattering away in Pinghua, the unfamiliar, Cantonese-like dialect of Guangxi Province in the south of China. They were a tour group who had chosen to travel to Dongbei in the winter so they could see snow for the first time.

Southern Chinese are fascinated by snow, as are South-east Asians, because it never falls where they live. That makes January Harbin's peak tourist season, as people from the more temperate regions of China flock to the city's ice festival in brand-new heavy coats, boots and scarves that are destined never to be used again. They brave temperatures that drop to -20 degrees Centigrade and below, as well as a wind so sharp it feels like your skin is being slowly stripped away layer by layer.

But snow wasn't a novelty for me. I had begun to dread the relentless weather, especially the forbidding, mostly sun-free sky of low-hanging, grey-white clouds. Of all the different legs of my journey around China's far edges, I found Dongbei the hardest. I was gripped by a lassitude I couldn't shake off – my reaction to the sub-zero temperatures and extreme landscape.

Winter in Heilongjiang is a black and white movie. Green fields disappear under a white blanket of snow, while the blue waters of lakes, rivers and streams are covered in dark ice. The closer we got to Russia, the emptier the countryside became, save for the increasing numbers of spindly and leafless pine trees which rose up the hills in the distance. There are no big cities in the northern borderlands, only towns and villages, and we could have been in Siberia rather than China.

On the train the heaters ran full blast, making it too hot to sleep in anything but a T-shirt. But it took only a trip to the unheated toilets with their frozen windows, or a smoke in the gaps between the carriages where ice covered the floor, to remind you of what it was like outside. It grew colder and colder as we meandered across the north-west of Heilongjiang, dipping briefly into neighbouring Inner Mongolia, until we were just a few hours from Mohe.

Now the rolling hills beyond the empty fields were far more thickly forested and the snow deeper. The train stopped at tiny stations where streets of wooden cabins started where the platforms ended. Smoke from their makeshift chimneys curled away towards the clouds that appeared to be descending lower the further north we went, while piles of timber as high as the houses themselves waited to be burned.

Mohe is the end of the line in every sense – China's far-northern outpost. It is also the coldest place in the country, and I stumbled off the train into a snowstorm. The town was coal black in the early evening, apart from the lights glowing in the windows of the apartment blocks. A taxi took me down the wide empty streets until I found a hotel, where I was greeted with confusion by a flustered receptionist. Few westerners make it to Mohe, and there was a quick consultation about whether I was allowed to stay.

I crunched through the snow in search of a still-open restaurant. Thick green blankets hung over its door, to keep out of the draughts, but inside it was deliciously warm, the windows shut tight, the air thick with cigarette smoke. I started peeling off sweaters, much to the amusement of two men downing glasses of *baijiu*. 'You're wearing too much,' said one, laughing. 'It's not that cold.'

He had the raw, wind-chapped face common to the people of northern Heilongjiang and was used to the extremes of the local climate. Winter in Mohe runs from early October to the middle of May and there are only three months a year when frost doesn't cover the ground. While I was there, the temperature never rose above −16 degrees Centigrade. In a town where the mercury has been known to plunge below -50, that is balmy weather, and plenty of people walked around during the day with their jackets wide open.

A waitress brought a menu containing a selection of typical Dongbei dishes. Thick stews of beef or donkey meat, sausage and roughly folded pork dumplings, nothing like the delicate little packages served in the south of China, provide insulation against the elements, as well as revealing the Russian influence on Heilongjiang's cuisine. I ate a lot of cabbage in the far north, one of the few vegetables that can be stored throughout the winter, and became accustomed to the lack of fresh fruit.

Mohe's residents, like those of most Chinese small towns, are friendly. They were both chuffed and intrigued to have a foreign visitor who wasn't a Russian from over the border eighty kilometres away. Mohe's quiet, surprisingly car-free streets too ensure it is far more pleasant than most places of an equivalent size in China. It is a modern town now, after an inferno in 1985 reduced most of its original wooden houses to ashes. Many of the new buildings are in a mock-Russian style, with peaked red roofs, domes and ornate façades.

Despite its isolation, Mohe is one of China's more unlikely tourist destinations. During the summer, when the sun shines for over twenty hours a day, it is the only place in the country where the northern lights are visible. Now, in an effort to attract visitors all year round, Mohe has appointed itself as the home of Father Christmas in China. Right on the border with Russia is the North Pole Village, and a section of it has been refashioned as a copy of the hamlet in Lapland that is Santa's 'official' residence.

China's rulers may dislike Christianity, but Christmas, along with other western holidays such as Halloween and Valentine's Day, is now part of the Chinese calendar. Retailers in the big cities view them as a chance to take advantage of the local fascination with the more obvious aspects of western culture. I was used to hearing Christmas carols in supermarkets in Beijing during December, but was surprised to discover Mohe following the trend.

Borderland kitsch was too good an opportunity to pass up, so I set off on the journey north to Santa's Chinese grotto and the frontier with Russia. Accompanying me were Zhu Guo and Zhang Lei, two twenty-one-year-old students and former high-school classmates from Guizhou Province in the south-west. Zhu Guo was a tiny, skinny, energetic girl studying engineering, Zhang Lei a thickset lad and trainee tenor. 'Peking opera is too hard to sing and too traditional, so I'm learning Italian opera,' he told me.

They spent their university holidays exploring their country. 'We're travel buddies, not boyfriend and girlfriend,' explained Zhu Guo. 'We go everywhere by train, always hard seat. We've been to lots of places, but Yunnan is my favourite. Good food, good weather and good fun.' Hard seat is the cheapest option on Chinese trains, its name an accurate description of the comfort level. I hadn't endured it on a long journey since 1988, and shuddered inwardly at the thought of twenty-one hours perching on the edge of a bench alongside migrant workers spitting, smoking and drinking their way north from Harbin.

Knowing they were travelling the tough way around China on a meagre budget prompted me to invite them to join my excursion to the North Pole Village. They are part of a new breed of Chinese travellers, and I admired their spirit. Their parents belong to the generation which join tour groups when they go on holiday; Zhu Guo and Zhang Lei were far more independent and confident.

Zhu Guo said they were planning a trip to Tibet the following year, but until then Heilongjiang was the next best thing. 'It's a bit of dream to come here because it's so cold and different from where we come from. I've seen snow before but never anything like this.' I hadn't either, because outside Mohe all signs of civilisation disappeared. In its place was a bleakly beautiful vista of pines, silver birches and virgin snow that lay across the land as if a pristine, never-ending white rug was unfurled every October, only to be rolled up the following spring.

Huddled together in a taxi against the cold, we drove north along a road of compacted snow overlying the ice beneath it. There was little traffic and we passed no villages or people. The first sign of life came when we turned on to a track which ended in front of a small wooden cabin. A man appeared and unlocked the door. Inside was a one-room museum dedicated to the prostitutes who had come to the region in the late nineteenth century.

For a few years from 1889, the area north of Mohe was the site of a gold rush. Chinese, Russian, Japanese and Korean prospectors, as well as a few westerners, flocked to Outer Manchuria to try and find their fortunes. In their wake came women also in search of more money, and this simple museum which I thought unique in China – a country which rarely acknowledges the existence of prostitution – is a poignant memorial to their lives. There are remnants of their clothes and jewellery and on the walls sepia photos of girls who looked no older than teenagers, staring straight at the camera as if daring it to judge them.

Behind the cabin, a small glade surrounded by pine trees made it clear why the museum is located here. Beneath the snow were the burial mounds of some of the women who had died of disease or unknown causes. A few crosses sticking up above the snow indicated the graves of Russians, but most were unmarked, their occupants forgotten as soon as they were underground. All cemeteries are austere, but the remoteness of this one, and imagining the lives of its occupants, reduced us all to silence.

North Pole Village wasn't exactly a winter wonderland either. A proper settlement of 2,000 people, despite its tourist-inspired, geographically inaccurate name, it has a neat grid of streets which are lined with solid wooden houses, as well as a few shops and restaurants, a school and a post office selling Santa stamps. Zhu Guo and Zhang Lei rushed in to send postcards as proof they had visited the far northern edge of China.

Father Christmas's home wasn't open and neither he nor his reindeers were around, but the setting was authentic enough. Beyond the streets were fields of snow, and when I ventured off the path through them, I sank down to my knees in it. As I struggled out, the sound of loud squeals announced the arrival of a tour group riding on horse-drawn sleighs. They glided swiftly past towards the north of the village.

Following them, I reached an imposing slab of stone covered in red characters announcing that this was the end of China in the north. Below was the Amur River, and a couple of hundred metres away on the other side of it were the pine-covered hills of Russia. There was only one way to reach the shore, the closest I could get to the border which runs through the middle of the river, and that was to body-toboggan down the banks.

Huge lumps of ice were backed up at the river's edge, like boats jostling for a mooring in a busy harbour. A few patches of ink-black water were visible, but soon the entire Amur would freeze and it would be possible to walk across it to Russia. The wandering bands of Manchu and Oroqen would have done so when both sides of the river were the same land. But no one travels between Heilongjiang and the Russian Far East from here now. The only place to cross the Amur legally is in Heihe. I would have to follow the river south.

25

Along the Amur

If Mohe is quiet at night, then Tahe is a graveyard: flurries of snow drifting aimlessly; the roads deserted apart from a few cars skidding slowly along; shuttered shops and restaurants. Finding a place to eat after dark was a struggle. I was always the only diner, and then it was just me trudging back to my chilly hotel room through the empty streets. It is as if a plague descends on Tahe every evening in the winter, leaving only a few survivors until morning.

Nearly 200 kilometres south-east of Mohe, Tahe endures a sub-Arctic climate too. Tahe, though, lacks the cachet that comes with being China's most northerly town. Hardly anyone visits, whether Chinese or foreign. But I had no choice. I needed a base while I searched for Heilongjiang's minorities in the outlying villages because, despite being as far north as you can go in China, Mohe is defiantly Han.

I had hoped to find Daur people, an ethnic group descended from Mongolians, in the area. But I discovered that almost all of the 130,000-odd Daur now live in Inner Mongolia, fifty kilometres to the west of Mohe, and I was going in the opposite direction. Nor would I find any Hezhen on the route I was taking. Distant relations of the Manchu, the fewer than 5,000 Hezhen live much further east along the Amur in the region of Heilongjiang that lies opposite Khabarovsk. There are more of them in Russia, where they are known as the Nanai, but in China intermarriage with the Han has resulted in their numbers shrinking dramatically.

Before 1949, it was ethnic cleansing which came close to annihilating the Hezhen completely. After the Japanese had occupied

Manchuria in 1931 they were rounded up and relocated far from their traditional fishing grounds by the Amur, or ended up as slave workers in mines. Many sought refuge in opium, and a combination of drug use and the brutality of the Japanese army all but wiped the Hezhen out. Some estimates claim that fewer than 500 were still alive by the time the Sino-Japanese War ended in 1945.

Along with the Daur, the Oroqen suffered under the Japanese too, some being conscripted into the army while others were used as forced labour. But the Oroqen were hunters, not a river people like the Hezhen, and many escaped into the forests that cover the Dongbei borderlands. Even so, there are fewer than 9,000 Oroqen left in China and almost all live around Tahe and in neighbouring Huma County.

Finding them was easier said than done. There are few Oroqen, whom the Chinese refer to as the Elunchuzu, in Tahe itself, and the local Han are not complimentary about those that do reside there. 'I don't like Elunchuzu people. The women are fat and drink *baijiu*,' one man told me dismissively. Asking exactly where the Oroqen villages are proved fruitless too; everyone in Tahe knows there are Oroqen living near by but no two people could agree on a place to direct me to.

Finally, I was advised to visit a small town named Shibazhan, south of Tahe and surrounded by boggy, unpromising land through which now frozen streams ran. Everyone appeared to be Han and, at first, I thought I had been given yet another erroneous tip. But soon I realised that Shibazhan is as divided as any Uighur or Tibetan settlement and that the Oroqen district was on the far southern edge of town.

Horse-drawn carts trotted through narrow alleys lined with one-storey brick and timber buildings all painted yellow and with red roofs, but there were few pedestrians. I wandered around until I was accosted by two men staggering like cartoon drunks. One was Han, his companion Ewenki, another of the minorities found in the former

Outer Manchuria. Linked ethnically and linguistically to the Oroqen, around 30,000 of them live in China, mostly in Inner Mongolia.

Both men reeked of *baijiu*, although it was not even midday. After they had discovered I was English, they kept shaking my hand, shouting 'Hello' and insisting I join them for a drink. As I struggled to extract myself from their clutches, two women emerged from a nearby house to see what all the fuss was about. Plump with pear-shaped bodies and round faces, they matched the Han stereotype of the Elunchuzu and, after I had asked, confirmed they were indeed Oroqen.

Conversation was difficult with the two drunks bawling in my ear, and the women soon got tired of standing outside. But before they returned to their house, they told me I should visit Baiyinna, a town in between Tahe and Huma, if I wanted to see Oroqen living in their traditional environment. 'There are lots of Elunchuzu in the villages around Baiyinna,' one said. 'Many more than there are in Shibazhan.'

Baiyinna is a few hours east of Tahe along roads lined with pine trees that lead to the border with Russia. It is designated as an Oroqen township because their numbers are too small to warrant them being assigned their own county. I was the only person to get off the bus and, as it pulled out, I looked around in dismay. Baiyinna is tiny, its main street no more than a few hundred metres long – an anonymous collection of box-like brick buildings and wooden structures.

Heavy snow was falling as the odd tractor chugged noisily up and down the road, their drivers wrapped up in thick green army great-coats and balaclavas, but everyone else was presumably hibernating inside their homes. I was burdened by my pack, having decided to abandon Tahe and move on to Huma, and wondered where to find someone to direct me to the Oroqen villages.

Pushing open the door to what I thought might be a restaurant I was confronted by well over a hundred people, jammed together around tables piled high with food and drink. The room was so crowded I couldn't see a path through to a spare seat, even if there was one, and I backed out in alarm just as I heard someone shout, '*Weiguoren*', or westerner. Before I could say a word, two people were standing on either side of me taking my arms and escorting me back inside. I was divested of my pack, a chair was found and I was seated at a table.

It was a wedding banquet and I was now the involuntary guest of honour. A bowl, chopsticks and a bottle of beer were put in front of me, and I was invited to start eating from dishes so numerous they were stacked on top of each other. The eyes of every single person in the room were on me and I could hear that I was the topic of conversation at each table. The Chinese can never contain their curiosity when they encounter a lone foreigner far from the big cities. Within minutes, many of the guests were gathered around the table firing questions at me. 'Where are you from?'; 'Why are you in Baiyinna?'; 'Why are you on your own?'

A capable young Han man named Jiang Feng, the restaurant owner, took it on himself to be my protector and started introducing me to the more important guests. They included the groom's mother, a cheerful lady in a black leather jacket with shocking, jagged stumps for teeth. I had to toast everyone I met, as well as those people I wasn't introduced to but who came up to me anyway because they wanted to be able to say they had drunk with the westerner.

Chinese toasts are formal affairs, with little glasses filled with either beer or *baijiu* held daintily between the thumb and forefinger and sometimes supported by the palm of the other hand. It is obligatory to down the glass in one with a shout of '*ganbei*', the Chinese equivalent of 'bottoms up', so I made sure to insist on drinking only beer, rather than risk getting catastrophically drunk on *baijiu*. Soon I was toasting so many people I had no time to eat.

My inadvertent arrival at the celebration resulted in the bride and groom, who had already departed, being summoned back. They were both very young: no more than twenty-one. The bride was pretty with her artfully curled hair and in the traditional red dress worn by Chinese women on their wedding day, her husband smart and self-conscious in a brand-new bright-blue suit.

We posed for photos together, with some of the other guests also recording the moment on their cellphones and a few filming it as well. The mantelpieces and walls of homes in and around Baiyinna are possibly still adorned with pictures of a scruffy, slightly drunk westerner standing next to a newly married couple. I felt embarrassed at being the centre of attention on their big day and told them so, as well as apologising for crashing their lunch. 'No problem,' said the groom. 'My mother is very pleased to have a foreign guest at my wedding.'

Most of the people were Han but a few were Elunchuzu, including one old man with twinkling eyes set deep in his round and lined, high-cheekboned face. He taught me how to say '*ganbei*' and 'hello' in Oroqen, information I forgot almost immediately. But the real surprise came near the end of the lunch, when a solidly built middle-aged man with blond hair, watery-blue eyes and a straggly moustache walked into the restaurant and sat next to me.

Hou Xue Ming was born and raised in a village near Baiyinna to parents who had moved across the border from the Russian Far East in the 1950s. I knew that enough ethnic Russians live in Heilongjiang, as well as some in Xinjiang, for them to be classified as an official minority numbering around 15,000 people. But I had never met one before. Just as I had gawped at Kamil, the Russian-looking Chinese Tatar I met in Urumqi, it was hard to take my eyes off Hou Xue Ming – a man so obviously western in appearance yet Chinese-born and bred.

Like all the minorities in Dongbei, the ethnic Russians are dying out as they intermarry with the Han. There are only a tiny number left who retain the blond or red hair of their ancestors. I was lucky to encounter Hou Xue Ming, and he seemed to believe it was more than just chance that had brought me to the wedding party. 'We are friends,' he said, raising another toast to me. 'You and I are Europeans.'

He had been at the banquet earlier, returning after he heard the news that I was here, and was already the worse for wear after too many beers and shots of *baijiu*. He spoke slowly and carefully, fighting against the alcohol to enunciate his words. I asked if he could speak Russian, or if he had ever been across the frontier, and he shook his head with what I interpreted as a gesture of regret.

As we carried on drinking, Hou Xue Ming grew more sentimental about his heritage. Later, I thought my presence had resurrected memories of his dead parents and the stories they must have told of their lives in Russia. They gave him a Chinese name, probably chosen with the assistance of the local CCP, to help him fit in. But it was easy to imagine how bizarre school must have been for a first-generation Chinese Russian surrounded by Han and Oroqen children who looked so radically different.

Yet his presence in Baiyinna would not have been considered strange in the days when there was no border and the different peoples of the former Outer Manchuria traversed across the region. And the journey his mother and father made mirrored those being taken by the new wave of Russian immigrants to China. Many will return home one day but, unless the Russian Far East's economic freefall is reversed, more than a few will remain in China for the rest of their lives.

By mid-afternoon, most of the guests had departed for home or, like Hou Xue Ming, to continue drinking next door in Baiyinna's only karaoke club. This too was owned by Jiang Feng, who was clearly the town's mover and shaker. I sat with him in a beer daze, while his crew of waitresses began the Sisyphean task of cleaning up the immense array of dishes and bottles littered across the tables and a floor ankle deep in debris.

I told Jiang Feng I had come to Baiyinna in search of a more authentic version of Oroqen life, and immediately he suggested we visit an Elunchuzu friend of his. It was a chance to show off his car, a newish Volkswagen he was obviously delighted with. We drove out of Baiyinna along tiny side roads, where snow was piled waist-high at their edges and tall pine trees bunched close together obscured the country behind them. Jiang Feng stopped by a frozen stretch of water. 'This is the Huma River. Isn't it beautiful?' I nodded my assent. I didn't want to say what I was thinking, which was how lifeless the Heilongjiang landscape is in winter.

His friend lived in a hamlet rather than a village. Icy tracks branched off the road running through it and along them were small wooden houses surrounded by high fences. Confined behind them are the Oroqen, a traditionally nomadic people. Until as recently as sixty years ago, the Oroqen were hunters who lived in the uplands of northern Heilongjiang and across the frontier in Russia. Animists who revered the Siberian tiger and the local brown bear, they moved from place to place in search of the animals which provided them with food and clothes, trading fur pelts with the Daur for other essentials.

After the communist takeover, the Oroqen's untethered existence in the wild had no place in the new China. Not only were they armed clans, and thus seen as resistance groups in the making, but their wandering lifestyle meant they could evade the strict controls on society introduced by the CCP. Itinerant hunters can't be tied to a work unit, or monitored by a neighbourhood official. Just as the CCP continues to fear the Khampa nomads of eastern Tibet, so the Oroqen were regarded as a threat.

From the early 1950s, the Oroqen were corralled in villages and their belief in shamans characterised as primitive superstition. To the Han, moving them into log cabins was progress; they were fulfilling the Confucian man's burden by giving the Elunchuzu permanent homes and replacing their animal skins with Mao jackets. China justifies its relocation of Tibetan nomads to isolated villages on the high plateau in the same way, insisting that they are lifting the Khampa out of poverty by getting them to substitute their tents for houses.

But neither the Oroqen nor Tibet's nomads have any tradition of being sedentary tillers of the land, and few have learned how to do so. The farmers around Baiyinna are all Han, leaving their Oroqen neighbours with few alternatives other than manual work. There is no obvious sign of tension between the Elunchuzu and the Han in Baiyinna, with both socialising together, but there is a marked income gap between them illustrated by the difference in their homes.

Jiang Feng's friend worked sporadically on building sites in Huma and more distant Heihe. He lived with his wife, their new baby and his parents in a two-room house with an outdoor toilet. His father was asleep when we arrived, and didn't stir despite us all sitting on the end of his bed. To supplement the family income, his wife and mother made wooden vanity boxes decorated with elaborate patterns imprinted on the soft wood by using the bone of an animal tapped with a small hammer. They sold them for 20 yuan (£2) and I bought one, out of guilt at intruding into their home and because I felt sorry for them.

When we left I asked Jiang Feng what he thought would happen to the Oroqen in the future. He shrugged and said there would be fewer of them. Their language has almost gone already, spoken only by older people like the man I had met at the wedding lunch. Jiang Feng's friend could understand what his parents said, but couldn't speak Oroqen fluently. His child would grow up speaking only Mandarin and, with so few Elunchuzu left, would likely marry someone Han. Before long, perhaps in less than thirty years, the Oroqen will be like the Manchu — a people in name only who have been absorbed by the Han.

Back in Baiyinna, Jiang Feng waited with me for the evening bus to Huma. He invited me to return one day and stay with him, and I told him I would try, although I knew I never would. Saying thank you for all his help seemed desperately inadequate, just as the hospitality shown to me when I walked by mistake into the wedding party was inconceivable to someone raised in a western culture. But for rural Chinese it is a natural thing to invite a strange Englishman to join them at an intimate celebration, an expression of both their conviviality and their belief that any foreigner who comes to their home deserves to be treated as a guest.

Huma was another Tahe, a small town becalmed on the border with Russia. I arrived in a swirl of snow. The following morning was crisp and bright – the sun shining, the snow clouds gone. But the heavy overnight fall had made the roads too dangerous to drive and the bus to Heihe had been cancelled. Along with a couple of locals, I found a taxi driver willing for a hefty fee to risk the ice hidden beneath the snow.

For the first time since I had left Yanji, there was blue sky above me. It was invigorating, the sun's rays glancing off the snow crystals so they sparkled like thousands of diamonds lining our route. We trailed the contours of the Amur, with the densely forested Russian side across from us, for much of the way, winding carefully around sharp corners for three hours until we entered Heihe.

Sean was waiting for me, a tall twenty-nine-year-old whose shaggy hair and casual clothes belied a sharp entrepreneurial streak. A friend of a friend, he had spent two years living in Luton as a student and four more in Brisbane designing websites – completely polarised experiences which had left him with a twangy Anglo-Australian accent. Han and originally from Bei'an, a city further south in Heilongjiang known for its high-security jail, large psychiatric facility and a preponderance of criminal gangs, he was now running his own English school in Heihe.

'There are lots of schools teaching Russian here but none teaching English,' said Sean, as we drove through Heihe towards the Amur in a new Japanese land cruiser. 'I did a lot of market research before I set up my school, and Heihe is perfect. It's smaller than other cities, but it's full of wealthy people because of the trade with Russia and they all want their kids to learn English so they can study abroad like I did.'

Cindy, Sean's stunning, big-eyed girlfriend, was at the wheel of the car. Her father was one of Heihe's new rich, the owner of a construction company erecting the riverside apartments being snapped up by those prospering from the city's proximity to Russia. Cindy was a former member of the PLA's elite dance troupe, a collection of beauties who tour military bases entertaining the soldiers, as well as performing at major state functions. When he wasn't screwing China, Mao used to select his mistresses from the dancers. I thought Sean had done well for himself in every sense.

Heihe's population is minute in Chinese terms, a mere 250,000 people, but like Pangshang in Wa State there are an awful lot of expensive vehicles jamming the roads and it took a while to reach the Amur. We walked along the promenade, looking down on the frozen river – wider here than at any other point I'd previously seen. A small pool had been carved out of the ice and a couple of hardy swimmers gave us a wave before jumping in. On the other side of the river, perhaps 500 or 600 metres away, was Blagoveshchensk.

The closest place to Russia of any size along the entire Heilongjiang–Russian border, Heihe is China's principal trading post with the former Outer Manchuria, just as Dandong is with North Korea. Russians come from Blagoveshchensk to take advantage of far cheaper prices, as well as for weekends of fun in the restaurants and clubs. Cyrillic signs are as common as those in Mandarin, and every foreigner walking into a shop is greeted by an assistant who can say at least a few words in Russian.

Only in the late 1980s did the frontier between Heihe and Blagoveshchensk reopen, after being closed for twenty years following the border clashes between the PLA and the Soviet Army in 1969. Back then, the commercial traffic headed north, as people from across Dongbei flocked to Russia to buy household items that were not available in China at the time.

That shopping spree ended soon after the fall of the Soviet Union and its subsequent break-up – a spectre that haunts Beijing as it nervously eyes the obstinate peoples of Tibet and Xinjiang. For the CCP, the collapse of the USSR, and Russia's rapid decline from global superpower to the gangster state it has become, is further justification for its unwillingness to tolerate either unruly minorities or dissent – a vast empire gone in a matter of months, its former leaders forgotten or reviled.

Now China has taken Russia's place as the world's second strongest nation. In Heihe, one of the signs of that status is Da Dao, literally 'Big Island' but in fact a promontory jutting into the Amur housing markets and warehouses. Set up solely to cater to Russians – Chinese are mostly barred from the shops here – Da Dao is the true heart of Heihe and the first stop for almost all the people who travel across the river.

Anything and everything is available at Da Dao – with coffee machines, cosmetics, furs, fishing equipment and liquor particularly popular. So cheap were the bottles of Jack Daniel's and Johnnie Walker on display that I assumed they must be fake. 'I don't think the Russians care if it isn't real,' said one store owner, guffawing when I asked him if the whisky was genuine.

Yang Chao's stall was doing a brisk trade in kitchen utensils and hairdryers. 'It's a much better business than my previous one, which was a clothes shop, and it's easier dealing with Russians than the Chinese,' she said. 'Russian people are quite honest and they buy things quickly. They pick up an item, decide if they like it and then pay for it. The Chinese spend ages trying to decide if they want it and then they start bargaining, which is tiring.'

So many Russians are in Heihe at any one time that the locals treat them more as a minority than as visitors, an odd-looking bunch who speak a different language but are part of the scenery. And just as the Han are always keen to demonstrate that they are in charge in the borderlands, so Heihe's government is not shy about letting the residents of Blagoveshchensk know that the balance of power has shifted to their side of the river.

Each evening at 11 o'clock sharp, the street lights of Heihe dim abruptly. The electricity that fuels them is instead diverted to the multitude of neon signs and displays on the buildings overlooking the Amur. A Dongbei version of the glittering Las Vegas Strip, it is an unsubtle boast of how Heihe is thriving at the expense of far less luminous Blagoveshchensk, a nightly show whose significance is understood by every Russian. 'This was all slums a few years ago,' one told me, as we stood on the promenade gazing up at the flashing, blazing lights.

26

An Empire Expanding

Heihe's apparently never-ending energy supply isn't the only way it likes to intimidate its neighbour. The Wujing at the border control by the Amur were the rudest I had ever encountered. They pushed and shoved the long lines of Russians waiting to return home with their shopping, making many open up their purchases only to look inside for a moment before walking away, leaving them struggling to reseal their boxes and bags.

Sean, who had come to see me off, was shocked. 'No wonder Russians say bad things about the Chinese.' In contrast, I was treated as a special guest. Hardly anyone crosses this frontier apart from Russians and Chinese. At the sight of my unfamiliar passport, I was waved through customs ahead of everyone else. The senior officer on duty left his office to usher me out of China and was charming with it.

I emerged on to the slippery, snow-covered banks of the Amur faced with having to persuade someone to take me to the other side. In the summer, boats ply between Heihe and Blagoveshchensk, while in the winter dinky little hovercraft make the run, skimming over the ice in a matter of minutes. But a rigid system of apartheid operates on the transport across the river, with some vessels for Chinese and others for Russians. I fell into neither category and had already been refused a ticket on a Chinese craft.

Russians, though, buy return tickets in Blagoveshchensk for specific boats, leaving little space for stray travellers. I traipsed up and down for half an hour before I found a hovercraft both willing to take me and with a spare seat. I handed over 200 yuan (£20) for the cramped five-minute ride, an unwelcome but salutary introduction to the difference in living costs between Russia and China.

At the Russian frontier post, I was greeted with a mixture of bewilderment and suspicion. Obstructive, vodka-grumpy Russian officials are less common now than they once were, but they still exist. Surprised by my arrival, they made me fill out numerous forms while my passport was examined minutely. I made sure to stay polite, sprinkling every sentence with *spasibo*, the Russian for 'thank you', and was eventually rewarded with an entry stamp.

My hotel room was typical of lodgings in the Russian Far East: a massively overpriced shoebox with a bed, furniture and TV dating from a couple of decades before. But it was very warm and the small window afforded me a sliver of a river view. I didn't stay long to enjoy it. Waiting for me downstairs were Elena and Anastasia, lecturers at the local university whose names had been passed on to me by a Russian journalist contact in Vladivostok.

Elena was a vivacious, middle-aged blonde, Anastasia younger and dark and pretty in a severe way. They asked what I wanted to eat. I suggested Russian food, which caused them to pause. 'Well there is one place we know,' said Elena. 'We mostly eat at Chinese restaurants. There are so many now and they are a lot cheaper than Russian ones.' Outside, it was bitter in the late afternoon, and after a few minutes the tip of my nose was tingling and my chin felt raw. 'It's frosty today,' said Anastasia, an understated way of describing a temperature of -26 degrees Centigrade.

Both were wrapped up in voluminous fur coats. I asked if they had bought them in Heihe. 'Of course,' they answered in unison. 'The only thing I buy in Russia is underwear,' said Anastasia. We walked along the riverfront, while Elena recalled how the Chinese used to broadcast deafening propaganda from Heihe twenty-four hours a day during the Cultural Revolution in an attempt to scare Blagoveshchensk's residents. Unlike in Dongbei, there were no teams of workers clearing away the snow. It was deep enough for some of the locals to take to snowboards towed by cars at night, a Russian winter alternative to waterskiing.

We passed the university Elena and Anastasia taught at, housed in an imposing redbrick former boarding school from the tsarist era. Blagoveshchensk, known to Russians as 'Blago', has a number of elegant nineteenth-century buildings, mostly lining the riverfront and its main street named after Lenin. Along with the city's ageing apartment blocks, they are the most obvious difference between Blago and Heihe which, like most Chinese cities, has been almost entirely rebuilt over the last two decades.

But Blago, despite appearing to be much older than its neighbour, is a relatively new creation. It was founded on the tsar's orders in 1858, the same year that the Treaty of Aigun confirmed Russia's appropriation of Outer Manchuria. Long before then, it was the site of a Manchu town and fort. And even after it became Blagoveshchensk, much of its population remained Manchu or Daur. Few Russians were willing to venture thousands of kilometres east from the country's European heartland to such an isolated spot.

Han migrants moved north to join the minorities. As in Vladivostok, another of the cities created in Russia's newly acquired lands in the second half of the nineteenth century, it was the Chinese who controlled much of the local trade. Well over a century before Da Dao in Heihe opened, imports from China to the Russian Far East already vastly outnumbered the goods sent south across the Amur.

That imbalance provoked jealousy and discontent among Blago's Russians. In the summer of 1900, the decision was taken to deport the entire Chinese community. Around 4,000 people were marched to the shores of the Amur and, with no boats to take them to the other side, were pushed in to drown or swim home. Those who struggled to stay on dry land were beaten to death by willing bands of Cossacks and locals. The massacre is the subject of a museum outside Heihe. It was closed when I was there, but Russians are banned from visiting it, an indication that the Chinese have not forgotten or forgiven what occurred over a century ago.

The slaughter by the banks of the Amur was the first notable expression of the schizophrenic attitudes towards China and the Chinese that continue to be held today by most Russians in the region. Elena and Anastasia, like everyone else in Blago, knew their lives would be far less pleasant without the presence of Heihe across the river to shop, eat and drink in. As academics, they were aware too that Chinese investment in the local construction and timber industries makes for a vivid contrast with the indifference displayed towards the Far East by their own government in far-off Moscow.

Yet they were typical too in their dislike and distrust of the Chinese migrants to Blago, who starting returning across the Amur in significant numbers from 2000 onwards, even if both women were happy to eat in their restaurants. 'Too many Chinese are here now. If too many come it won't be beneficial to Russia,' stated Anastasia, picking her words carefully. Elena had a problem with their personal habits. 'They spit and smoke everywhere and they eat too much garlic,' she said.

In part, Anastasia and Elena were merely being Russian. Intolerance of immigrants is something of a national trait, notwithstanding the fact that Russia is the largest country in the world, as well as being hugely under-populated. 'I think Russians in general don't really like foreigners. Here it's the Chinese. In other parts of Russia it's people from the Caucacus or Serbs or Africans,' one of Anastasia's students named Sergei told me. 'A lot of Chinese walk around Blago like they own the place, and many unemployed Russians resent that they take jobs away from them because they'll work for lower salaries.'

Nikolay Kukharenko, the engaging head of the local Confucius Institute, a Beijing-funded scheme to encourage the learning of Mandarin and present a softer side of China to the world, disagreed. 'I know lots of Russian businessmen who'll tell you how they will pay 30,000 roubles [£550] a month to a Russian and they work for a month and then they start drinking. The Chinese don't drink, work hard and they'll accept 20,000 roubles [£370] a month. You know, it's a lot easier for a western Russian politician to say the Chinese are taking jobs than it is for them to create jobs.'

Nationalist deputies in the Duma, the Russian parliament, crack jokes about how Blago is so dominated by Beijing that the city government includes Chinese officials. None of the migrants from Dongbei are laughing, as that only feeds the anger of the local xenophobes. 'I think the Russians are prejudiced towards the Chinese,' said Zhang Li Na, a thirty-five-year-old woman from Harbin. 'Sometimes we are afraid to go out at night because the young Russian guys get drunk and beat the Chinese up. But the police don't care if a Chinese person gets attacked.'

Zhang and her husband are typical of the Chinese in Blago, who are mostly small-time traders. Their business is selling clocks. 'We buy the clocks in southern China, in Guangzhou and Yiwu, and then assemble them here using Chinese workers. Russians are no good at working hard. They drink too much and they're lazy and inefficient,' she said. 'I don't really like Russians, although the old people are friendly, and the Russians don't like us being here. But they can't live without us. The only real Russian industries are all heavy manufacturing. They can't make clothes or clocks or anything like that cheaply.'

Most of the stall owners at the main market are Chinese and they were happy to put up with my tone-uncertain Mandarin, rather than having to communicate in the pidgin Russian they use normally. There are now around 10,000 full-time Chinese residents of Blago, with another 10,000 or so coming to work on a seasonal basis on farms and building sites. In total, the Chinese make up about 10 per cent of the population. That is more than enough to confirm the greatest fear of the locals, which is that China wants to reclaim Outer Manchuria and is colonising the Far East by stealth.

Beijing's ambitions in the region are the subject of TV documentaries and newspaper columns in Russia, and are the subtext to every conversation about the Chinese in Blago. 'Here in the Far East, people feel neglected by Moscow and we are detached from the rest of Russia. You can't be sure it won't happen in the future because the Russian population is declining and the Chinese need room because there are so many of them,' said Sergei the student.

It is the dwindling number of Russians in the Far East that truly alarms the politicians in Moscow. There are around six and a half million people in an area that covers six and a half million square kilometres, down from just over eight million in 1991 when the Soviet Union expired. Across the Amur, over 100 million Chinese live in far smaller Dongbei alone. Faced with such an overwhelming numerical superiority, the paranoia of Blago's residents is understandable. Many are convinced the arrival of Chinese workers in the Far East over the last decade is the first step in China's plan to extend its boundaries in the north-east.

Adding to the temptation for Beijing are the region's abundant natural resources. Rich in everything from coal to timber, as well as untapped minerals and a huge salmon-fishing industry, China is already buying up as many local companies as it can. And every Russian with even a tenuous grasp of history knows that the Far East was once Manchu territory. For the conspiracy theorists, resurrecting the Manchurian Empire would allow China to solve some of its energy needs and give its people access to a fresh supply of both land and jobs.

Arresting the decline in the Far East's population is probably an impossible task. In the days of the USSR, many of the country's cleverest citizens were encouraged to move east by higher salaries and subsidised flights back to European Russia. Now those incentives are gone and their descendants are leaving in their droves. Just as bright as their parents and grandparents were, they are unwilling to put up with low wages and living so far from the centre of the country.

So expensive is the eight-hour flight to Moscow that it is cheaper for Blago's residents to cross the Amur and hop on a plane to the beaches of Sanya on Hainan Island, China's southernmost point, for a holiday in the sun. Many of the young people in the Far East have never even been to western Russia. Instead of looking for jobs in the capital or St Petersburg, more and more of them are now migrating south. Almost all of Elena and Anastasia's students wanted out of Blago, and China is increasingly their destination of choice.

They grow up visiting Heihe as often as twice a month. Moving to the country they know already is the logical next step. 'I used to want to go to America or the UK and that's why I worked so hard at my English. But then I started to study Chinese and now I've decided my future lies in China. It's much easier for me to get to China than it is to get a visa for America,' said Eugenya, a smart and tall twenty-one-year-old with flaming red hair. Her Mandarin is already almost fluent. 'Some people in Russia think being so close to China is dangerous because of the history, but I think it's an opportunity for me.'

Despite the Russians fleeing the Far East, and the ominous pronouncements from Moscow about China's intentions, it is improbable that Beijing will literally retake the territory it lost to Russia. But, as North Korea already is, the region is set to become an economic colony of Dongbei. 'In ten years' time there'll be far more Russian resources owned by China,' said Nikolay Kukharenko, the most rational of the Russians I met in Blago when it came to their neighbour. 'What reason is there for the Chinese to come physically if they can just take our resources?'

Some of the people of Blago will be absorbed into the Chinese realm too, like the Manchu, Oroqen and Hezhen before them. It is the nature of empires to contract and expand, to attract and repel. Eugenya's determination to travel south and find a future in China is simply part of a natural process, just the latest wave of migration in Outer Manchuria – a land so vast that maps are automatically arbitrary.

China's borderlands mutate constantly. They are permanently restless, forever in flux. Different peoples have always moved in both directions between China and its neighbours. All that changes are the reasons that pull or push them beyond the frontiers. In Blago, especially late at night, the contrast with the opposite bank of the Amur is so great that is enough to make anyone want to move on. Standing on the riverfront with the darkened buildings of the tsar's Russia at my back, even I could feel the neon lights of Heihe calling me towards China.

Further Reading

Bailey F. M. *Mission to Tashkent* (Oxford University Press, 1946)

Bailey F. M. *No Passport to Tibet* (Rupert Hart-Davis, 1957)

Becker Jasper *Hungry Ghosts: Mao's Secret Famine* (Simon & Schuster, 1997)

Bickers Robert *The Scramble for China: Foreign Devils in the Qing Empire 1832–1914* (Allen Lane, 2011)

Cha Victor *The Impossible State: North Korea, Past and Future* (The Bodley Head, 2012)

Chang Jung and Jon Halliday *Mao: The Unknown Story* (Jonathan Cape, 2005)

Chang Leslie T. *Factory Girls: From Village to City in a Changing China* (Spiegel & Grau, 2008)

Colquhoun Archibald Ross *Amongst the Shans* (Field & Tuer, 1885)

Colquhoun Archibald Ross *The 'Overland' to China* (Harper & Brothers, 1900)

Crossley Pamela Kyle, Helen F. Siu and Donald S. Sutton (eds), *Empire at the Margins: Culture, Ethnicity and Frontier in Early Modern China* (University of California Press, 2006)

Davis Sara L. M. *Song and Silence: Ethnic Revival on China's Southwest Borders* (Columbia University Press, 2005)

Demick Barbara *Nothing to Envy: Real Lives in North Korea* (Granta Books, 2010)

Dikötter Frank *The Discourse of Race in Modern China* (C. Hurst, 1992)

Evans Grant, Christopher Hutton and Kuah Kung Eng (eds), *Where China Meets Southeast Asia: Social and Cultural Change in the Borderlands* (Palgrave, 2000)

Fleming Peter *News from Tartary* (Jonathan Cape, 1936)

Fleming Peter *One's Company* (Jonathan Cape, 1934)

French Patrick *Tibet, Tibet: A Personal History of a Lost Land* (HarperCollins, 2003)

Gifford Rob *China Road: One Man's Journey into the Heart of Modern China* (Bloomsbury, 2007)

Goullart Peter *Forgotten Kingdom* (John Murray, 1957)

Hopkirk Peter *The Great Game: The Struggle for Empire in Central Asia* (Kodansha Amer, 1992)

Johnston Reginald Fleming *From Peking to Mandalay* (John Murray, 1908)

Kynge James *China Shakes the World: The Rise of a Hungry Nation* (Weidenfeld & Nicolson, 2006)

Ma Jian *Red Dust: A Path through China* (Chatto & Windus, 2001)

Pomfret John *Chinese Lessons: Five Classmates and the Story of the New China* (Henry Holt, 2006)

Scott James C. *The Art of Not Being Governed: An Anarchist History of Upland Southeast Asia* (Yale University Press, 2009)

Shakya Tsering *The Dragon in the Land of the Snows: A History of Modern Tibet since 1947* (Pimlico, 1999)

Spence Jonathan D. *The Search for Modern China* (Hutchinson, 1990)

Thubron Colin *To a Mountain in Tibet* (Chatto & Windus, 2011)

Tyler Christian *Wild West China: The Untold Story of a Frontier Land* (John Murray, 2003)

Wang Lixiong and Tsering Shakya *The Struggle for Tibet* (Verso, 2009)

Acknowledgements

All travellers are reliant on the kindness of strangers. A travel writer is even more so. I owe a great debt to the many people who spoke to me about their lives and assisted with introductions. Aba, Angelina, Billy, Christina, Julia, Li Qingmei, Mr Kim, Nang, Paul, Pemba, Piao, Rayila, Samphel, Tenzin and Yu Shumei were especially central to the writing of this book. Sadly, given the sensitivity of the subject matter, I am unable to print their real names. I wish I could.

My agent Ben Mason has been a huge support over the years. The excellent advice of Michael Fishwick, Anna Simpson and Peter James at Bloomsbury was crucial in turning a mere manuscript into a book worthy of publication. Needless to say, any mistakes, or shortcomings, are all mine. My family and friends have been an ongoing source of encouragement.

The following people aided me in different but vital ways in my seven and a half years in China, during my research and travels and as I wrote this book – thanks to you all: Anastasia Arkharova, Paul Atherley, Jasper Becker, Natalie Behring, Andrew Chant, Rayhan Demytrie, Laurent Dupin, Peter Foster, Colin Hinshelwood, Jiang Feng, Jin Guangzhu, Jin Ni, Kakharman Khozhamberdi, Justin Kiersky, Nikolay Kukharenko, Eva Li, Lily Li, Zoe Li, Elena Mezhakova, Malcolm Moore, Peter Simpson, Richard Spencer, Chris Taylor, Piero Vio, Samara Yawnghwe, Sean Yu and Xiao Yu.

Index

education system, Chinese, 33, 106–8, 181, 263
elderly, care of, 228–9
environmental degradation, 8, 165–6
   see also deforestation
Everest National Park, 157
Ewenki people, 290

face, concept of, 40
famine and starvation, 107, 261–2
Father Christmas, 285, 287
Federated Shan States, 199
Fleming, Peter, 5
Fleming Johnston, Reginald, 235
football, 15, 202, 223, 258–9
Friendship Highway, 128, 131

gambling, 165, 173, 192, 194, 228, 234
Gandhi, Mahatma, 155
Ganesha, 144–5
Ganges River, 147
Gansu Province, 1–2, 67, 84, 93, 246
gaokao (university entrance exam), 18, 247
Garuda Valley, 152
gender imbalance
   among Chinese, 228, 237
   among Koreans, 273–4
Genghis Khan, 246
Ghez, 65
Gobi Desert, 2
gold rush, Manchurian, 287
Golden Triangle, 163–4, 184–7, 189, 191, 193, 208
   and Dai diaspora, 199–200
   and drugs trade, 194–6, 204–6, 209–10, 234
Golmud, 82, 84, 86, 88
Gorbachev, Mikhail, 52
Gorno-Badakhshan, 66
Great Game, the, 4, 53, 56, 59, 69
Great Leap Forward, 107, 260–2
Great Wall of China, 1, 8, 246, 252
guang guan (bachelors), 228
Guangdong Province, 30
Guangxi province, 248, 283
Guangzhou Province, 305
Guanlei, 185–8, 191–2
Guizhou Province, 135, 268–70, 286
Gyantse, 125–8, 130, 132

Hainan Island, 109, 307
Halloween, 285
Han Chinese
   and ethnic minorities, 2–3, 5–7, 19, 96, 114, 172, 174
   and Hui, 8–9
   insensitivity to religions, 81, 153
   and Koreans, 256–8, 272
   and Manchu, 27, 248
   migration to Xinjiang, 10, 14, 20, 22, 24
   and nationalism, 31–2
   and Oroqen, 290–1, 296
   sexual reticence, 161–2
   and Uighurs, 13–19, 28–9, 39, 44–5, 49, 70–1
   and Zhuang, 248
Han dynasty, 189
Hani people, 163
Harbin, 278–83, 305
Harrer, Heinrich, 99
hashish, 4, 59–60
healthcare, in China, 33, 263
Hedin, Sven, 147
Heihe, 282, 288, 296–304, 307–8
Heilongjiang Province, 56, 245, 260, 278–89, 293, 295
Heilongjiang (Black Dragon) River, 279
Helong, 259
heroin, 66, 186–7, 195–6, 199, 206, 210, 213, 216, 223, 234, 236
Hexi Corridor, 9–10, 84
Hezhen (Nanai) people, 279, 282, 289–90, 307
Highway 219, 74, 126, 131, 135, 152, 156
Hindu Kush Mountains, 67
Hindus, 144–5, 147, 155
HIV/AIDS, 234
Hong Kong, 53
Hotan, 74–9, 81–2, 234
   Han Chinese minority in, 75–6
housing costs, 33
Hsipaw, 193
Hu Jintao, 139
Huang Di, Emperor (the Yellow Emperor), 31
Huatugou, 84–7
Huay Xai, 204
Hui people, 8–9, 53, 82, 103

315